WRITTEN FOR US

WRITTEN FOR US

RECEIVING GOD'S WORDS IN THE BIBLE

PETER ADAM

Inter-Varsity Press
Norton Street, Nottingham NG7 3HR, England
Email: ivp@ivpbooks.com
Website: www.ivpbooks.com

First published 2008

British Library Cataloguing in Publication Data
A catalogue record for this book is available from the British Library.

ISBN: 978–1–84474–208–0

Set in Monotype Garamond 11/13pt
Typeset in Great Britain by Servis Filmsetting Ltd, Manchester
Printed and bound in Great Britain by Ashford Colour Press Ltd, Gosport, Hampshire, UK

Inter-Varsity Press publishes Christian books that are true to the Bible and that communicate the gospel, develop discipleship and strengthen the church for its mission in the world.

Inter-Varsity Press is closely linked with the Universities and Colleges Christian Fellowship, a student movement connecting Christian Unions in universities and colleges throughout Great Britain, and a member movement of the International Fellowship of Evangelical Students. Website: www.uccf.org.uk

1. To those who pray for me and for my ministry. Thank you for 'wrestling in prayer' for me. I am deeply grateful to God for your fellowship in Christ, and for your loving and costly support. I am constantly sustained and strengthened by your prayers to our gracious Heavenly Father.

2. To fellow workers in the gospel in Australia as we stand 'firm in one spirit, [wrestling] side by side with one mind for the faith of the gospel' (Phil. 1:27). I am constantly encouraged by your godliness, faithfulness, and fruitfulness in ministry in Christ Jesus.

CONTENTS

PREFACE

I am grateful to Dr Philip Duce, Theological Books Editor at Inter-Varsity Press, for his encouragement and help, and for the support of the IVP staff. Many thanks also to the Council of Ridley College for granting me two months' study leave to write the book, and to Lindsay Wilson for serving as Acting Principal over that time.

This book continues a long-term interest of mine, and follows two other books, *Speaking God's Words* (1996) and *Hearing God's Words* (2002).

Soon after I was converted to Christ in 1963, I went to study at Melbourne University, and there I met a theological student who had moved away from his earlier conservative views on the Bible, and who was eager to win me from my newfound confidence in Scripture. We engaged in many debates together. So I have been working through the issues of the nature of the Bible for many years. Over that time I have faced many difficulties and problems in understanding the Bible, but in the long term I have gained a greater trust in the Scriptures, and have benefited more and more from them.

I have been privileged in the many opportunities I have had to preach and teach God's words, and to help to train others for this vital ministry. Working hard to prepare a talk or Bible study has been of great benefit to me. Then my confidence in the Scriptures has also grown as I have seen people and churches transformed by the power of God as they have received and trusted his words in the Bible.

I am glad to be able to say that writing this book has given me greater confidence and trust in God. I continue to learn from God's holy writings.

I am very grateful to many who have contributed to my thinking about this topic, and so to the writing of this book. Many did so by hearing some material from this book in other forms. These have included sermons and conference addresses at St Jude's Carlton, Ridley College, the Timothy Institute, the Melbourne University Christian Union, the Sydney Missionary and Bible College, the Proclamation Trust in England, pastors' conferences in India and Pakistan, and the Eliza Ferrie Lecture for 2006 at the Presbyterian Theological Centre in Sydney. Many perceptive questions and comments have been of enormous influence in my long-term reflection on the issues tackled in this book. The books in the Bibliography have also stimulated my thinking, even if I have not quoted directly from them. I am grateful to those who wrote them.

Thanks to those who have responded to early drafts of this material, especially to members of the Ridley College Graduate Seminar, and to Andrew Malone, Tim Patrick, Lindsay Wilson, Tim Anderson, Alison Flynn, and David Broxholme.

I am also very grateful to my colleagues and friends Ruth Millard, Nicole Harvey, and Peter Angelovski for practical help in this project.

Peter Adam

INTRODUCTION

This book develops the theme of the Bible as 'written for us' by expounding the summary phrase 'Receiving God's words written for his people by his Spirit about his Son'. This is a summary of what the Bible claims about itself, and of how God wants us to use it. This book is not a defence of those ideas, but a summary of them.

It is an important topic to tackle, because many descriptions of the Bible argue from what needs to be the case, or from what we assume to be the case, without a careful study of what the Bible teaches about its own nature. As we should pay attention to what the Bible teaches on other subjects, we should not neglect its teaching on this basic topic.

Even correct theologies of the Bible are often expressed in non-biblical categories, which give the impression that these theologies come from non-biblical sources, and so may more easily be dismissed as culturally determined. They may leave a sense of unease, because an extra-biblical foundation seems to have been introduced, or because a few verses have been milked for meaning, without reference to the wider biblical evidence. While it may seem a curiously circular exercise to try to work out what the Bible says about the Bible, it is in fact an issue of central importance. For it would be foolish to believe of the Bible what it does not claim for itself, implicitly or explicitly.

I have assumed that the Bible has a coherent theology about itself. My defence is that one way to test or prove that idea is to attempt the project, and hope that it is successful!

This book complements two previous books. In *Speaking God's Words*, I described a practical theology of preaching, the theology and process of speaking God's words to others. In *Hearing God's Words*, I showed how the Bible functions as a means of spirituality, and how it helps us to understand the nature of good spirituality.

So here is a biblical theology of the Bible, based on the summary phrase, 'Receiving God's words written for his people by his Spirit about his Son'. The theology of the Bible depends on the four theological themes of this phrase: a doctrine of receiving God's verbal revelation ('Receiving God's words'), a doctrine of the people of God, or ecclesiology ('written for his people'), a doctrine of the Holy Spirit, or pneumatology ('by his Spirit'), and a doctrine of Jesus Christ, or Christology ('about his Son'). These four doctrines are fundamental to the Bible's implicit and explicit teaching about itself. I hope this book will help us recognize what a great gift God has given us in the Holy Scriptures, and receive that gift with faith, obedience, and praise to God.

The methodology I have used here is to search the Scriptures to find their answer to the question of their identity and use. In Part 1 there is an overview of biblical thought on each of the four elements in the phrase 'Receiving God's words, written for his people, by his Spirit, about his Son'. In Parts 2–5 we have studies of sections of the Bible which cover these four foundations. In Part 6 we will see how Jesus authenticated the Old Testament and New Testament, and that these four foundations of the doctrine of Scripture are present in his teaching.

The summary phrase is itself composed of words from the Bible. These are not, I hope, taken out of context. We will see many of these sentences and phrases in their own contexts throughout this book, and find in them the theological foundation of what we believe about the Bible.

Receiving God's words

The author of Proverbs wrote: 'I looked and received instruction' (Prov. 24:32).

Jesus said to his Father about his disciples: 'The words that you gave to me I have given to them, and they have received them' (John 17:8).

Paul wrote to the Thessalonians: 'you received the word with joy inspired by the Holy Spirit' (1 Thess. 1:6), and 'when you received the word of God that you heard from us, you accepted it not as a human word but as what it really is, God's word' (1 Thess. 2:13).

James instructed his readers, 'Welcome with meekness the implanted word that has the power to save your souls' (Jas 1:21).

Written for his people

Moses said: 'Hear, O Israel . . . Keep these words that I am commanding you today in your heart' (Deut. 6:4, 6).

'Moses wrote down all the words of the LORD'. '[Moses] received living oracles to give to us' (Exod. 24:4; Acts 7:38).

Paul wrote: 'These things happened to them to serve as an example, and they were written down to instruct us, on whom the ends of the ages have come' (1 Cor. 10:11).

Paul wrote: 'For whatever was written in former days was written for our instruction, so that by steadfastness and by the encouragement of the scriptures we might have hope' (Rom. 15:4).

By his Spirit

Jesus said: 'David himself, by the Holy Spirit, declared . . .' (Mark 12:36).

Jesus said: 'The Advocate . . . the Spirit of truth . . . will testify on my behalf' (John 15:26–27).

The author of Hebrews wrote: 'Therefore, as the Holy Spirit says . . .' (Heb. 3:7).

Paul wrote: 'All Scripture is inspired by God and is useful for teaching, for reproof, for correction, and for training in righteousness' (2 Tim. 3:16).

Peter wrote: 'Men and women moved by the Holy Spirit spoke from God' (2 Pet. 1:21).

About his Son

Jesus said: 'These are my words that I spoke to you while I was still with you – that everything written about me in the law of Moses, the prophets, and the psalms must be fulfilled' (Luke 24:44).

Peter said: 'All the prophets testify about [Jesus Christ] that everyone who believes in him receives forgiveness of sins through his name' (Acts 10:43).

Peter wrote: 'Concerning this salvation, the prophets who prophesied of the grace that was to be yours made careful search and inquiry, inquiring about the person or time that the Spirit of Christ within them indicated, when it testified in advance to the sufferings destined for Christ and the subsequent glory' (1 Pet. 1:10–11).

John wrote: 'But these are written so that you may come to believe that Jesus is the Messiah, the Son of God, and that through believing you may have life in his name' (John 20:31).

This book comprises a survey of what the Bible teaches about itself, a study of over twenty-four chapters of the Bible, and a survey of Hebrews. I could have considered the topic in the light of historical or systematic theology, but that would have produced a different book. My intention has been to let the Bible speak for itself, so that we may discover what the Bible teaches about the Bible.

Part 1

RECEIVING GOD'S WORDS, WRITTEN FOR HIS PEOPLE, BY HIS SPIRIT, ABOUT HIS SON

1. RECEIVING GOD'S WORDS

In this chapter we focus on receiving God's powerful words as one of the many gifts he gives us.

'Then God said' (Gen. 1:3)

God has spoken

God is the God who speaks, and uses human language to achieve effective communication.[1] He is God who speaks, and who has made human beings in his image and likeness as speaking beings (Gen. 1 – 2). The Old Testament shows us that God can speak in human language. Of course God does not have vocal cords, but he can imprint human words in our consciousness, or produce the sounds of human words for our ears, or speak to us by humans who speak his words. The effect is of God using human words.

God is often described as speaking directly and personally to individuals or to his people. Every time God uses human language, his words are both divine and human, 'God's word in human language'.[2] He addressed Abram with

---

1. Adam, *Hearing*, chapter 2.
2. Goldsworthy, *Hermeneutics*, p. 280.

command and promise (Gen. 12:1 – 3). He spoke both to Moses and to the people at Mt Sinai (Exod. 19 – 24, 25 – 40). The speaking ministry of angels and prophets in both Old and New Testament shows that God used human words.

It would indeed be a bizarre situation if God could not speak. When reluctant and stammering Moses claimed to be slow of speech, the Lord replied, 'Who makes man's mouth? . . . Is it not I, the LORD?' (Exod. 4:11 [my trans.]). How extraordinary to think that God who made humans with the capacity to speak would not himself be able to speak, to convey words to humanity.[3] God is not dumb, but can speak: 'I have spoken, and I will bring it to pass; I have planned, and I will do it' (Isa. 46:11). And again: 'Who told this long ago? Who declared it of old? Was it not I, the LORD?' (Isa. 45:21). As Jürgen Moltmann wrote, 'Thus theology as *speaking about God* is possible only on the basis of *what God himself says*'.[4]

God and human language

Is it possible for our transcendent God to use human language? Some think that God cannot bridge the gap. However, the God of the Bible is so great that he can use human language without compromising his transcendence. The gap between the infinite God and finite humanity can be bridged by God, if not by humanity. As John Webster wrote, 'revelation is God's self-presentation to us'; 'revelation is God's eloquence, God's speaking-out'.[5]

God is also able to achieve non-verbal communication by his actions. However, he usually communicates the meaning of his actions by his words. God uses human language, and so builds relationship and communicates effectively with humanity. The infinite God uses finite words to communicate with finite beings.[6]

This pattern of self-revelation by using words is similar to ordinary human self-revelation. We use words to communicate who we are, what we think, what we like, and what we want others to learn of us. They respond by listening, and the more they listen attentively, the more they will understand both what we mean by our words, and also what kind of people we are. Words communicate meaning, words reveal the person who speaks them, and words build relationships. The appropriate response to someone speaking to us is to trust

---

3. For a defence and explanation of the claim that God can speak, see Helm, *Revelation*; Swinburne, *Revelation*; and Wolterstorff, *Discourse*.
4. Moltmann, *Crucified God*, p. 66.
5. Webster, *Word and Church*, p. 27.
6. I have developed this theme in Adam, *Speaking*, chapter 1.

their words, and so learn to trust the person. God speaks, and people learn to trust him as they trust his words.[7]

As the use of language is a fundamental feature of mature full human community, so it is the best way for God to communicate his relationship with us through his Son. The infinite God uses finite human language to achieve effective communication.[8]

The words of God's covenant (Deut. 29:1)

The idea that God makes covenants assumes that God uses human language, for a covenant is a spoken or written agreement and promise. 'Write these words; in accordance with these words I have made a covenant with you and with Israel' (Exod. 34:27). Moses described God's relationship with his people in Deuteronomy in terms of God's words: 'He declared to you his covenant, which he charged you to observe, that is, the ten commandments; and he wrote them on two stone tablets' (Deut. 4:13), and 'Therefore diligently observe the words of this covenant, in order that you may succeed in everything that you do' (29:9).

For the word 'covenant' implies 'words of the covenant'. Similarly, 'law' implies 'words of the law'; 'promise' implies 'words of promise'. Furthermore, 'witness' often implies 'words of witness', 'steadfast love' often implies 'words of steadfast love', and 'revelation' often implies 'words of revelation'.

The tensions of the spoken covenant between God and David are clearly expressed in Psalm 89. First we hear of that covenant, or spoken promise. Notice how the themes of God's protection, steadfast love and faithfulness, and covenant come together: 'I have found my servant David . . . My faithfulness and steadfast love shall be with him . . . For ever I will keep my steadfast love for him, and my covenant with him will stand firm' (89:20, 24, 28).

Even if David's descendants break the laws and commandments of the covenant, God promises that he will not break his words:

If his children forsake my law
    and do not walk according to my ordinances,
if they violate my statutes

---

7. See further McDonald, *I Want to Know*, pp. 10–23.

8. See Morris, *I Believe*; Jensen, *Revelation*; Packer, 'The Adequacy of Human Language' in *Honouring*, pp. 23–50; and Adam, *Speaking*, pp. 15–24.

and do not keep my commandments,
  then I will punish their transgression with the rod
    and their iniquity with scourges;
  but I will not remove from him my steadfast love,
    or be false to my faithfulness.
I will not violate my covenant,
    or alter the word that went forth from my lips.
Once and for all I have sworn by my holiness;
    I will not lie to David.
  (89:30–34)

Then comes the contrast between the promise of God and the present situation of God's people:

But now you have spurned and rejected him;
    you are full of wrath against your anointed.
You have renounced the covenant with your servant;
    you have defiled his crown in the dust.
  (89:38–39)

The psalm ends with a plea that God would put into practice his promised love and faithfulness: 'Lord, where is your steadfast love of old, which by your faithfulness you swore to David?' (89:49). God showed his love and faithfulness in the words of the covenant made with David. God will be steadfast in his promised covenant love for his people, and faithful to his words.

So we relate to God by relating to his words. Moses explained that to 'love God' with heart, soul, and might is to 'keep these words . . . in your heart', and 'recite them to your children and talk about them' (Deut. 6:4–7).

God also promised the new covenant to be fulfilled in Christ. In Paul's words about Jesus Christ: 'For in him every one of God's promises is a "Yes"' (2 Cor. 1:20).

'My word . . . shall accomplish that which I purpose' – powerful words (Isa. 55:11)

God's words are powerful because God is powerful. God's words are powerful as God's actions are powerful. This theme of the power of God's word is common throughout the Bible. In Isaiah we read: 'By myself I have sworn, from my mouth has gone forth in righteousness a word that shall not return', and 'my word . . . shall not return to me empty, but it shall accomplish that which I purpose' (45:23; 55:11). And in Zechariah 1:5: 'Your ancestors, where are they? And the prophets, do they live for ever? But my word and my statutes, which I commanded my servants the prophets, did they not overtake your ancestors?'

So the word and gospel of God is living and active. We read in Romans that the gospel is 'the power of God for salvation to everyone who has faith' (1:16), and 'God . . . is able to strengthen you according to my gospel and the proc-lamation of Jesus Christ' (16:25).

We see the power of the word in the Gospels: 'The sower sows the word . . . The kingdom of God is as if someone would scatter seed upon the ground . . . the kingdom of God . . . is like a mustard seed' (Mark 4:14, 26, 30–31). 'You have already been cleansed by the word that I have spoken to you' (John 15:3). As J. I. Packer wrote:

> In the New Testament the Word of God – that is, the Gospel – is declared to be the means by which God searches hearts (Heb. 4:12), creates faith (Rom. 10:17, cf. John 17:20), effects new birth (James 1:18, 1 Pet. 1:23), cleanses (John 15:3, Eph. 5:26), sanctifies (John 17:17), gives wisdom (Col. 3:16), builds up Christians in faith and brings them to their final heritage (Acts 20:32) – in short, saves their souls (James 1:21).[9]

What is true of the word and gospel of God is specifically true of Scripture. So in the summary of Joshua: 'Not one [word] has failed of all the good words that the LORD your God has promised concerning you; all have come to pass, not one has fallen to the ground' (Josh. 23:14 [my trans.]).

Paul assures us that 'It is not as though the word of God had failed' (Rom. 9:6), and wrote to Timothy about 'the sacred writings that are able (*ta dynamena*) to instruct you for salvation through faith in Christ Jesus' (2 Tim. 3:15). As Calvin wrote: '[Paul] calls God true, not only because he is prepared to stand faithfully on his promises, but also because he really fulfils whatever he declares; for he so speaks, that his command becomes a reality.'[10]

We may describe this in theological terms as the power of God in 'the word of God' (the gospel) in 'the words of God' (the Bible). Luther commented, 'He who wants to hear God speak should read Holy Scripture.'[11]

---

9. Packer, *Honouring*, p. 105.

10. Calvin, *Commentaries*, 19, p. 116, on Rom. 3:4.

11. As quoted in Thompson, *Sure Ground*, p. 57.

God's acts in all ways (as far as we know) by speech. as they're revealed

God's powerful words are effective secondary causes. God is the primary cause of everything in the universe. Sometimes he works without using human language. Sometimes he uses human language as a 'secondary cause' to achieve his will, just as sometimes he uses human beings as 'secondary causes'. His words achieve his relational and revelatory purposes. God uses these words to reveal who he is, as God, Father, Son and Holy Spirit. He uses words to explain what he wants human beings to think, to do, and to know. He uses these words to explain the world, to interpret reality, and to promise a future. He uses words to warn and judge, to encourage and elicit faith, to forgive and give assurance. God's effective 'secondary causes' can be described as God's 'instruments'. Calvin wrote: 'The word is the instrument by which the Lord dispenses the illumination of the Spirit to believers.'[12] Thomas Cranmer put the same truth in more vivid words. He described how much carpenters and masons value their tools, then added: 'as mallets, hammers, saws, chisels . . . be the tools of their occupation, so be the books of the prophets and apostles, and all Holy Writ inspired by the Holy Ghost, the instruments of our salvation.'[13]

Indeed, the words of God convey the power of God so completely that we can claim that God is present in his speech, in his words, just as he is present in his other actions. 'In the readings . . . God speaks to his people, reveals to them the mysteries of redemption and salvation, and provides them with spiritual nourishment; and Christ himself, in the form of his word, is present in the midst of the faithful.'[14]

We find in 1 Peter 1 a compelling description of the role of the word as God's instrument. The original cause of new birth is the mercy of God, and its historical cause is the resurrection of Christ: 'Blessed be the God and Father of our Lord Jesus Christ! By his great mercy he has given us a new birth into a living hope through the resurrection of Jesus Christ from the dead' (1:3). How is the power of the new birth applied to humans? Peter's answer is 'the word of God'. For he wrote: 'You have been born anew, not of perishable but of imperishable seed, through the living and enduring word of God' (1:23). God uses the instrument or means of his word to bring about new birth for his people.[15]

Similarly, we will see in chapter 3 that the Scriptures are holy. Holy means that they have holy power, power to make holy. Just as God's words are the

---

12. Calvin, *Institutes*, 1.9.3, p. 96.

13. Cranmer, 'Preface to the Great Bible', in Bray, *Documents*, p. 237.

14. Flannery, *Vatican Council*, pp. 170–171.

15. Adam, *Hearing*, pp. 105–108.

means by which he brings new birth, so they also make God's holy people more holy. God's words are holy power, powerfully holy.

We need to make it clear that God's human words are instruments or means of revelation, because there is an unhelpful strand of teaching which claims that God's revelation happens independently of words, and that words are either just God's pointers to that non-verbal revelation, or else merely human attempts to make sense of that non-verbal revelation. John Spong taught that the 'Bible is the means by which I hear, confront, interact with the Word of God. No, the words of the Bible are not for me the words of God.'[16] What a contrast to Jesus' claim, 'The words that I have spoken to you are spirit and life', and to Peter's reply, 'You have the words of eternal life' (John 6:63, 68). God's powerful words are revelation, and do not just point to revelation. Austin Farrer wrote: 'the inspiration is to be found in the very words and nowhere else'.[17]

Here is the great reformer Martin Luther, speaking about the Reformation in Europe:

> All I have done is to put forth, preach and write the word of God, and apart from this I have done nothing. While I have been sleeping, or drinking Wittenberg beer with my friend Philip and with Amsdorf, it is the word that has done great things . . . I have done nothing: the word has done and achieved everything . . . I have let the word act . . . it is all powerful, it takes hearts prisoner, and when they are taken prisoner, the work that is done comes from the word itself.[18]

My word in your mouth

God's words in the mouth of prophet and apostle

The fact that God is able to use human words is reinforced by the way the Bible speaks of human words coming from God's mouth and then being found in human mouths. Of course God does not have a mouth: this language means that God is able to communicate to us using human words, so his words can be found in our mouths.

The first example of God putting his words in human mouths in the Bible is found in the vivid narrative of the call of Moses. It is especially striking because

---

16. Spong, *Rescuing*, p. 249.

17. Farrer, *Interpretation*, p. 12.

18. Ebeling, *Luther*, pp. 66–67.

several points that are significant for us come from Moses' objections to his call. He first complains that he is unable to speak for God: 'O my Lord, I have never been eloquent, neither in the past nor even now that you have spoken to your servant; but I am slow of speech and slow of tongue' (Exod. 4:10). The Lord's reply, as we have seen, made it clear that he creates human mouths, and so is able to enable speech on his behalf: 'Who makes man's mouth? Who makes them mute or deaf, seeing or blind? Is it not I, the LORD?' (4:11 [my trans.]). Even more significantly, God is able to teach Moses what to say: 'Now go, and I will be with your mouth and teach you what you are to speak' (4:12).

As Moses still objected, God told Moses to use Aaron his brother as his spokesman, and that God's words would be given to Moses to pass on to Aaron: 'You shall speak to him and put the words in his mouth; and I will be with your mouth and with his mouth, and will teach you what you shall do. He indeed shall speak for you to the people; he shall serve as a mouth for you, and you shall serve as God for him' (4:15–16).

The similarity of relationship between God and Moses, and Moses and Aaron, is remarkable, and shows that God's words can indeed be found in the mouths of Moses and Aaron.

This point is reinforced in the account of God's call of Jeremiah: 'Now I have put my words in your mouth' (Jer. 1:9),[19] as it is in the words of Acts 3:18 (my trans.): 'In this way God fulfilled what he had foretold through [the mouth of] all the prophets, that his Messiah would suffer', as also in Acts 15:7, when Peter said, 'God made a choice among you, that I should be the one [from whose mouth] the Gentiles would hear the message of the good news and become believers.' God's words fit human mouths. No wonder the widow of Zarephath said to the prophet Elijah, 'Now I know that you are a man of God, and that word of the LORD in your mouth is truth' (1 Kgs 17:24). As Calvin wrote: 'The word *goeth out of the mouth* of God in such a manner that it likewise "goeth out of the mouth" of men; for God does not speak openly from heaven, but employs men as his instruments, that by their agency he may make known his will.'[20]

God's words in our mouths
However, the great miracle of the Bible is not only that the word of God can be found in the mouths of his special messengers, prophets in the Old Testament and apostles in the New Testament, but also that the word can be found in the mouths of all of God's people. We read in Deuteronomy:

---

19. Adam, *Hearing*, pp. 73–79.
20. Calvin, *Commentaries*, 8, p. 170, on Isa. 55:11.

> Surely, this commandment that I am commanding you today is not too hard for
> you, nor is it too far away. It is not in heaven, that you should say, 'Who will go
> up to heaven for us, and get it for us so that we may hear it and observe it?' Neither
> is it beyond the sea, that you should say, 'Who will cross to the other side of
> the sea for us, and get it for us so that we may hear it and observe it?' No, the word
> is very near to you; it is in your mouth and in your heart for you to observe.
> (Deut. 30:11–14)

The word is 'in your mouth', because God called all his people to love him by
meditating on his words, and by speaking of them 'when you are at home and
when you are away, and when you lie down and when you rise' (Deut. 6:7). This
word is of course what God has revealed, for 'The secret things belong to the
LORD our God, but the revealed things belong to us and to our children for
ever, to observe all the words of this law' (Deut. 29:29).

The revealed word is 'in your heart for you to observe', because of God's
grace expressed in Deuteronomy 30:6 in terms of God's circumcision of the
hearts of his people. In the words of Paul Barker, 'Faithful obedience is possible because the word is near, that is in the heart, the heart circumcised by
God.'[21] As J. A. Thompson wrote, 'Even if there were secrets still to be
revealed, Israel could now enjoy life by loving God and by loyally obeying his
covenant.'[22]

The apostle Paul quoted these words from Deuteronomy 30, and applied
them to the immediacy of the gospel.

> But the righteousness that comes from faith says, 'Do not say in your heart, "Who
> will ascend into heaven?" ' (that is, to bring Christ down) 'or "Who will descend into
> the abyss?" ' (that is, to bring Christ up from the dead). But what does it say?

> 'The word is near you,
>   on your lips and in your heart'

> (that is, the word of faith that we proclaim); because if you confess with your lips that
> Jesus is Lord and believe in your heart that God raised him from the dead, you will be
> saved. (Rom. 10:6–9)

God's word of the gospel must be in our mouths if we are to 'confess with
(our) lips that Jesus is Lord'. For 'faith comes by hearing, and hearing comes

God - Father at interpersonal.

---

21. Barker, *God*, p. 92.
22. Thompson, *Deuteronomy*, p. 286.

through the word of Christ' (Rom. 10:17 [my trans]). As James Dunn observed, in Paul's mind Deuteronomy 30 'points to that deeper level of obedience now called for in the gospel's call to faith'.[23]

God's words should be found in our mouths as a witness to our faith in Christ, to encourage other believers, and to bring others to know Christ. In Peter's words, 'Whoever speaks must do so as one speaking the very words of God' (1 Pet. 4:11).

We too can speak God's human words.

Jesus said, 'My words will not pass away' (Mark 13:31)

The significance of Jesus' words

John 6 begins with the miracle of the feeding of the five thousand, but it was the teaching that Jesus gave after this miracle which was hard to understand. Jesus compared himself with the manna that God gave to his people in the desert in the time of Moses, and claimed, 'I am the living bread that came down from heaven. Whoever eats of this bread will live for ever; and the bread that I will give for the life of the world is my flesh' (6:51). The Jews wondered how he would be able to give them his flesh to eat (6:52). In reply Jesus told them: 'Very truly, I tell you, unless you eat the flesh of the Son of Man and drink his blood, you have no life in you' (6:53). It is no surprise that many of his disciples said that this teaching was difficult, and wondered who could accept it (6:60). Jesus replied, 'The words that I have spoken to you are spirit and life' (6:63). It was possible to eat the bread that Jesus had provided, and miss the meaning found in his words.

To understand the sign meant to listen to Jesus' words, for it was by his words that he explained who he was ('the bread of life', 6:48), the incarnation ('the living bread that came down from heaven', 6:51), the cross ('the bread that I will give for the life of the world is my flesh', 6:51), the absolute necessity of eating his flesh and drinking his blood (6:52–58), and fact that 'no one can come to me unless it is granted by the Father' (6:65). So it is by hearing, receiving, and believing the words of Jesus that people can truly eat his flesh and drink his blood.

No wonder that at this point many of his disciples 'turned back and no longer went about with him' (6:66). Jesus then asked the twelve if they too wished to go away. Peter replied: 'Lord, to whom can we go? You have the words of eternal life' (6:68).

---

23. Dunn, *Romans*, p. 615.

This shows the vital role of Jesus' teaching, his words, in his incarnate revelation.

If nothing else, Jesus was a teacher, a rabbi; and by believing the words that he taught, people came to know that he was much more than a rabbi. By Jesus' words they knew the meaning of his signs, and that he truly was the Word made flesh. Now God's words came immediately through the vocal cords of his Son.

Incarnation and inspiration

What should we make of Jesus' claim to speak divine words? God's capacity to accommodate to human language is shown too in the incarnation of Christ. If God is not able to use human words, or if human words are too fragile to communicate divine meaning, then we must regard Jesus' teaching and communication as merely human, and his claim to communicate divine words as a delusion.

To deny that God can use human language to communicate divine truth is to imperil the incarnation of God in Christ. If God can be incarnate, surely God's thoughts can be expressed in human words. This is an argument from the greater (incarnation) to the lesser (inspiration). If God cannot use human words, then the incarnation of God's Son, Jesus Christ, seems less likely. 'Indeed the words of God expressed in the words of men, are in every way like human language, just as the Word of the eternal Father, when he took on himself the flesh of human weakness, became like men.'[24]

There are also some useful similarities between our view of incarnation and our view of inspiration. When God uses human words, they are both fully divine and fully human, not merely appearing to be one or the other, and not a mixture which ends up being neither divine nor human.

Furthermore, incarnation and inspiration are linked in that when the incarnate Lord Jesus spoke in human words, the divine and human Lord spoke words that were, like the Scriptures, divine in origin and human in form.

Jesus' teaching about the Scriptures

Furthermore, followers of Christ accept the Scriptures as God's words because we follow his teaching.

Jesus did not come to displace the message of the Old Testament, to make it redundant, or to replace it, but to fulfil it. This fulfilment meant that he achieved what was promised in the Old Testament, and shaped his life and

---

24. Flannery, *Vatican Council*, p. 758.

ministry and actions to show the full meaning of its message. So he claimed that he himself was the fulfilment of the Old Testament – that, for example, Moses 'wrote about me' (John 5:46).

However, this fulfilment did not mean that his disciples could now disregard it or think of it as a merely historical document. It remained a living text for Jesus and his disciples. We see this clearly in the account of the temptation of Jesus in the wilderness. When tempted by the devil to make stones into bread to feed his hunger, he answered, as we have seen: 'It is written, "One does not live by bread alone, but by every word that comes from the mouth of God"' (Matt. 4:4).

He showed his continued dependence on the Old Testament by his use of the quotation from Deuteronomy 8:3 rather than by using his own words in reply, emphasizing that dependence by introducing that quotation with the words 'It is written', and by stating a truth which is generally true for all believers. The words of the quotation make it clear that the words that come from God's mouth include words from the Old Testament. The context of these words in Deuteronomy is also illuminating, because there Moses explains that this message was the point of the gift of manna (Deut. 8:2).

Jesus stated that Scripture cannot fail: 'and the scripture cannot be annulled' (John 10:35). Furthermore, he taught that he himself was the fulfilment of Scripture: 'Today this scripture has been fulfilled in your hearing' (Luke 4:21), and that he was consciously doing what was written of him in the Old Testament: 'Everything that is written about the Son of Man by the prophets will be accomplished' (Luke 18:31). He said of the Law of the Old Testament: 'For truly I tell you, until heaven and earth pass away, not one letter, not one stroke of a letter, will pass from the law until all is accomplished' (Matt. 5:18). He told the Sadducees: 'You are wrong, because you know neither the scriptures nor the power of God', and 'Have you not read what was said to you by God . . . ?' (Matt. 22:29, 31). He quoted Old Testament narrative as God's words, even though in the narrative God was not identified as the speaker (Matt. 19:4–5).

Jesus also taught his disciples to follow his own words and teaching: 'Everyone then who hears these words of mine and acts on them will be like a man who built his house on rock' (Matt. 7:24). He taught the permanency of his own teaching: 'Heaven and earth will pass away, but my words will not pass away' (Matt. 24:35). He warned of the danger for those who are embarrassed by his words: 'Those who are ashamed of me and of my words in this adulterous and sinful generation, of them will the Son of Man also be ashamed when he comes in the glory of his Father with the holy angels' (Mark 8:38). And he called his disciples his friends: 'I have called you friends, because I have made known to you everything that I have heard from my Father' (John 15:15).

He sent the Holy Spirit of truth, who would teach the disciples and guide them into all the truth (John 14:26; 16:13–14). The words that Jesus spoke to the disciples were words that he had received from the Father (17:8); he believed that the Father's word 'is truth' (17:17), and promised that the Holy Spirit would tell the disciples what he heard from the Father and the Son (16:13–15). His apostles were his teachers in the early church (1 Cor. 15:1–11; 7:40; Eph. 2:22; 3:5–6; 2 Pet. 3:2; Jude 17). No wonder that the first converts on the day of Pentecost devoted themselves to 'the apostles' teaching' (Acts 2:42).

Receiving God's words

Receiving from God

As created beings, we receive everything from the hand of God, our creator and the creator of everything. As Paul wrote, 'What do you have that you did not receive?' (1 Cor. 4:7). It is God's great joy to give, and our great joy to receive. As we read of God's people in Psalm 24, 'They will receive blessing from the LORD, and vindication from the God of their salvation' (24:5). This means that we must learn to receive whatever God gives: 'Shall we receive the good at the hand of God, and not receive the bad?' (Job 2:10).

As we receive the blessings of creation, so too we are called to receive the blessings of salvation. In Jesus' words, 'Truly I tell you, whoever does not receive the kingdom of God as a little child will never enter it' (Luke 18:17). And fundamental to receiving the blessings of salvation is receiving and welcoming the Lord Jesus Christ. He is the true light, and we must not refuse him, but receive him, and in receiving him, receive abundant grace. 'The true light, which enlightens everyone, was coming into the world . . . He came to what was his own, and his own people did not accept him. But to all who received him, who believed in his name, he gave power to become children of God . . . From his fullness we have all received, grace upon grace' (John 1:9, 11–12, 16).

No wonder Jesus encouraged his disciples to ask, search, and find: 'For everyone who asks receives, and everyone who searches finds, and for everyone who knocks, the door will be opened' (Matt. 7:8).

Receiving Christ's messengers and message

To receive and welcome Christ is to receive and welcome God: 'whoever receives me receives the one who sent me' (Matt. 10:40). So also to refuse to receive Christ is to reject the one who sent him: 'whoever rejects me rejects the one who sent me' (Luke 10:16). As Christ has been sent by God, so too Christ's disciples and apostles have been sent by Christ, so that Christ said to his disciples: 'Whoever receives you receives me, and whoever receives me receives the one who sent me' (Matt. 10:40).[25] On the other hand, there is great danger in rejecting Christ's messengers and their message: 'If anyone will not welcome you or listen to your words, shake off the dust from your feet as you leave that house or town' (Matt. 10:14). For to listen and receive the message of the disciple of Christ is to listen to and receive the message of Christ. To refuse the messenger is to refuse the one who sent the messenger, and so to refuse God. As Jesus' disciples passed on the message that he told them, receiving the words of Christ's disciples during his life on earth was equivalent to listening to the words of Christ.

This was also true after the resurrection of Christ. Jesus told the disciples to make disciples of all nations, and to teach them 'everything that I have commanded you' (Matt. 28:16–20). So the apostles of the risen Christ have the same authority, and their words have the same significance. To receive the message is to receive the one who sent messenger and message. Paul, that late addition to the apostles, claimed that 'the gospel that was proclaimed by me is not of human origin; for I did not receive it from a human source, nor was I taught it, but I received it through a revelation of Jesus Christ' (Gal. 1:11–12). As Martin Foord has argued, we should add to the apostles their fellow workers, those who jointly wrote some of the letters, and the prophets of the New Testament church.[26]

The apostles were called to pass on what they had received, and people must in turn receive their message. If they do this, they will have fellowship with Jesus Christ, and with the Father who sent him.

> We declare to you what was from the beginning, what we have heard, what we have seen with our eyes, what we have looked at and touched with our hands, concerning the word of life – this life was revealed, and we have seen it and testify to it, and declare to you the eternal life that was with the Father and was revealed to us – we declare to you what we have seen and heard so that you also may have fellowship with us; and truly our fellowship is with the Father and with his Son Jesus Christ. (1 John 1:1–3)

It is by handing on this gospel, as an apostle of the risen Christ, that Paul has served both Christ and his church. Paul wrote to the church at Thessalonica

---

25. These three quotations are my translations.
26. Foord, *Weakest Link*, p. 11.

that they had received both the word and those who brought the word: 'you received the word with joy inspired by the Holy Spirit . . . For the people of those regions report about us what kind of welcome we had among you' (1 Thess. 1:6, 9).

Paul was thankful for their conversion to Christ, that they had received message and messenger, and had recognized the message for what it was, God's powerful word. 'When you received the word of God that you heard from us, you accepted it not as a human word but as what it really is, God's word, which is also at work in you believers' (1 Thess. 2:13).

And this word passed on, this tradition, brings about not only conversion, but also Christian maturity. Paul later called the believers at Thessalonica to live according to his teaching: 'Now we command you, beloved, in the name of our Lord Jesus Christ, to keep away from believers who are living in idleness and not according to the tradition that they received from us' (2 Thess. 3:6).

The authority of the apostles came not only from the fact that they were apostles of the risen Christ, but also from the fact that their message was authenticated from the Old Testament: 'I stand here, testifying to both small and great, saying nothing but what the prophets and Moses said would take place: that the Messiah must suffer, and that, by being the first to rise from the dead, he would proclaim light both to our people and to the Gentiles' (Acts 26:22–23).

Just as Jesus fulfilled the Old Testament, so his apostles fulfilled the Old Testament as they obeyed him. Their words had a double authentication.

Receiving God's words is of course not just a matter of understanding them, or using them as convenient daily mottoes. It is a matter of mind, heart, and life. It involves understanding, submission, and integration. It requires patience, energy, and love. It means reading to understand, reading to make the words part of ourselves, and also letting the words read us. As we will see from Psalm 1, it means delighting in the word of God, and then meditating on it day and night. Receiving God's words is nothing less than receiving God.[27]

What is it like to receive God's words?

Psalm 119 gives us a rich and broad view of receiving God's words.[28]

To receive God's words is to delight in them, and know God's goodness in them: 'I delight in the way of your decrees as much as in all riches' (verse 14);

---

27. Recent books that fill out what it means to receive God's words are Peterson, *This Book*, and Spriggs, *Feasting*.

28. Adam, *Hearing*, pp. 62–63.

'How sweet are your words to my taste, sweeter than honey to my mouth!' (103); 'Your word is a lamp to my feet and a light to my path' (105); 'The sum of your word is truth; and every one of your righteous ordinances endures for ever' (160).

To receive God's words is to ask for more understanding: 'Open my eyes, so that I may behold wondrous things out of your law' (18); 'Make me understand the way of your precepts, and I will meditate on your wondrous works' (27); 'Deal with your servant according to your steadfast love, and teach me your statutes' (124).

To receive God's words is to ask God to act on his promises: 'My eyes fail with watching for your promise; I ask, "When will you comfort me?"' (82); 'My soul clings to the dust; revive me according to your word' (25); 'I implore your favour with all my heart; be gracious to me according to your promise' (58); 'I am severely afflicted; give me life, O LORD, according to your word' (107).

To receive God's words is to trust God: 'Let your steadfast love become my comfort according to your promise to your servant' (76); 'My soul languishes for your salvation; I hope in your word' (81); 'The LORD exists for ever; your word is firmly fixed in heaven' (89); 'You are my hiding-place and my shield; I hope in your word' (114).

Furthermore, as we would expect, there is great power in God's words. In Psalm 19 we read of the transformative power of God's word in human lives:

> The law of the LORD is perfect,
>   reviving the soul;
> the decrees of the LORD are sure,
>   making wise the simple;
> the precepts of the LORD are right,
>   rejoicing the heart;
> the commandment of the LORD is clear,
>   enlightening the eyes;
> the fear of the LORD is pure,
>   enduring for ever;
> the ordinances of the LORD are true
>   and righteous altogether.
> More to be desired are they than gold,
>   even much fine gold;
> sweeter also than honey,
>   and drippings of the honeycomb.
>   (19:7–10)

The result of the power of God's word, reviving, making wise, rejoicing the heart, enlightening the eyes, is that those words become more and more attractive, more and more desirable.

These ideas are expressed even more richly in the New Testament, where we learn that receiving God's promises means we share in the power and life of God.

> His divine power has given us everything needed for life and godliness, through the knowledge of him who called us by his own glory and goodness. Thus he has given us, through these things, his precious and very great promises, so that through them you may escape from the corruption that is in the world because of lust, and may become participants in the divine nature. (2 Pet. 1:3–4)

What are the qualities of God's words?

Modern discussions of the qualities of God's word usually focus on issues like authority, inerrancy, and infallibility. It is fascinating to see that these issues are of secondary interest in the Bible itself. They are consequences of more fundamental and important statements about God's words.

We have just read in Psalm 19 that God's words are perfect, right, and pure (19:7–9). Psalm 119 celebrates these qualities and more. We often find that God's words share the qualities of God, whose words they are. So God and his words are both sure and righteous: 'The LORD exists for ever; your word is firmly fixed in heaven' (verse 89), and, 'You are righteous, O LORD, and your judgements are right' (137). Furthermore, truthfulness and eternity are closely linked. What lasts is true: 'Your righteousness is an everlasting righteousness, and your law is the truth' (142), and 'The sum of your word is truth; and every one of your righteous ordinances endures for ever' (160). As Allan Harmon wrote, 'The totality of God's words (Hebrew, "the head of your words", i.e. the sum of them . . .) is absolutely sure, for all his words are trustworthy (verses 86, 138), true (verses 142, 151, 160) and eternal (verses 89, 111, 142, 144, 152).'[29]

For what is true is trustworthy and reliable, like the promises of God. 'Yet you are near, O LORD, and all your commandments are true' (verse 151). Not only are God's words eternal, right, righteous, and true, but they have a limitless perfection. 'I have seen a limit to all perfection, but your commandment is exceedingly broad' (96). As Wayne Grudem comments, 'God's written words are unlimited in their perfection; no other words can be assessed in that way.'[30]

---

29. Harmon, *Psalms*, p. 399.
30. Grudem, in Carson and Woodbridge, *Scripture*, p. 34.

These powerful themes are reinforced in the New Testament. Jesus said to the Father: 'Your word is truth' (John 17:17), and he claimed of his own teaching, 'Heaven and earth will pass away, but my words will not pass away' (Mark 13:31). Paul asserts that 'the law is holy, and the commandment is holy and just and good' (Rom. 7:12), and Peter wrote of 'the living and enduring word of God' (1 Pet.1:23).

We see in 2 Corinthians 4 a moving sequence of expressions that Paul used to describe God's words about Christ: 'God's word' (verse 2) is the same as 'the truth' (2), the same as 'our gospel' (3), the same as 'the gospel of the glory of Christ' (4), the same as 'the light of the knowledge of the glory of God in the face of Jesus Christ' (6), which is the same as 'this treasure' (7). In 2 Timothy Paul wrote: 'Guard the good treasure entrusted to you, with the help of the Holy Spirit' (1:14).

Jesus spoke of living by 'every word that comes from the mouth of God' (Matt. 4:4). Words that come from the mouth of God are likely to share his qualities. Words that are 'perfect', 'right', 'true', 'truth', 'eternal', are likely to be authoritative, reliable, and infallible. Words that are 'perfect', 'right', 'true', 'truth', 'eternal', 'a treasure', are unlikely to be imperfect, unrighteous, untrustworthy, temporary or worthless. Bishop Westcott described Hebrews' view of the Old Testament in words that we can apply to the New Testament as well: 'the words spoken by the prophet in his own person are treated as divine words', and 'the record is the voice of God; and as a necessary consequence the record is itself living'.[31]

This chapter has shown us that God is able to use human language. God made human language, and uses it, as we do, to create and build relationships. The covenant God is faithful to his covenant words and promises, and also promised a new covenant, to be fulfilled in Jesus Christ. We found that God's words are powerful in Old and New Testament alike, that they are effective and achieve God's gospel purpose. They are effective secondary causes, God's instruments. We also found that God's human words can also be found in the mouths of prophets, apostles, and ordinary members of God's people in both Old and New Testament times. Furthermore, the great miracle of the incarnation supports the possibility of the lesser miracle of God using human words. We also found that Jesus Christ's claim to speak God's words supports the idea that God can use human language, and that he authenticated his own words and other words of the Bible. Finally we saw that we receive many gifts

---

31. Westcott, *Hebrews*, pp. 474–475.

from God, including the gifts of creation and salvation, and that we receive
God's words through his representatives: his prophets, his Son, and his apos-
tles.[32] We have seen from the Bible some of the richness found in receiving
God's words, and also the qualities of God's words.

Wolf-Dieter Zimmerman was a student at the Confessing Church seminary
run by Dietrich Bonhoeffer at Finkenwalde in the 1930s. He described the
impact of the practice of meditating on the Bible: 'We had not known what it
means that the word preaches itself . . . Only through long times of waiting
and quiet did we learn that the text "may be our master".'[33]

---

32. Adam, *Speaking*, pp. 89–91.
33. Zimmerman and Smith, *Bonhoeffer*, p. 108.

Does this book look implications/applications to be helpful for church?

Addressing church or academia?

'Fellow-heirs, members of the same body, and sharers in the promise in Christ Jesus' (Eph. 3:6)

One people of God

The Bible makes sense as the accumulated and long-term words of God. These words have been addressed to the one people of God in different ages, written down and brought together for all the people of God in the last days. This unity of God's people is not just a contemporary unity at any one time, but also a historical unity, a common family history, and a common gospel hope.

So there are not two branches of the people of God, the Old Testament people of God and the New Testament people of God. I can remember thinking when I first became a Christian that God had Plan A with the Jews in the Old Testament, and that that plan failed, and so he then brought in Plan B in the New Testament, this time with the Christians!

It didn't take much Bible reading to realize that this was not the case! For I found Christians described as those who 'belong to Christ' and so are 'Abraham's offspring' (Gal. 3:29), 'the Israel of God' (Gal. 6:16). Paul claimed that Old Testament believers 'drank from the spiritual rock that followed them, and the rock was Christ' (1 Cor. 10:4). Peter said to his Jewish hearers: 'You are the descendants of the prophets and of the covenant that God gave to your ancestors, saying to Abraham, "And in your descendants all the families of the earth shall be blessed"' (Acts 3:25).

The people of God in the Old Testament also lived 'by faith', as did Christian believers, and served as useful examples to us (Heb. 11). Christ was described in Old Testament terms, as a 'paschal lamb . . . sacrificed' for us (1 Cor. 5:7), as 'the Lion of the tribe of Judah' (Rev. 5:5), and as 'a great priest' (Heb. 10:21), who brought cleansing and forgiveness through his blood, shed on the cross (Heb. 9:14). So God has one people, and Gentiles have become 'fellow-heirs, members of the same body, and sharers in the promise in Christ Jesus through the gospel' (Eph. 3:6).

It then makes sense that Christian believers should inherit the Scriptures of the Old Testament. 'These things happened to them to serve as an example, and they were written down to instruct us, on whom the ends of the ages have come' (1 Cor. 10:11).

Jesus showed the unity of God's people, and their corporate habits of mind, in these words:

> 'Woe to you, scribes and Pharisees, hypocrites! For you build the tombs of the prophets and decorate the graves of the righteous, and you say, "If we had lived in the days of our ancestors, we would not have taken part with them in shedding the blood of the prophets." Thus you testify against yourselves that you are descendants of those who murdered the prophets. Fill up, then, the measure of your ancestors . . . Therefore I send you prophets, sages, and scribes, some of whom you will kill and crucify, and some you will flog in your synagogues and pursue from town to town, so that upon you may come all the righteous blood shed on earth, from the blood of righteous Abel to the blood of Zechariah son of Barachiah, whom you murdered between the sanctuary and the altar. Truly I tell you, all this will come upon this generation.' (Matt. 23:29–32, 34–36)

Ephesians 1 is a great celebration of the unity of God's people. It begins with God's blessings on his Old Testament people given in Christ, in itself an amazing claim about the unity of God's people. 'Blessed be the God and Father of our Lord Jesus Christ, who has blessed us in Christ with every spiritual blessing in the heavenly places, just as he chose us in Christ before the foundation of the world to be holy and blameless before him in love' (1:3–4). Then Paul describes the way in which God extended this blessing to all the nations: 'In him you also, when you had heard the word of truth, the gospel of your salvation, and had believed in him, were marked with the seal of the promised Holy Spirit; this is the pledge of our inheritance towards redemption as God's own people, to the praise of his glory' (1:13–14).

As Chris Wright has shown, the mission of God is the basis of the Bible, and the Bible is the product of God's mission to the world.[1] The Bible is God's message to the world, as well as to those whom he has added to his people.

One book for one people

What evidence is there that God intended some of his verbal revelation not just for those to whom it was originally spoken or written, but also to subsequent generations of the people of God?

God's earliest words include promises about the future, a future beyond the lifetime of those to whom the words were originally addressed. Here is God's promise to Abram: 'Now the LORD said to Abram . . . "I will make of you a great nation, and I will bless you, and make your name great, so that you will be a blessing. I will bless those who bless you, and the one who curses you I will curse; and in you all the families of the earth shall be blessed"' (Gen. 12:1–3).

We hear the words of Peter, 'The promise is for you and for your children, and for all who are far away' (Acts 2:39). We read in John's Gospel that Jesus did many other signs, but, in addition to the Scriptures of the Old Testament, 'these are written so that you may come to believe that Jesus is the Messiah, the Son of God' (John 20:30–31; see also 21:24–25). This record was written not for those who were there when Jesus performed these signs, but for others. Here we see not only the selection of what is written, but also the purpose of that selection.

Are all God's words recorded in the Bible? Why are some recorded and others not? God spoke many words that are not recorded in the Bible, through his prophets, through his Son, and through his apostles. Those words are as surely God's words as are his words in the Bible, but they had a limited purpose, being addressed to those people who originally heard them, and not to later generations. The words of God recorded in the Bible were addressed to the original hearers, but were also preserved by God for future generations of God's people.

Jesus said of the Old Testament Scriptures, 'they witness to me', and, 'If you believed Moses, you would believe me, for he wrote about me' (John 5:39 [my trans.], 46).

We cannot understand the New Testament without the Old Testament. What can we make of Christ as 'the last Adam', without knowing something of 'the first man, Adam' (1 Cor. 15:45)? Why did Moses and Elijah appear with

---

1. C. Wright, *Mission*, pp. 48–51.

Christ at the transfiguration (Mark 9:4)? What did Jesus mean by 'my blood of the covenant' (Mark 14:24)? Why did John write that the saints 'sing the song of Moses, the servant of God, and the song of the Lamb' (Rev. 15:3)? These are not just remote literary references, but depend for their meaning on a profound theology of the unity of God's people. Nor can we understand the Old Testament without the New, as we shall see.

In the remarkable words of John Donne, poet, and Dean of St Paul's Cathedral in London in the seventeenth century: 'The Scriptures are God's voice, the church is his echo.'[2] For as God speaks to the church by the Scriptures, so those same Scriptures should echo in the life, worship, teaching, and proclamation of God's people. And just as God's great acts of salvation are complete, so his verbal revelation that accompanied that salvation is also complete.

The Bible is the record of the witness of the people of God to the revelation of God, and it is made up of parts of that revelation. As the works of God (salvation history) are complete until the return of Christ, so the cumulative words of God (biblical theology) are also complete. For God uses the Scriptures to produce the church. In the words of David Jackman, 'The Spirit of God still uses the Word of God [that is, the Bible] to produce the people of God.'[3]

Receiving or refusing God's words

Receive or refuse

The great invitation of God in the Old Testament is: 'Hear, O Israel . . . Keep these words that I am commanding you today in your heart' (Deut. 6:4, 6).[4] The great tragedy of the Old Testament is the refusal of God's people to hear and receive the words of God. In refusing God's words, they are refusing God.

> But they refused to listen, and turned a stubborn shoulder, and stopped their ears in order not to hear. They made their hearts adamant in order not to hear the law and the words that the LORD of hosts had sent by his spirit through the former prophets . . . Just as, when I called, they would not hear, so, when they called, I would not hear, says the LORD of hosts. (Zech. 7:11–13)

---

2. Donne, *Sermons*, 6, p. 223, modernized.

3. Jackman, *I Believe*, p. xiii.

4. See Adam, *Hearing*, pp. 52–56.

For Moses had accepted God's words of revelation: 'I went up the mountain to receive the stone tablets, the tablets of the covenant that the LORD made with you' (Deut. 9:9). However, there were many signs that God's people refused to receive God's words:

> The LORD, the God of their ancestors, sent persistently to them by his messengers . . . but they kept mocking the messengers of God, despising his words, and scoffing at his prophets, until the wrath of the LORD against his people became so great that there was no remedy. (2 Chr. 36:15–16)

Jesus warned his hearers that if they refused to receive Moses' witness to him, then Moses himself would be their accuser (John 5:45–46); and if they refused to receive his own words, then they would be judged by those words (John 12:48).

The king who received, and the king who refused

We have in the Old Testament two remarkable stories about receiving and refusing God's words. These are the stories of two kings of Judah, Josiah and his son Jehoiakim.

The first is King Josiah, who received the written words of God in the book of the covenant. We read in 2 Chronicles 34 of Josiah's plan to restore the temple, which resulted in the discovery of the book of the covenant. Josiah's response was to read the book, to fear the consequences of not obeying the words of the book, to read the book publicly to God's people, and to make a public covenant to perform the words written in the book.

> The king went up to the house of the LORD, with all the people of Judah, the inhabitants of Jerusalem, the priests and the Levites, all the people both great and small; he read in their hearing all the words of the book of the covenant that had been found in the house of the LORD. The king stood in his place and made a covenant before the LORD, to follow the LORD, keeping his commandments, his decrees, and his statutes, with all his heart and all his soul, to perform the words of the covenant that were written in this book. Then he made all who were present in Jerusalem and in Benjamin pledge themselves to it. And the inhabitants of Jerusalem acted according to the covenant of God, the God of their ancestors. (2 Chr. 34:30–32)

What a remarkable story of a king who read and received the words of God written down for his people so many years before! How productive for him and his people when he received those words of God! How moving to read of the powerful effects of God's words written for his people!

The second story is of his son Jehoiakim, whose response to the written word of God was very different. King Jehoiakim received the scroll on which were written the words of the prophet Jeremiah, but burned it, as a way of refusing God's words.

> Now the king was sitting in his winter apartment (it was the ninth month), and there was a fire burning in the brazier before him. As Jehudi read three or four columns, the king would cut them off with a penknife and throw them into the fire in the brazier, until the entire scroll was consumed in the fire that was in the brazier. (Jer. 36:22–23)

However, though the King refused to receive the words of God, and had them burned, Jeremiah dictated another scroll with the same words and more. These words were fulfilled in the coming of the Babylonians to destroy Jerusalem and take God's people into exile.

> Then Jeremiah took another scroll and gave it to the secretary Baruch son of Neriah, who wrote on it at Jeremiah's dictation all the words of the scroll that King Jehoiakim of Judah had burned in the fire; and many similar words were added to them. (Jer. 36:32)[5]

So too, those who do not accept Jesus' words will be judged by those words. 'The one who rejects me and does not receive my word has a judge; on the last day the word that I have spoken will serve as judge . . . What I speak, therefore, I speak just as the Father has told me' (John 12:48, 50).

'Written down to instruct us, on whom the ends of the ages have come' (1 Corinthians 10:11)

The words that God intends for future generations were 'inscripturated' or written down. So the Bible is a cumulative revelation, each part illuminates each other part, and there is also a development and growth in revelation, as promise finds its fulfilment in Jesus Christ. So 'Moses wrote down all the words of the LORD', 'Moses wrote down this law' (Exod. 24:4; Deut. 31:9), and Jeremiah was told, 'Take a scroll and write on it all the words that I have spoken to you' (Jer. 36:2). Habakkuk was instructed, 'Write the vision' (Hab. 2:2). Daniel read in Jeremiah the length of the exile in Babylon (Dan. 9:2). John was told, 'Write in a book what you see' (Rev. 1:11).

---

5. Adam, *Hearing*, pp. 73–79.

Not all words of God are preserved for future generations, but the gathered and lasting words of God interpret the past, present, and future acts of God. God uses these words to relate to his people, to reveal who he is, who they are, and how he wants them to live. God's enduring written teaching comes in different stages of revelation from promise to fulfilment, but with the final message of the gospel fulfilled in Jesus Christ.[6] The long-term and accumulated teaching of God not only helps God's people to know God in Christ, but also ensures the unity and coherence of the people of God in every age.[7]

It is so remarkable when the Old Testament language is used theologically in the New Testament without any reference to its context, for this means that the author assumes that he and his readers share a common world of meaning. So when we read of Jesus in Revelation, we are meant to connect with the Old Testament allusions: 'Do not be afraid; I am the first and the last, and the living one. I was dead, and see, I am alive for ever and ever; and I have the keys of Death and of Hades' (1:17).

By the way, when we are reading the historical narrative parts of the Bible, like the Gospels, it is worth concentrating on the purpose of the writer. It is often more useful to ask, 'What was Luke trying to teach Theophilus?' rather than trying to put ourselves in the sandals of the disciples: to treat ourselves as readers, rather than hearers.[8]

The Bible is the sufficient collection of God's enduring words, God's Spirit-words about his Son.[9] As Paul wrote, 'These things happened to them to serve as an example, and they were written down to instruct us, on whom the ends of the ages have come' (1 Cor. 10:11). Paul explained the same truth to Felix:

---

6. F. F. Bruce describes the progress of revelation: '[The author of Hebrews] is thinking . . . of that special revelation which He has given in two stages: first, to the fathers through the prophets, and finally in His Son. These two stages of divine revelation correspond to the Old and New Testaments respectively. Divine revelation is thus seen to be progressive – but the progression is not from the less true to the more true, from the less worthy to the more worthy, or from the less mature to the more mature . . . the progression is one from promise to fulfilment.' Bruce, *Hebrews*, p. 2.

7. John Macquarrie describes this accumulated message contained in and communicated by the Bible as the 'primordial revelation' of God: Macquarrie, *Principles*, pp. 7–8 .

8. This is because Luke will have made the connection for us from what happened originally, and what he wrote for Theophilus.

9. Adam, 'The Preacher'.

'But this I admit to you, that according to the Way, which they call a sect, I worship the God of our ancestors, believing everything laid down according to the law or written in the prophets' (Acts 24:14).

'Scripture' was used of the Old Testament writings, as we have seen. It is also used of a written gospel tradition of Jesus' words in 1 Timothy 5:18 ('the scripture says . . . "The labourer deserves to be paid"' [cf. Luke 10:7]), and of Paul's writings in 2 Peter 3:16, where Paul's letters are like 'the other scriptures'.

The ways in which the Bible writers refer to the Old Testament offer ample evidence that they believed in not only its divine origin, but also its ongoing relevance. In Peter's words: 'It was revealed to them that they were serving not themselves but you, in regard to the things that have now been announced to you through those who brought you good news by the Holy Spirit sent from heaven – things into which angels long to look!' (1 Pet. 1:12).

'He received living oracles to give to us' (Acts 7:38)

There is a common pattern of gathered and enduring verbal written revelation in every part of the Bible, which comes together to form the Bible.

The whole Bible is a working out of the promises to Abraham, Isaac and Jacob, as Abraham's descendants form the people of God, believe God's promises, and live in God's promised land. We find, too, that these promises are fulfilled in Jesus Christ, and so Abraham's descendants are those who live by faith in Jesus Christ. The history and promises of God form a verbal revelation which remains relevant all through the Bible.

The law of Moses is part of this gathered revelation, whether we think more narrowly of the verbal revelation and instructions given at Sinai, or of the whole of the books Genesis to Deuteronomy. We find the law of Moses celebrated in the Psalms, applied in the Prophets, and fulfilled in the New Testament. Within the Wisdom books we also find an accumulating revelation, as wisdom was passed on from generation to generation by wise men and wise women.

The prophets of the Old Testament not only applied the law of Moses, but also built up a tradition of prophetic words which continue to address God's people. The priests of the Old Testament taught and applied the requirements of the law to God's people. The historical books show how the Law, the Prophets, and Wisdom were sometimes put into practice and sometimes neglected by God's people.[10]

---

10. For example, see Neh. 8; Dan. 9:2; Hag. 2:10–19; Zech. 1:4.

The gathered verbal revelation we call the Old Testament is fundamental to the New Testament. As the Old Testament ends with only partial resolution, and needs the New Testament for its fulfilment, so too the New Testament cannot stand alone without the foundation of the Old Testament. The creation, fall, and flood are fundamental to the New Testament as well as the Old, and creation is a promise which will reach complete fulfilment only in the New Creation at the return of Christ.[11]

The same pattern continues in the New Testament. Jesus' teaching grew out of the Old Testament, fulfilled it, and also provided accumulated words for the future. The writings of the apostles and their followers show how the hopes and expectations of the Old Testament were fulfilled in Christ, and also provide a definitive revelation for the future post-apostolic people of God. The task of the evangelists, teachers and preachers of the New Testament churches is to use the Holy Scriptures to explain the gospel to bring people to faith in Jesus Christ, to build up the church, to edify God's people, and to teach those people to encourage each other and to speak to others about the Lord Jesus.

Henry Bullinger, the sixteenth-century Swiss Reformer, summarized this truth in these words:

> The word of God is the speech of God, that is to say, the revealing of his good will to mankind, which from the beginning, one while by his own mouth, and another while by the speech of angels, he did open to those first, ancient, and most holy fathers; who again by tradition did faithfully deliver it to their posterity. Here are to be remembered those great lights of the world, Adam, Seth, Methuselah, Noe, Sem, Abraham, Isaac, Jacob, Amram, and his son Moses, who, at God's commandment, did in writing comprehend the history and traditions of the holy fathers, whereunto he joined the written law, and exposition of the law, together with a large and lightsome history of his own lifetime. After Moses, God gave to his church most excellent men, prophets and priests; who also, by word of mouth and writings, did deliver to their posterity that which they had learned of the Lord. After them came the only-begotten Son of God himself down from heaven into the world, and fulfilled all, whatsoever was found to be written of himself in the law and the prophets. The same also taught a most absolute mean how to live well and holily: he made the apostles his witnesses; which witnesses did afterwards first of all with a lively expressed voice preach all things which the Lord had taught them; and then, to the intent that they should not be corrupted, or clean taken out of man's remembrance,

---

11. See Dumbrell, *Creation*.

they did commit it to writing: so that now we have from the fathers, the prophets, and apostles, the word of God as it was preached and written.[12]

So we have in the Bible the accumulated verbal revelation of God from these different stages in salvation history. These are the 'Holy Scriptures' of the Old and New Testaments, the Holy Scriptures of the one people of God. As Paul wrote: 'For whatever was written in former days was written for our instruction, so that . . . by the encouragement of the scriptures we might have hope' (Rom. 15:4).

God's people and God's holy writings (Rom. 1:2)

The Bible writers were members of the people of God; so was the Bible then a product of God's people, or does God use the Bible itself to create, sustain, and correct his people, and bring them to maturity in Christ? Is the Bible 'the book that came from the people', or is the church 'the people that came from the book'?

The evidence is that the Bible documents were God's way of correcting and training his people. In Ezekiel 34 God's words are against the leaders or shepherds of God's flock, in the Gospels the disciples are usually slow to learn, and in the epistles churches are constantly being corrected. We find a constant picture in the Bible that the people of God naturally resist God's words, and follow false prophets and teachers. Again and again the words of God come to correct and reform his people. So although these words of God to his people come through members of the church, such as prophets and apostles, their authority does not come from the church but directly from God. The church has not made up the Bible, but recognized God's authority and truth in the Bible.

However, we know that the church finally decided which Scriptures or writings would be the Holy Scriptures, and be accepted into the 'canon'. This occurred in two stages, first the recognition of the Old Testament canon, then the New Testament canon.[13]

---

12. Bullinger, *Decades*, pp. 55–56.

13. The Old Testament canon was effectively finalized by the first century, and the New Testament canon in AD 367 (East) and 397 (West). In both cases this was recognition of the books that were widely accepted. See Bruce, *Canon*; Jackman, *I Believe*, pp. 75–87; and Foord, *Weakest Link?*

The words of God in the Bible correct and build up the people of God. Furthermore, God uses his Spirit-given words to bring about new birth, as we shall see in James and 1 Peter below, and so creates the people of God by his words. In Luther's words: 'It is not God's word just because the church speaks it; rather, the church comes into being because God's Word is spoken. The church does not constitute the Word, but is constituted by the Word.'[14]

As P. T. Forsyth wrote: 'For the books of the Bible were given *to* the Church, more than *by* it, and descended on it rather than rose from it. The canon of the Bible arose from the Church, but not its contents.'[15]

We need to explain the Bible in theological terms, not just sociological terms, just as we need to describe the church in theological terms, not just as a sociological phenomenon.[16]

However, it is also true that the church has greater value than the Bible, for the Bible is a means to achieve an end, and that end or purpose is the creation of God's church. The church is composed of people, who are made in God's image. The Bible contains and conveys God's powerful words. We are made in God's image, and are being transformed into the image of the Lord Jesus.

Paul points to the ironic relationship between God's people and God's words: 'Because the residents of Jerusalem and their leaders did not recognize him or understand the words of the prophets that are read every sabbath, they fulfilled those words by condemning him' (Acts 13:27).

Francis Turretin clarified the relationship between church and Bible. He explained why we trust the Bible: 'I do so on account of the Scriptures itself', because 'the Holy Spirit produces that belief in me', and 'through the church which God uses in delivering the Scriptures to me'.[17]

What responsibilities does the church have for the Scriptures? To read, teach, remind, explain, interpret, practise, pray, apply to the life of the church, explain to those who are not yet believers, and translate into new languages, that the word of God may bear fruit, that God's people may learn from his words, and trust him, that we may know God through Jesus Christ.

---

14. Quoted in M. D. Thompson, *Sure Ground*, p. 122.

15. Forsyth, *Jesus Christ*, pp. 140–141.

16. Webster, *Word and Church*, chapter 1.

17. Turretin, *Institutes*, 1, p. 87.

'Your word is truth' (John 17:17): a circular argument?

Church and Bible

We believe what we believe about the Bible because of the teaching of the Lord Jesus Christ. He authenticated Old and New Testament alike. We need to realize that great authority is recognized, not granted. The Reformer Martin Bucer used the example of testing whether a coin is valid currency. Recognizing that a coin is valid currency rather than a counterfeit does not mean granting it validity, but recognizing it as valid currency.[18]

If you ask me for the best book on clocks, then I will tell you of the book that seems to me to carry the greatest authority. I have not granted the book that authority, but recognized it. We test the value of an authoritative book by constantly testing it, using it, and putting it into practice. Either it will show its great value, or it will be shown to fail. We learn to trust a book as we learn to trust a person. In learning to trust words, we learn to trust the one who spoke or wrote the words.

In the Bible God speaks to us. We should accept God's words, and constantly put them into practice, as we believe, trust, obey, implement, pray, and use those words for others. We do not need to believe in the divine origin of Scripture to read it. However, as we read it, pray it, meditate on it, obey it and use it, we will find that it works: more than that, we will find ourselves addressed by God, and learning how to relate to God, and trusting him more and more. As we do this, we will come to trust the Bible more and more, and find that it is the word of God in the inspired words of God.[19]

So the process that the church undertook, and that we undertake, is to recognize the God-given status of the Bible, not authorize it. We receive a gift which has God's authority, we acknowledge and submit to it, rather than create or grant it authority.[20]

It is as if God appeared before us, and said, 'Trust me.' We could not find another greater authority to tell us to trust God, because no greater authority exists. In the words of Kenneth Cragg: 'Canonising does not confer authority on the text. It acknowledges authority already present.'[21]

Of course, if we have dismissed any possibility of any external authority, then we will have great difficulty with the Bible, and with God. Today the

---

18. Stephens, *Bucer*, p. 141.

19. See Helm, 'Faith Evidence', in Carson and Woodbridge, *Scripture and Truth*, pp. 301–320.

20. Webster, *Word and Church*, pp. 38–41.

21. Cragg, *Credentials*, p. 126.

authority of reason or experience rules with great power in many lives.[22] It is increasingly obvious that, as we were made to serve God, when we break free we do not find freedom, but become servants of alien lords.

The historian Edwin Hatch wrote about Philo, the Jewish author of Bible times, and described his view of God's verbal communication in words that we could also use of our own view. 'The good man trusts God . . . To trust God was to trust His veracity [truthfulness] . . . Belief in this sense is the highest form of conviction . . . It is the full assurance that certain things are so, because God has said that they are so.'[23]

In this book we are finding out what the Bible claims it is, including its divine origin through the Holy Spirit. We can then put that teaching into practice, and then find that it works, and that what God has said is trustworthy. In the words of Elizabeth Achtemeier, 'The Christian church is the community that expects to hear God speaking through its Scriptures.'[24]

Varied styles of God's authority

It is important to recognize the variety of styles of God's authority in Scripture. God's authority sometimes comes in the form of a direct command ('You shall have no other gods before me', Exod. 20:3); but also as information that will lead to a good choice ('These things occurred as examples for us', 1 Cor. 10:6); encouragement to observe consequences of actions ('Those who guard their mouths preserve their lives', Prov. 13:3); entreaty or appeal ('I appeal to you', Rom. 15:30); stories of the past ('Remember Lot's wife', Luke 17:32); parables ('A sower went out to sow', Mark 4:3); appeals not to demean ourselves ('Do you not know that your body is a temple of the Holy Spirit?', 1 Cor. 6:19); warnings ('Weep for yourselves and for your children', Luke 23:28); and promises of a better future within the will of God ('Let the believer who is lowly boast in being raised up', Jas 1:9). We find this variety in God's direct words, in the words of prophets and apostles, and in the ministry of Jesus Christ. It is important to take notice of this variety.[25] Otherwise we can tend to read one style of authority ('Do this because God told you to do it') into every part of the Bible, and so misrepresent God.[26] We might also

---

22. Jackman, *I Believe*, pp. 18–21.
23. Hatch, *Greek Ideas*, pp. 311–312.
24. Quoted in S. H. Webb, *Divine Voice*, p. 199.
25. Adam, *Hearing*, pp. 67–73.
26. Notice too the motivations used in Ps. 1 in chapter 8 below.

tend to adopt this one-style authority ourselves, which would mar God's image in us.[27]

Scripture says, God says

The argument so far in this book has been that God has spoken, and that some of God's words have been written down in the Scriptures. I now need to clarify that we can rightly describe the Bible as God's words not only when God is directly quoted in the Bible, but also when others are quoted, and when the Bible narrative is quoted. We will also see that ancient texts are referred to as God's contemporary words.[28]

David said, Moses said, God said

The Bible assumes and teaches that words spoken by humans can also be rightly described as spoken by God. In Mark 7, Jesus referred to the law as both the commandment of God and as what Moses said: 'Then he said to them, "You have a fine way of rejecting the commandment of God in order to keep your tradition! For Moses said, 'Honour your father and your mother.'"' (Mark 7:9–10).

The words of Isaiah were introduced in Matthew with the words, 'All this took place to fulfil what had been spoken by the Lord through the prophet' (Matt. 1:22). Zechariah said of God, 'He spoke through the mouth of his holy prophets from of old' (Luke 1:70; see also Acts 3:18, 21; Rom. 1:1–2; 1 Pet. 1:11; 2 Pet. 1:21).

Jesus and his apostles taught that David's words were the Spirit's words. So Jesus quoted from Psalm 110 with this introduction: 'David himself, by the Holy Spirit, declared . . .' (Mark 12:36); the apostles in Acts 4 prayed, 'Lord . . . you who said by the Holy Spirit through . . . David' (Acts 4:24–25); and Hebrews referred to Psalm 95 with these words: 'As the Holy Spirit says . . . saying through David . . .' (Heb. 3:7; 4:7).

Paul quoted from the Psalms with these words: '[God] has also said in another Psalm' (Acts 13:35), even though in Psalm 16 these were words addressed to God, rather than spoken by God. We see here that words of human speakers or writers are also regarded as words of God. In Romans 3 Paul asked the question, 'What advantage has the Jew?' His answer is that 'the

---

27. See also C. Wright, *Mission*, pp. 48–58.

28. See the detailed evidence for this section in Warfield, *Revelation*, chs. 5, 8, and 9, and Grudem, 'Scripture's Self-Attestation', pp. 19–59.

Jews were entrusted with the oracles of God' (Rom. 3:1–2), just as we read in Acts 7:38 that Moses 'received living oracles to give to us'.

The narrative is also God's word

When Jesus taught about divorce, he described God as both the one who made Adam and Eve and the one who spoke the narrative words of Genesis 2:24. 'Have you not read that the one who made them at the beginning "made them male and female," and said, "For this reason a man shall leave his father and mother and be joined to his wife, and the two shall become one flesh"?' (Matt. 19:4–5). Paul, speaking to Felix, said: 'According to the Way . . . I worship the God of our ancestors, believing everything laid down according to the law or written in the prophets' (Acts 24:14). Remember that 'the law' (of Moses) includes much more than commands: Genesis, Exodus, Numbers, and Deuteronomy contain a lot of narrative.

'He [God] said', 'Scripture says', 'it says', 'it is written'

It is fascinating to see how the New Testament quotes the Old Testament.

'God said' is used to refer, as we have seen, both to direct quotations from God and also to the rest of the Old Testament. God is frequently described as the speaker of the words of the Old Testament: 'For he [God] says' (2 Cor. 6:2), and, 'For he [God] says to Moses' (Rom. 9:15). (We know that the 'he' is God from the context.) See also Hebrews chapter 1, where words of the Old Testament are quoted as words of the Father to the Son: for example, 'But of the Son he [the Father] says, "Your throne, O God, is for ever and ever"' (Heb. 1:8).

'It is written' occurs over 100 times. The phrase assumes and asserts the authority of the words of the Old Testament Scriptures, for what 'is written' is the word of God. So we find: 'Jesus answered him, "It is written . . ."' (Luke 4:4); 'What is written must be fulfilled in me' (Luke 22:37 [my trans.]); 'As it is written, "The one who is righteous will live by faith"' (Rom. 1:17); 'For it is written in the book of Psalms . . .' (Acts 1:20); and 'For it is written, "You shall be holy"' (1 Pet. 1:16).

Similarly, 'Scripture', which means 'something written', or 'writing', is used over fifty times: 'But let the scriptures be fulfilled' (Mark 14:49); 'And the scripture cannot be annulled' (John 10:35); 'This was to fulfil what the scripture says' (John 19:24); and 'What does the scripture say?' (Rom. 4:3). We also find the phrases 'it is said' and 'it says', presumably as a way of saying 'God says' or 'Scripture says'.[29] So we read, 'For it is [or God] said . . .' (1 Cor. 6:16);

---

29. Warfield, *Revelation*, pp. 283–332.

'Therefore it is [or God] said . . .' (Eph. 4:8), and 'Therefore it [or God] says . . .' (Jas 4:6).

Sometimes a quotation is introduced with the words 'scripture says' when in fact the original speaker was God: 'The scripture . . . declared the gospel beforehand to Abraham' (Gal. 3:8), and 'The scripture says to Pharaoh' (Rom. 9:17). This second example is especially interesting, for here Paul uses the introductory words 'he [God] says to Moses' and 'the scripture says to Pharaoh' in close proximity (9:15, 17).

We find a great sequence of equivalent references to the Old Testament in Galatians 3: 'the scripture . . . declared' (verse 8); 'it is written' (10, 13); 'he [i.e. God] says' (16);[30] 'the law' (21); and 'the scripture' (22).

Similarly, the Old Testament is referred to in terms of its main section, as 'the law', 'the law and the prophets', or 'the prophets'. Jesus referred to 'the law' (or 'Moses') 'and the prophets' (Matt. 7:12; Luke 16:16, 29, 31; etc.). In Acts 3, Peter referred to 'all the prophets', 'his holy prophets', 'Moses', and 'all the prophets from Samuel on' (18, 21, 22, 24). In Acts 26:22, Paul referred to 'the prophets and Moses', and in Romans 1:2 he wrote of 'the gospel [God] promised beforehand through his prophets', and in 3:21 of the fact that 'the law and the prophets' testify to God's righteousness in Jesus Christ.

The words 'He [God] said', 'scripture says', 'it says', and 'it is written' refer to the same reality: that the words of the Old Testament are God's words. 'Scripture' is shorthand for 'God through Scripture', just as 'it is written' is shorthand for 'God caused these words to be written', etc.

What God said then he still says now

God, the author of the Old Testament, lives for ever, and so Old Testament words are God's contemporary speech. Jesus, referring to the words of God in Exodus, said, 'Have you not read what was said *to you* by God?' (Matt. 22:31), and speaking of the Old Testament, he says, 'the scriptures . . . *witness* to me' (John 5:39 [my trans.]). Similarly, in Acts 10:43, Peter says, 'All the prophets *testify* about him that everyone who believes in him receives forgiveness of sins through his name.' Paul asked, 'But what does the scripture *say*?' (Gal. 4:30); he wrote, 'Whatever the law *says*, it *speaks* to those under the law' (Rom. 3:19), and 'For the scripture *says* . . .' (1 Tim. 5:18). Hebrews often refers to the Old Testament as God's present words: 'As the Holy Spirit *says*' (Heb. 3:7, with Ps. 95:7); 'the Holy Spirit also *testifies* to us . . . *saying* . . .' (Heb. 10:15, with Jer. 31:33); and 'Have you forgotten the exhortation that *addresses* you as children?'

---

30. 'He' because of the reference to promise in verse 16.

(12:5, with Prov. 3:11–12). God lives and endures for ever, and therefore so do his words, whenever they were spoken. Peter wrote of 'the living and enduring word of God', and 'the word of the Lord [that] *endures* for ever' (1 Pet. 1:23, 25).

So we learn that all kinds of words in the Old Testament can rightly be described as God's words; that the Scriptures, what is written, are the words of God; and that just as God lives, so do his words, even though spoken long ago.

We will see in Part 6 that we can trust the authority of the Bible because of the example and teaching of the Lord Jesus Christ. For Christ authenticated the Bible as he taught about the Old Testament, referred to his own teaching, and promised the ministry of the Holy Spirit of truth and the ministry of his own apostles and their associates.[31]

We have seen in this chapter that a theology of the one people of God is fundamental to a theology of the Bible. For the Scriptures are the accumulated record of God's words to his people, recorded and preserved for his universal people. This unity of 'Scripture' also derives from the unity of the works and words of God in his providential care, his works of salvation history and his verbal revelation that makes up biblical theology. I include God's providential care here because parts of Scripture, such as the book of Proverbs and Psalm 104, are based on observing God's general care for his world, and seeing his wisdom in the basic structures and patterns of nature, animals, and people. The Bible is a self-referencing and self-interpreting collection of books. We found that the people of God did not create the books of Bible but recognized their God-given origin and authority. We also observed the varied ways in which the authority of God over his people is expressed in the Bible, and the ways in which each part of the Old Testament was recognized in the New Testament as words of God. The Holy Scriptures were truly 'written for us'.

---

31. Foord, *Weakest Link*, p. 11.

3. BY HIS SPIRIT

'As the Holy Spirit says' (Heb. 3:7)

The Spirit and human words

Just as God uses human words, and Jesus gave words of eternal life to his disciples, so too the Holy Spirit uses human words. Jesus spoke of the future work of the Holy Spirit in these terms: 'The Holy Spirit . . . will teach you' (John 14:26), 'the Spirit of truth . . . will testify' (John 15:26), 'the Spirit of truth . . . will guide you into all the truth' (John 16:13). As the transcendent God and the divine Christ are not compromised by using human words, so too the Holy Spirit not only 'searches . . . the depths of God' but also communicates these in words 'taught by the Spirit' (1 Cor. 2:10, 13).

It is very clear from the New Testament that the Holy Spirit can use human words. In Luke we meet Zechariah, who 'was filled with the Holy Spirit and spoke this prophecy' (Luke 1:67). Of Simeon in the temple, we read that the Spirit 'rested on him', 'revealed to him', and 'guided' him (Luke 2:25–27). Jesus promised his disciples that when they face trials for their faith, 'the Holy Spirit will teach you . . . what you ought to say' (Luke 12:12); and he said, 'David himself, by the Holy Spirit, declared . . .' (Mark 12:36). We find the same idea in Acts: '[God] . . . said by the Holy Spirit through our ancestor David . . .' (Acts 4:25); 'The Holy Spirit was right in saying to your ancestors through the prophet Isaiah . . .' (Acts 28:25). In Acts, the Spirit 'said to Philip, "Go over to this chariot"'' (8:29); the Holy Spirit instructed the church at Antioch, 'Set apart for me Barnabas and Saul' (Acts 13:2); Paul and Timothy were 'forbidden by the Holy Spirit' to go to Asia (16:6); and the prophet Agabus said, 'Thus says the Holy Spirit . . .' (21:11). In the letters of Peter we read: 'The prophets . . . inquiring about the person or time that the Spirit of Christ within them indicated' (1 Pet. 1:10–11), and 'Men and women moved by the Holy Spirit spoke from God' (2 Pet. 1:21). In 1 Timothy 4:1 we read, 'The Spirit expressly says . . .', and in Hebrews 10:15, 'the Holy Spirit also testifies to us . . . saying'. We have in the Bible the content of the Spirit's verbal witness to God and to Christ.

John Donne, poet and preacher, wrote of Moses as 'the principal [i.e. first] secretary of the Holy Ghost', of the Holy Spirit as 'the author of all these books, the Holy Ghost', and therefore of the Bible as the place where 'Christ's flock hearken to his voice, his word'.[1]

Some assume that the Spirit's revelation is always 'too deep for words' (Rom. 8:26), that the Spirit is too ethereal or otherworldly to use mere human words, or that the Spirit gives us experiences of God, but that we have to find the words to describe those experiences.[2] However, there is no reason why the Spirit should be unable to speak human language. Why should we limit what the Spirit may do? God speaks through the Holy Spirit. This idea is central to Christian faith, and is no new invention. In the words of the Nicene Creed, 'We believe in the Holy Spirit, the Lord and giver of Life . . . who spoke by the prophets.' As Kevin Vanhoozer has written: 'The Spirit speaking in Scripture continues the three-fold office of Christ (as Prophet, Priest and King); witnessing to the truth of the living and written word; executing the . . . force of Scripture so that it reigns in the hearts and lives of believers; mediating the personal presence of Christ through the words that testify to him to bring about personal union with Christ.'[3]

These words come by the Spirit. So what God expects from our reading of the Bible is the 'fruit of the Spirit', and not the 'works of the flesh' (Gal. 5:16–26). Our response should not come from the 'evil intentions' of 'the human heart' (Mark 7:21–23), or from our rebellious and hostile minds (Rom. 8:7–8). Furthermore, our response to Scripture is a response to the Holy Spirit. We must not 'grieve the Holy Spirit', or 'lie to the Holy Spirit', or find ourselves

---

1. Donne, *Essays*, pp. 11, 40–41, 48–49.

2. A common version of this view is that the Bible writers experienced God, and then did their best to describe their experiences for their day. Now we too experience God, and so we should follow their example, and try to put into words our own experiences.

3. Vanhoozer, *Drama*, p. 210.

'opposing the Holy Spirit' (Eph. 4:30; Acts 5:3; 7:51). Our response to the Bible is our personal response to God the Holy Spirit.

The internal witness of the Spirit

As Calvin explained, God used the Spirit to create the Scriptures, and also uses the Spirit to illuminate our minds with the Scriptures: '[God] sent down the same Spirit by whose power he had dispensed the Word, to complete his work by the efficacious confirmation of the Word.'[4] So the Spirit through whom God inspired both the human authors of the Scriptures and their written words also brings those words home to our minds, hearts, and lives, witnesses to their divine origin, and illuminates the Scriptures as we read and receive them. In the words of G. C. Berkouwer: 'We believe the Scripture because of the witness of Christ, and through the witness of the Spirit.'[5]

It is most helpful to see that the Spirit witnesses to the God-given authenticity of the Scriptures, witnesses to the Christ revealed in those Scriptures, and witnesses to our spirits that we are truly adopted into God's family. It is the same witness of the Spirit that assures us of Christ, the Bible, and our place in God's family.[6]

God has spoken, the Lord Jesus has the words of eternal life, and the Holy Spirit is our teacher and guide.

'Holy Spirit', 'Holy Scriptures' (2 Timothy 1:14, 3:15)

The Holy God

God is holy, the Holy One of Israel (Ps. 89:18). When he acts 'his right hand and his holy arm have gained him victory' (Ps. 98:1).

We might think that God is holy, and that nothing else and no one else can be holy. However, God wants to communicate his holiness to others. God wanted to make a holy nation (Exod. 19:6). God wanted his people to be holy: 'You shall be holy, for I the LORD your God am holy' (Lev. 19:2).

So too in the New Testament, God's plan was to make a holy people through the blood of Christ. We are God's holy temple (1 Cor. 3:17), 'made

---

4. Calvin, *Institutes*, 1.9.1, p. 95.

5. Berkouwer, in McKim, *Word*, p. 168. See also Berkouwer, 'The Testimony of the Spirit', in McKim, pp. 155–181; Calvin, *Institutes*, 1.7, pp. 74–81, and 3.2, pp. 33–37; and Berkouwer, *Scripture*, chapter 2.

6. For similar ideas see Berkouwer in McKim, *Word*, pp. 166–168.

holy in Christ Jesus' (my trans.), and also 'called to be saints' (1 Cor. 1:2). We even dare to believe that, by the mercies of God, we can present our bodies as 'a living sacrifice, holy and acceptable to God' (Rom. 12:1).

God can make people holy, and God can make things holy. Moses stood on 'holy ground' when God spoke from the burning bush (Exod. 3:5). The Sabbath day must be kept 'holy' (Exod. 20:8). The ark of the covenant (the mercy-seat) was to be placed in the 'most holy place' (the holy of holies) (Exod. 26:34). Sacrifices offered to God can be described as 'holy' (Lev. 7:1, 6). God's people worship at God's 'holy' mountain, for 'the LORD God is holy' (Ps. 99:9).

Holy words

God also makes human words holy, to serve his holy purpose. In the Old Testament we read of God's 'holy promise' (Ps. 105:42), God's 'holy name' (1 Chr. 16:35), and God's 'holy words' (Jer. 23:9). Elisha, a prophet who will speak God's words, is described as a 'holy man of God' (2 Kgs 4:9). In Daniel 11 we read of an evil king that 'his heart shall be set against the holy covenant' (Dan. 11:28).

In the New Testament we read of God's 'holy covenant' (Luke 1:72), 'a holy angel' (Acts 10:22), and 'holy prophets' (Luke 1:70; Acts 3:21; 2 Pet. 3:2). The Scriptures are described as 'holy scriptures' (Rom. 1:2; 2 Tim 3:15), and Paul speaks of 'the holy promises made to David' (Acts 13:34). The commandment of God is 'holy' (Rom. 7:12; 2 Pet. 2:21), and we are to build each other up in our 'most holy faith' (Jude 20).

The words of God are holy because they were spoken by the Holy Spirit: 'men and women moved by the Holy Spirit spoke from God' (2 Pet. 1:21). The Holy Spirit communicates holiness to God's people through his words. It is the Holy Spirit, the Spirit of truth, who will guide the disciples into all the truth (John 14:26; 16:13). The Holy Spirit brings holy words of holy truth, to show us the holy Son of God, his sanctifying sacrifice on the cross, and to make us holy people.

Holy Scripture

What does it mean to call the Bible 'Holy Scripture'? John Webster describes the sanctification of the Bible (making Scripture to be Holy Scripture) as the Holy Spirit's work in using the writers, the books, and the selection of the books into the Bible.[7] Here the holiness or sanctification of

---

7. Webster, *Scripture*, pp. 17–18. His idea of the sanctification of Scripture also included its 'canonization'; Webster, *Word and Church*, pp. 32–42. I have developed the idea of the sanctification of Scripture in slightly different ways.

Scripture includes taking human words and setting them apart as holy, and collecting these words into the Holy Scriptures received by the people of God. We should not think, however, that the human authors wrote their books independently of God, and then God decided to adopt these books as 'holy'. This would not allow enough room for God's initiative in the writing of the books of the Bible. For the ideas, thoughts, and words of Scripture come from the mind of God. The Scriptures are God's holy speech; they are holy because God has made them holy; they are holy because they are the product of the Holy Spirit.

As we think of the Scriptures as 'holy', we should remember that there are few more dangerous sins than that of misusing holiness. Aaron's sons, Nadab and Abihu, committed a great sin when they offered 'unholy fire' before the LORD, and they were consumed by a fire that came out from the presence of the Lord (Lev. 10:1–2). The Levites were warned, 'You shall not profane the holy gifts of the Israelites, on pain of death' (Num. 18:32). Uzzah died when he touched the ark of the covenant (1 Chr. 13). Paul warned that because the church is the holy temple of God's Spirit, 'if anyone destroys God's temple, God will destroy that person' (1 Cor. 3:16–17).

Just as God is offended when holy places are defiled, so God's Holy Spirit is personally hurt when we sin. We read the warnings: 'They rebelled, and grieved his holy spirit; therefore he became their enemy; he himself fought against them' (Isa. 63:10). We take to heart the words of Peter to Ananias, 'Why has Satan filled your heart to lie to the Holy Spirit?' (Acts 5:3). We heed the words of Hebrews: 'Therefore, as the Holy Spirit says, "Today, if you hear his voice, do not harden your hearts"' (Heb. 3:7).

So it is our duty and joy to believe God's holy promises, receive God's holy words, read and understand the Holy Scriptures, the gift to us given through men and women moved by God's Holy Spirit, and build each other up in our most holy faith. Careful and loving reception of the ministry of the Spirit in the words of Scripture is a way of loving God. This is why, in Eugene Peterson's words, 'Exegesis is an act of love', and, 'Exegesis is an act of sustained humility.'[8]

The desire of our holy God is to keep on making us holy through the words of the Holy Spirit given us in the Holy Scriptures. As we saw in chapter 1, God's words are powerful in bringing new birth, and they are also powerful in making holy. Their power is a holy power.

---

8. Peterson, *Eat this Book*, pp. 55, 57. Exegesis is the explanation of the content and meaning of the text of Scripture.

'The Holy Spirit says . . . through David' (Heb. 3:7; 4:7): God's words and human authors

In this work of the Holy Spirit, the humanity of the authors is never bypassed. Jeremiah always sounds like Jeremiah and not like Haggai. Paul writes like Paul, Peter like Peter, and John like John. Every word achieves God's communicative purpose, and yet he manages to use the ordinary humanness of the authors. This is an extraordinary sign of God's transcendent power, and of his great respect for our personal humanity. In a similar way, God gives us good works to do, and empowers us to do them, but the way we do those good works is always personal to us, and expresses our humanity. God uses human beings with all their frailties and sins, and still achieves what he wants to achieve.[9]

Inspiration

John Calvin claimed that the apostles 'were sure and genuine scribes of the Holy Spirit, and their writings are therefore to be considered oracles of God'.[10]

What should we understand by the claim that Scripture is 'inspired'? The text commonly used to support the inspiration of Scripture is 2 Timothy 3:16.[11] By itself it cannot carry the weight some put upon it. It is not helpful to derive our doctrine of Scripture from that one verse: it is better to look at wider evidence, such as the relationship between the Holy Spirit and Scripture, and the 'holiness' of Scripture, as we have seen.

The traditional idea of inspiration is especially relevant to those times when prophets received a direct word from God, and passed it on to their hearers. Inspiration is not the same as dictation, for inspiration describes what happened, and dictation how it happened on some occasions, but not all. The model of inspiration that we usually assume is that of artistic inspiration, when words are given directly from God to a person, either taking over their creativity, or bypassing their consciousness. Another common model is that of God dictating, while the human author records God's words. The first model is appropriate in cases like Jeremiah receiving words from God, or John receiving his visions and words from God in the book of Revelation. The second model is true in the account in Exodus of Moses writing down the words of the law at God's dictation.

---

9. Adam, *Speaking*, pp. 104–109.

10. Calvin, *Institutes* 4.8.9, p. 1157.

11. 2 Pet. 1:18 is about the Spirit-carried writers, not the Spirit-inspired words.

If we are to use the word 'inspiration' to describe the process by which God produces the Bible, then it must have a broad meaning. It will include those times when God dictated his instructions, as when the Lord spoke the law to Moses (Exod. 20–23), and gave Moses instructions about the materials and building of the tabernacle (Exod. 25–31). It also included the speeches of Job's friends, which to God's mind were not true (Job 42.7, 'You have not spoken of me what is right'). It included the Cretan proverb quoted by Paul, 'All Cretans are always liars, vicious brutes, lazy gluttons' (Titus 1:12), as well as the sayings of the pagan philosophers, 'For in him [God] we live and move and have our being' (Acts 17:28). These very human words have been adopted or sanctified for a divine purpose. It included the words of Satan, 'Does Job fear God for nothing?' (Job 1:9), as also the prophets' words about God and about themselves and their feelings, as well as the words they received from God (e.g. Jer. 20:7–18; 21:3–14). Inspiration also described the research done by Luke (Luke 1:1–4), Paul's struggle in finding the right words to write to the church at Colossae (Col. 2:1), observation of what God's providential care looks like in the world around us (Proverbs), descriptions of how the writer of a psalm felt on a bad day (Ps. 88), and the receiving of a revelation by John (Rev. 1:1–4).

The danger of taking one biblical word and making it cover the many different ways in which God caused the Bible to be written is that it imposes one model on all situations, and extends the meaning of the word to cover ideas not found in its original contexts. Inspiration will include the work of the Spirit in human authors as well as their writings.

It is not helpful to suggest that God is present in the Bible in the way in which God was present in Christ, or that the Bible is both divine and human in the way in which Christ was divine and human. For Christ is divine in substance, rightly worshipped as God: the Bible is the product of the divine Spirit, but not itself divine. It effectively conveys divine truths, but it is not God.

John Webster rightly warns us that 'some doctrines of inspiration deny the naturalness of the texts, and propose an immediate relation between God and the texts. "Inspired" short-circuits all historical processes.'[12] This commonly happens when we treat the Bible as God's direct word to us, and forget that it was first God's word to God's people in the past and must be read in that historical and biblical theological context, before it applies to us. We must read Corinthians as a book addressed to Corinth, before it applies to us. We must read Leviticus as part of the Law of the Old Testament, before we can work out how it applies to us. The Bible was written 'to them, for them; and to us, for us'.

---

12. Webster, *Word and Church*, p. 30.

However, the misuse of the idea of inspiration does not mean that it is not true. Notice how John Stott combined divine and human authorship: 'The Bible is both divine and human in its authorship. Therefore we must neither affirm its divine authorship in such a way as to deny the free activity of the human authors, nor affirm their active cooperation in such a way as to deny that through them God spoke the word.'[13]

'Inspiration' need not and did not short-circuit historical processes.

As we noted above, the inspiration of human words is a lesser miracle than the incarnation of the Son of God. If God incarnate retains his complete divinity while taking on full humanity, it must be possible for the Holy Spirit to bring us his truth clothed in our words. If God was able to cause Mary to become pregnant with his Son, then he was certainly able to communicate his words to humanity.

Double authorship

We must take both divine and human authorship into account when we read the Scriptures.

We respect divine authorship when we recognize that the words of the Bible come with God's grace, compassion, power, truthfulness, and authority, and that we must receive and welcome them, delight in them, and obey them.

We respect its human authorship when we read it in its historical context, take note of its literary genre, read it in its context in God's providential care and salvation history and in biblical theology, are aware of its cultural context, take note of whether it claims to be direct speech of God or a human reaction to God or to life, and observe whether in its context it claims to be true or false, history or parable, exaggeration or plain truth, symbolic language, proverb, general summary, or historical record.

Notice how Paul described the role of God in Romans 1:1–2, when he wrote of 'the gospel of God, which he promised beforehand through his prophets in the holy scriptures'. God promised this gospel, and Paul states both the means God used, 'through his prophets', and also where that promise is to be found, 'in the holy scriptures'.

Did the authors of Scripture know that they were inspired? I suspect that inspiration is rather like guidance. When we read of God guiding us, we think that it must mean that we will feel guided. It may often mean that God guides us through our perplexities and indecision, and directs us to the right conclusion. It may be that we assume a nineteenth-century Romantic idea of inspiration,

---

13. Stott, *Truth*, p. 61.

that of 'genius, touched with emotion',[14] the driven artist, like Beethoven. Bach was equally 'inspired' when he used the gifts God gave him to write another cantata because he needed the money to feed his large family! The fact that the Bible writers were inspired need not mean that they felt inspired.

We should follow God's example in respecting the humanity of the authors of Scripture. In the nineteenth century J. C. Ryle wrote: 'I believe that in some marvellous manner the Holy Ghost made use of the reason, the memory, the intellect, the style of thought and the peculiar mental temperament of each writer of the Scripture . . . there is both a Divine and a human element in the Scripture, and . . . while the men who wrote it were really and truly men, the book they wrote and handed down to us is really and truly the Word of God.'[15]

The conviction that God used the words of ordinary humans and still perfectly achieved his revelatory purpose is only one example of the general fact that God can use humans for many different purposes, and still achieve his will. It is a particular example of our common experience of God's grace in our lives: 'I . . . though it was not I, but the grace of God' (1 Cor. 15:10). For our God is so powerful and so delicate that he can achieve perfect work through us, without distorting or destroying us. In Peter's words: 'Whoever speaks must do so as one speaking the very words of God; whoever serves must do so with the strength that God supplies' (1 Pet. 4:11).

Austin Farrer wrote: 'We must attend to the homely phrases, the soaring poetry, the figures of speech, and the changes of mood; for these are the alphabet of the divine utterance.'[16]

'In many and various ways' (Heb. 1:1): the variety of Scripture

Respecting the way in which God has caused the Scriptures to be written also means recognizing that they come in many different forms: history, parable, saying, prophecy, argument, story, letter, revelation, prayer, song, and gospel.

Does the fact that the Bible comes in a variety of 'genres', or styles of writing, make it too difficult to understand? No, for anyone reading a newspaper has to cope with a variety of literary 'genres', such as a news story, an editorial, an advertisement, a notice of birth or death, a funny story, a gossip column, a comic strip, a sports report, a crossword, or a public disclaimer. We

---

14. McDonald, *I Want to Know*, p. 15.

15. Ryle, 'Is All Scripture Inspired?', as quoted in Wellings, *Evangelicals*, p. 37.

16. Farrer, *Interpretation*, p. 12.

do the same in everyday conversation, where we easily distinguish between an outburst of emotion, an imagined story, a joke, a story from the past, a complaint, telephone marketing, and a proposal of marriage. We make mistakes, but we try to learn from them!

Some believe that the Bible is basically propositional revelation: that is, true statements about reality, like 'God is love', or 'Jesus is the saviour of the world.' Others see the Bible as basically story or narrative, the story of God's creation and then his rescue of humanity. I think both that there are propositions in the Bible, and that there are stories. The challenge is to see each for what it is, cope with the variety, and not make the mistake of reading Job as if it were a series of propositional truths, or Romans as if it were a story.

The Bible includes many propositions, such as 'The Son of Man is lord of the Sabbath' (Matt. 12:8) and 'There is one God; there is also one mediator between God and humankind, Christ Jesus, himself human, who gave himself a ransom for all' (1 Tim. 2:5–6). However, there are many other forms of communication in the Bible, including historical statements, exclamations, parables, questions, prayers, complaints, requests, and proverbs. The message of the Bible should not be reduced to propositions, since God chose a wider range of styles of communication, and we should value that variety, and not try to reduce it or limit it. However, the Bible does include many propositions, and we should not dismiss or ignore them. We should not think that propositional revelation is less personal than other forms of revelation. Our ordinary personal communication is often in terms of propositions: 'I am her husband', 'I am a doctor', 'She is my daughter', and 'That bottle contains poison' are all expressed in the form of propositions. And our statements or propositions can be relational. In the words of Paul Helm: 'There is no antithesis between believing a proposition and believing a person if the proposition is taken to be the assertion of some person.'[17]

Is the lasting verbal revelation of God in the form of a story? Yes, there is a big storyline to the Bible, about the promise and then the fulfilment of God's plan to send his Son. And there are many smaller stories in the Bible, including historical stories and non-historical parables. However, as with a propositional view of Scripture, we should not reduce everything in the Bible to the category of story. If propositions are popular with people with a 'scientific' or 'modern' viewpoint, then stories are equally popular with people of a 'postmodern' viewpoint. We may like stories because we think that they are naturally more ambiguous, more indirect. Some Bible stories are ambiguous and

---

17. Helm, *Revelation*, p. 178.

indirect, but others have plainer meaning, which is sometimes included in the story. We should not try to push the Bible into any one literary straitjacket. Our culture may help us relate to some parts of the Bible, and make it more difficult to relate to other parts. We should not respond by trying to make all parts of the Bible fit our cultural expectations.

It is a sign of God's great desire to relate to different sorts of people from every human background and culture that he uses such a rich variety of literary forms and styles in the Scriptures. What we don't like, someone else will like, and what we find hard to read, others will read easily and naturally. We should rejoice in the varied literary forms of the Scriptures.

Every part of the Scriptures will lead us to know God and serve God. Every part of the Scriptures will lead us to other parts of the Bible to help our understanding. Every part of the Scriptures will lead us to Jesus Christ. Every part of the Scriptures will help us to belong to the one people of God, and every part of the Scriptures will be useful in bringing the gospel of Christ to the men, women and children of our world.

We should not think that we can achieve complete understanding of the Bible at one reading. Its message is ultimately clear, but we need to read and study it many times, compare Scripture with Scripture, learn from others, find the fundamental cohesion and unity, and understand each part in the light of the whole of the Bible.[18]

Recently I was asked if it was better to use the gospel of Romans, or the idea of the spiritual quest, to help young people today become believers. I gave two answers.

The first was that God has given us many different ways of helping people come to faith in Christ, including the gospel of Romans, the search for wisdom in Proverbs or Ecclesiastes, the stories of the Gospels, the warning of the prophets, and the powerful visions of the book of Revelation (along with many others). We should use all of these in turn if we want to help all kinds of people come to Christ. God would not have given us so many ways if they were not necessary. The danger of using one way is that we will win only one kind of person. Ring the changes!

The second was that we should not only use all these different ways, but also make sure that we use each way according to its use in Scripture. If we use Romans 1–8, we should make sure we apply it as Paul does in Romans 9–16. If we use the idea of the 'unknown God' from Acts 17, we should make sure we mention the day of repentance of Acts 17:30–31.

---

18. Thompson, *Clear and Present Word.*

In this chapter we have investigated the role of the Holy Spirit in the verbal revelation of God called the Holy Scriptures. We have seen that the Spirit uses human words, and that our response to Scripture is a personal response to the Spirit. We found that the Scriptures are 'holy' because they are the product of the Holy Spirit. We have noticed that inspiration came in varied forms, and that the Bible contains varied literary forms. We have seen that divine authorship does not preclude human authorship, and that this cooperative work is just one example of God's grace working through human beings to achieve his perfect purposes. In the words of Bernard Ramm, 'The Scriptures function in the ministry of the Spirit of God, and the Spirit functions in the instrument of the Word.'[19] Or, in the vivid words of Martin Luther, 'the Bible is the very language of the Spirit'.[20]

---

19. From Ramm, *Pattern of Authority*, as quoted in McDonald, *I Want to Know*, p. 129.
20. As quoted in McDonald, *I Want to Know*, p. 125.

4. ABOUT HIS SON

The early preachers of Acts certainly believed that the message of the Old Testament was about God's Son, Jesus Christ: 'Therefore let the entire house of Israel know with certainty that God has made him both Lord and Messiah, this Jesus whom you crucified' (2:36); 'This Jesus is "the stone that was rejected by you, the builders; it has become the cornerstone." There is salvation in no one else, for there is no other name under heaven given among mortals by which we must be saved' (4:11–12); and 'All the prophets testify about him that everyone who believes in him receives forgiveness of sins through his name' (10:43).

However, a more complete and correct version of our heading would be: 'God's words written for his people, through his Son, by his Spirit, about himself and his Son'. For Christ the Son is the mediator between God and ourselves, and he also sent the Holy Spirit; and the Bible is about God. We must beware of Christomonism, of being so Christ-centred that we neglect God the Father and God the Spirit.[1] Furthermore, in chapter 5 I make the point that the Bible is not only about the Son, but he is also the key to its interpretation, and authenticates and fulfils its message. In addition, as Jesus is the mediator of the knowledge of God (1 Tim. 2:5), God's revelation came *through* him, as

---

1. See Greidanus, *Preaching Christ*, pp. 111–124, 163–176, 178.

well as being *about* him. To expand our phrase further: 'Receiving God's words written for his people, through his Son, by his Spirit, and about himself, his Son, and his Spirit'.

For the sake of simplicity, however, we will focus on one of these truths, in claiming that the Bible is about God's Son, Jesus Christ.

Jesus said, 'These are my words that I spoke to you . . . everything written about me . . . must be fulfilled' (Luke 24:44): the Bible interprets itself

The Bible is self-interpreting

There is no book of the Bible, no unit of verbal revelation, which can be understood apart from the other books of the Bible. Esther and Ruth make sense only in the light of the promises to Abraham. Ecclesiastes perfectly expresses life after Genesis 3. James shows what the wisdom tradition looks like in the New Testament. Leviticus is fulfilled in Hebrews. 1 and 2 Timothy and Titus explain what life will be like after the apostles, as do Jude and 2 Peter. Jesus described his death and resurrection in terms of 'the law of Moses, the prophets, and the psalms' (Luke 24:44). These three terms referred to the three main parts of the Old Testament, the Law, the Prophets, and the Wisdom writings. Paul understood his gospel mission as a fulfilment of God's promise to his servant in Isaiah, 'I have set you to be a light for the Gentiles, so that you may bring salvation to the ends of the earth' (Acts 13:47).[2]

The death and resurrection of Christ is explained in terms of the creation of Adam, the promise to Abraham, the exodus from Egypt, the manna in the wilderness, the bronze snake in the desert, the sacrifices and priests of the tabernacle and temple, the Passover lamb, the innocent sufferer of the Psalms, the servant of the Lord of Isaiah, the shepherd of Ezekiel 34, and the return from exile. Life in Christ is explained in terms of Abraham's faith, the Passover and unleavened bread, entry into the promised land, the life of wisdom, fulfilling the righteousness of the law and the prophets, living by faith like the heroes of the Old Testament, the prophets, and Job; and avoiding the sins of Esau, those who fell in the desert, Jezebel, and the sins of Cain, Balaam and Korah. Just as the world was destroyed by water in the flood, so it will be destroyed by fire at the end. Just as God struck Egypt with plagues in the past,

---

2. Adam, *Hearing*, chapter 4, for a study of Calvin's theology of one covenant, one people of God, and one Word of God.

so he will strike the whole world with plagues in the future. Just as God chose and built Jerusalem, so he will build the new Jerusalem, and we will sing the song of Moses and the song of Lamb.

These interconnections between the sixty-six units of biblical revelation are not optional extras, but are fundamental to their meaning. None of them makes full sense apart from these interconnections. In the words of 1 Peter: 'It was revealed to them that they were serving not themselves but you, in regard to the things that have now been announced to you through those who brought you good news by the Holy Spirit sent from heaven – things into which angels long to look!' (1:12).

The more we study the Bible, the more we find out about the unity of God's people, not just across the two Testaments, but also within each Testament.

The story of Esther made sense only in the light of God's promise to Abram to bless his descendants, and to bring blessing to the nations through those descendants (Esth.; Gen. 12:1–3). Ecclesiastes ('Vanity of vanities!', Eccl. 1:2) makes sense as the experience of Genesis 3 death and futility. The prophets apply the law of Moses. The gospel of grace is found in Deuteronomy.[3] Wisdom is found in 'the fear of the LORD': that is, in the fear of Yahweh of the covenant (Prov. 1:7). The story of Joseph is both a narrative of the fulfilment of the promises to Abraham, Isaac, and Jacob and an account of the practice of wisdom.[4]

The 'Holy Scriptures' come from the common life of the one 'people of God', and those Scriptures reflect the one mind of God expressed in successive generations of God's people. Northrop Frye has described the Bible as the 'Great Code', by which he means that 'the Bible is clearly a major element in [the Western] imaginative tradition'.[5] The Bible became the 'Great Code' for the West only because it had already been the Great Code for the Christian church. We have what has been called an 'enscripturalized identity'. However, before all this, the Bible has also been its own 'Great Code'. For the best book to help us understand the Bible is the Bible itself: it is its own interpreter.

Accumulated learning in accumulated Scriptures

In many instances what the Bible assumes is as important as what it asserts or teaches. 'Recognized prior learning' is a key to reading the Bible, and that prior

---

3. Barker, *Grace.*

4. Wilson, *Joseph.*

5. Frye, *Code*, p. xviii.

learning is the revelation that God has already given in the Scriptures. So the New Testament assumes the Old Testament: Jesus does not need to teach that God exists, that there is one God, that there is one definitive revelation, or the salvation history or biblical theology of the Old Testament, for he assumes all this knowledge and understanding. To make the same point another way, it is perilous to read the New Testament without having read and understood the Old Testament. For to do so is to miss the interpretative clues which God has provided for us. The Bible is God's syllabus for the human race; it is his educational agenda for us.

This also means that we should pay attention to what the Bible assumes, as well as to what it aims to teach us. For assumptions form a substantial part of a world-view, of a 'Great Code'. When Jesus said, 'David himself, by the Holy Spirit, declared, "The Lord said to my Lord, 'Sit at my right hand, until I put your enemies under your feet'"' (Mark 12:36), the main point he was making was about the identity of David's Lord, namely, himself. However, his reference to the Holy Spirit showed his view of God's inspiration of David, and perhaps also the inspiration of the words of Psalm 110. It certainly showed that he thought that the Holy Spirit could work with human words. It is the common world of accumulated gathered meaning which is our quest.

Furthermore, unacknowledged quotations from the Old Testament are powerful evidence of this 'Great Code' in operation. When Paul wrote, 'At the name of Jesus every knee should bend, in heaven and on earth and under the earth, and every tongue should confess that Jesus Christ is Lord, to the glory of God the Father' (Phil. 2:10–11), he must have had Isaiah 45 in mind, and must also have assumed that his readers would make the same connections. For there God said, 'To me every knee shall bow, every tongue shall swear' (Isa. 45:23). In Paul's mind, the divinity, dignity, and glory of Christ are clearly and powerfully expressed by the application of these words to Jesus Christ.

One of our difficulties is that we often use the word 'text' to refer to one verse of the Bible. This means that we easily focus on a few words out of context. In fact there are sixty-six texts in the Bible, for each book of the Bible is a text. And no book of the Bible can be read in isolation from all the other books in the Bible.

Jesus showed the coherence of Scripture when he read from Isaiah in the synagogue at Nazareth, and then began his sermon with the words, 'Today this scripture has been fulfilled in your hearing' (Luke 4:21). No wonder we read in the next chapter of Luke that 'the crowd was pressing in on him to hear the word of God' (Luke 5:1).

Wisdom or folly? (Proverbs 1:20–22)

This common world of meaning, this 'Great Code', includes a tradition of truth and a tradition of error. The truth of God is found in the certain promises and words of God, in hanging on to the words of God, and in finding light and truth in these words. It includes accepting people like Moses as the leader appointed by God, and in Joshua following the commands of God given to Moses. It means trusting the words of God's priests, prophets, and wise men and women, as they point to the true worship of God in obedience to God. Then it means accepting Jesus Christ and his teaching about himself, about God, about God's people, about the need to repent and believe the gospel, and about what God will do in the future. It means accepting those apostles chosen and sent by Christ, and so believing in the 'faith that was once for all entrusted to the saints' (Jude 3).

If we are to believe Moses, then we must turn away from those who rebel against him. If we are to accept the true prophets of God, then we must also refuse the false prophets. If we are to accept the teaching of Jesus, then we must turn aside from those whom he corrects and refutes. If we are to believe the apostles of Christ, then we must reject false prophets, false apostles, and false gospels. If there is a revelation for the last days, then the last days are also the times when the great beast, the false prophet, performs signs and wonders to deceive the elect, and to draw men and women to worship the Satan, the great dragon. The common world of meaning, the 'Great Code', includes errors and lies to be avoided as well as truths and promises to be believed.

We find this distinction between truth and error clearly expressed in Malachi, in the stark contrast between what Old Testament priests were meant to do, and what the priests of Malachi's day were doing: 'My covenant with him [Levi] was a covenant of life and well-being, which I gave him; this called for reverence, and he revered me and stood in awe of my name. True instruction was in his mouth, and no wrong was found on his lips . . . But you have turned aside from the way; you have caused many to stumble by your instruction; you have corrupted the covenant of Levi, says the LORD' (Mal. 2:5–6, 8).

We are sometimes told that the two-way contrast between truth and error is the product of our modern, rationalistic Western minds, which we tend to read into the Bible. In fact the Bible itself contains and conveys the most powerful binary contrasts, such as wisdom and folly in Proverbs, and light and darkness in the writing of John in the New Testament. In the Bible the contrast is even more powerful than in Western rationalism and modernism.

For the contrast is not about the apprehension of abstract qualities, but between serving God's truths and serving Satan's lies. There is no neutral ground. We were created to believe God, and if we do not believe God, we will believe other words and serve other gods, as we will see in our study of John 8.

In the Scriptures, truth is not a mere human construct, but the powerful and convincing revelation of the personal God. And the Bible's concern with words is not the product of a modern logocentricity, but based on the fact that words effect revelation, either true or false. So, as we will see in John 17, we can be sanctified by the truth, and in John 14 – 16 and 1 Corinthians 2 – 3, that the Holy Spirit deals in human words of revelation. The Holy Spirit of truth is a wordsmith, and his role is to lead us to Christ and glorify Christ, who is the way, and the truth, and the life.

We should not only refuse to receive alien words that come from sources other than God; we should also oppose those who 'falsify God's word', misquote or misinterpret God, or change his words so that they have alien meanings (2 Cor. 4:2). Otherwise we will be led astray from 'a sincere and pure devotion to Christ' (2 Cor. 11:3). Spiritual chastity means exclusive loyalty to God's words. Our great and mighty God loves those who love his words and receive them in humility.

> Thus says the LORD:
> Heaven is my throne
>   and the earth is my footstool;
> what is the house that you would build for me,
>   and what is my resting-place?
> All these things my hand has made,
>   and so all these things are mine,
>   says the LORD.
> But this is the one to whom I will look,
>   to the humble and contrite in spirit,
>   who trembles at my word.
> (Isa. 66:1–2)

We find the same message in the New Testament: 'Everyone who does not abide in the teaching of Christ, but goes beyond it, does not have God; whoever abides in the teaching has both the Father and the Son. Do not receive into the house or welcome anyone who comes to you and does not bring this teaching; for to welcome is to participate in the evil deeds of such a person' (2 John 9–11).

We should then heed the advice of Thomas Cranmer, 'Let us diligently search for the well of life in the books of the New and Old Testament, and not run to the stinking puddles of men's traditions.'[6]

One integrated message: 'the word of God' (Acts 12:24)

The word of God

There is an overall shape and purpose of this gathered and interconnected verbal revelation. Just as the verses and chapters come together to form the shape and purpose of each book of the Bible, so the sixty-six books of the Bible come together in one overall message, one big purpose, one common aim: the words come together to become one word. This is a book about God, a book about the people of God, a book about Jesus Christ, a book about the gospel of Christ. The Bible itself uses a variety of words to describe this one message. These words include: 'the kingdom of God', 'the gospel of Christ', 'the word of truth', 'the truth', 'the message of salvation', 'the Lord Jesus Christ', 'the grace of God', 'the word of life', 'the revelation of Jesus Christ', 'the word of God', or simply 'the word'. The context of the whole Bible is the mission of God, as Chris Wright has shown:[7] this is why our interpretation of the Bible must be 'gospel-centred'.[8]

This biblical gospel is not only powerful enough to bring individuals to faith in Jesus Christ; it is also powerful enough to transform them and bring them to maturity in Christ, to plant and establish churches, to bring these churches to maturity in Christ, and to transform the world.

This is the message of Old and New Testament alike. When Paul addressed Festus, he claimed: 'I stand here, testifying to both small and great, saying nothing but what the prophets and Moses said would take place: that the Messiah must suffer, and that, by being the first to rise from the dead, he would proclaim light both to our people and to the Gentiles' (Acts 26:22–23).

The book of Revelation reveals 'the word of God', which is the same as 'the testimony of Jesus Christ' (Rev. 1:2).

Jesus and the Bible

The interpretative key to the Bible is Jesus Christ. For the subject of his constant debates in the synagogues and with the leaders of God's people of his

---

6. Cranmer, *Sermons*, p. 2, modernized.

7. See Wright, *Mission*.

8. See Goldsworthy, *Hermeneutics*.

day was about the meaning of the Old Testament. Jesus claimed that his interpretation was right, and that the Scriptures promised his coming.

As we find in Luke 24, Jesus summarized both the message of the Old
Testament and his own message in these words: 'The Messiah is to suffer and
to rise from the dead on the third day, and . . . repentance and forgiveness of
sins is to be proclaimed in his name to all nations, beginning from Jerusalem'
(24:46–47). Jesus said of the Old Testament Scriptures, 'They witness to me'
(John 5:39 [my trans.]).

Paul and the other New Testament writers continued this argument, for the
argument about the identity of Jesus Christ and the argument about the
meaning of the Old Testament could not be separated. If the Old Testament
points to Jesus Christ, then so does the New Testament, for the writers of the
New Testament record and express the message of the apostles of Christ: they
are his messengers, and he is their message.

It is biblical theology that explains the unfolding revelation of God in the
Bible. It follows the pattern of revelation that God used. For God did not reveal
in topics or abstract ideas, but in a gradual historical revelation which follows
salvation history and God's providential care, from creation to new creation.
Biblical theology expresses both the common shape of the life of faith of God's
people, and also the increasing and cumulative clarity of that revelation. It is theology as interpreted story, the unfolding of the gospel of Christ. Biblical theology tries to do justice to every part of the Bible, and also to show how every
part comes together to give verbal witness to Jesus Christ and his gospel.[9]

What kind of unity?

However, this does not mean that the Bible fits easily together, or that there are
not paradoxes and varied voices within Scripture. The tensions between Psalm
1 and Job are very fruitful, as are varied links between sin and sickness in John 5
and 9. We should enjoy having four Gospels, and make the most of their diversity. The variety of Scripture comes from its gradual revelation, the freedom and
tension of God in his responses to human action (Hos. 11), the variety of human
conditions, the varied humanity of its authors, and its variety of contexts.[10]

---

9. For useful reading on biblical theology, see Clowney, *Mystery*; Dumbrell, *Israel*;
   Goldsworthy, *According to Plan*, and *Whole Bible*; Motyer, *Rock*; Vos, *Redemptive
   History*; and Wright, *Knowing Jesus*. See also Adam, *Speaking*, pp. 109–112, and Adam,
   Hearing, pp. 42–43, 119–138.
10. See Carson, 'Unity and Diversity in the New Testament', in Carson and
    Woodbridge, *Scripture*, pp. 777–795.

It is illuminating to work out the relationships between 'contradictions' in the Bible. For example, contrast 'Honour your father and your mother' (Exod. 20:12) and 'Whoever comes to me and does not hate father and mother . . . cannot be my disciple' (Luke 14:26). Or contrast 'Whoever is not with me is against me' (Matt. 12:30) and 'Whoever is not against us is for us' (Mark 9:40). Or contrast Romans 13:1, 'Let every person be subject to the governing authorities', and Acts 5:29, 'We must obey God rather than any human authority.' In each case both are true, but they are true in different ways. As Oliver O'Donovan wrote, 'Reading for contrast . . . can be wonderfully illuminating of the text.'[11] So too it is better to look at the distinctives of the four Gospels, rather than to amalgamate them.

Yet this diversity does not preclude unity. This is not a scientific unity, nor a lowest-common-denominator unity, but a unity of purpose and of themes, ultimately finding its focus in Jesus Christ and the gospel.[12]

There is one word of God, one gospel, promised in the Old Testament, and fulfilled in the New Testament. And from that promise and fulfilment, we have the accumulated revelation for the one people of God, that serves God's gospel plan in Jesus Christ, through the church. These long-term accumulated words come together to point to Jesus Christ.

One God, one gospel, one book

The unity of the Bible derives from our monotheistic faith. There is one God, and all times, all places, and all people come under his rule and providence. It is instructive to see that the great Old Testament statement about the oneness of God is followed by the requirement to love this one God by reflecting on his words: 'Hear, O Israel: The LORD is our God, the LORD alone. You shall love the LORD your God with all your heart, and with all your soul, and with all your might. Keep these words that I am commanding you today in your heart' (Deut. 6:4–6).

Just as there is one God, so there is one gospel, calling people to believe in the only Son of this one God, Jesus Christ. For, as God promised in the Old Testament:

> There is no other god besides me,
> a righteous God and a Saviour;
> there is no one besides me.

---

11. O'Donovan, *Articles*, 57.

12. As Richard Bauckham says, the Bible's unity is more postmodern than modern in style. See Bauckham, *Bible and Mission*.

Turn to me and be saved,
   all the ends of the earth!'
(Isa. 45:21–22)

There is one God, one Saviour, one mediator, one Holy Spirit, one gospel truth, one people of God, and one message of salvation. Paul wrote that there is 'one body and one Spirit . . . one hope of your calling, one Lord, one faith, one baptism, one God and Father of all' (Eph. 4:4–6).

The unity of the Scriptures comes from the one mind and plan of the one true and living God, and teaches his one gospel about the one and only Saviour, Jesus Christ, our Lord. 'All of Scripture is but one book, uttered by the One Holy Spirit.'[13]

'For us', as Paul wrote, 'there is one God, the Father, from whom are all things and for whom we exist, and one Lord, Jesus Christ, through whom are all things and through whom we exist' (1 Cor. 8:6).[14]

Through many human authors, writing at different times and places, in different circumstances and for different purposes, and in different styles and genres, the one divine author achieved his one gospel purpose, to reveal himself as God, Father, Son, and Holy Spirit.[15]

How should we think of the relationship between the words of God that comprise the Bible, and the Word, Jesus Christ, the Word made flesh? Of course, Jesus the Word of God is central to our understanding of God, as God the Son reveals God to us. And Jesus is the one mediator between God and humanity, and we rightly worship him as God, the Word made flesh. However, it is also the case that to call Jesus the Word is to use metaphorical language.[16] It means that the Son reveals the Father: Jesus is 'the natural voice of God', 'God's perfect speech'.[17] However, Jesus is not often described as 'the Word', and the most common use of the idea of God speaking in the Bible is that of God using human words.[18] Furthermore, we should note that without the

---

13. Cyril of Alexandria, quoted in Schökel, *Inspired Word*, p. 83.

14. See Wright, *Mission*, pp. 121–135.

15. See Carson, 'Unity and Diversity in the New Testament', in Carson and Woodbridge, *Scripture*, pp. 65–95.

16. For those who think that the idea of God speaking human words is itself a metaphor, describing Jesus as the Word of God is the metaphorical use of metaphorical language!

17. Webb, *Divine Voice*, pp. 69, 132.

18. Jensen, *Revelation*, pp. 47–49.

Bible, and our confidence that the Bible contains the words of God, we would not have understood that God is Trinity, that Jesus is the Son of God and the Word of God. The defence of the divinity of Christ in the early church was based on the right interpretation of the Bible verses about Christ. Without the Bible, our experience of God would only lead us to mystical Unitarianism. We needed Bible clarity to understand God the Father, God the Son, and God the Spirit. In the words of Kevin Vanhoozer, 'Jesus Christ is both the material and the formal principle of the canon: its substance and its hermeneutic'.[19]

One God, one gospel

The message of the Bible is God, and the gospel of his Son Jesus, revealed and applied through the Holy Spirit. It is worth thinking very carefully about the gospel, lest we miss the intention of the Scriptures, and so miss receiving God's words.

Here is Paul's famous summary of the gospel in 1 Corinthians 15:3–5: 'For I handed on to you as of first importance what I in turn had received: that Christ died for our sins in accordance with the scriptures, and that he was buried, and that he was raised on the third day in accordance with the scriptures, and that he appeared to Cephas, then to the twelve.'

Notice that there are three ingredients in this gospel statement: what Christ did (salvation history), what it meant (biblical theology), and how we know what happened and what it meant (Scripture). Each of these three is found in Holy Scripture (see Table 1).

Note the following:

Table 1

What happened	What it meant	How we know what happened and what it meant
'Christ died' 'He was buried'	'For our sins'	'In accordance with the Scriptures'
'He was raised on the third day'		'In accordance with the Scriptures'

What happened: 'Christ died'; 'he was buried'; 'he was raised on the third day'
The gospel is about what happened in history, what Christ did in history. We see in the Gospels that the death of the Messiah, the Christ, was a scandalous

---

19. Vanhoozer, *Drama*, p. 195.

idea to Jesus' disciples.[20] The death and resurrection of Christ are at the heart of the gospel.

The three statements go together. He died, and so he was buried. He was buried, to show that he really had died. His burial confirmed both his death and the miracle of his resurrection from the dead. He died 'for our sins', and his resurrection demonstrated that his death had been effective.

We so easily move to claims about the present: 'Christ loves us', 'God rescues us', 'God calls us', 'Christ cares for us', etc. These are true, but we know that they are true because of what happened to Christ. The present power of Christ's love was once for all expressed at the cross, and all the benefits he brings to us, such as forgiveness of our sins, freedom from God's condemnation, peace with God, free access to God, adoption as God's children, the gift of the Spirit, etc., are benefits that he won for us in his death and resurrection.

What it meant: 'For our sins'

Christ died *for our sins*, that is, both 'on our behalf', and 'to deal with our sins'.[21] Christ died for our benefit, and that benefit was to deal with our sins. He dealt with our sins by being our priest and sacrifice, by atoning for our sins by bearing them in his own body on the cross, dying as our substitute, in our place. In Jesus' words: 'This is my blood of the covenant, which is poured out for many for the forgiveness of sins' (Matt. 26:28). Or as Peter wrote: 'You know that you were ransomed from the futile ways inherited from your ancestors, not with perishable things like silver or gold, but with the precious blood of Christ, like that of a lamb without defect or blemish' (1 Pet. 1:18).

Christ died for *our* sins. We often think and say that Christ died for me, for you. There is only one place in the New Testament where Paul writes of 'the Son of God, who loved me and gave himself for me' (Gal. 2:20). Otherwise it is about Christ's death and resurrection for many, for his people, for the world, for the nations: 'The Son of Man came . . . to serve, and to give his life a ransom *for many*' (Mark 10:45); 'The good shepherd lays down his life *for the sheep*' (John 10:11); 'God so loved *the world* . . .' (John 3:16); and 'Repentance and forgiveness of sins [will] be proclaimed in his name to *all nations*' (Luke 24:47).

When we individualize the gospel we reduce its significance, confirm people's natural self-obsession, and lessen the convert's commitment to world mission. No wonder some Christians think that they can be followers of Christ without belonging to a church, that church membership is an optional extra,

---

20. E.g. Matt. 16:21–23.
21. Barrett, *1 Corinthians*, p. 338.

when they have been fed an individualized gospel. No wonder we find it difficult to interest people in God's great mission to the world, when they have become Christians with such a reduced gospel as 'Christ died for you'. 'For our sins' explains the meaning of his death, just as the rest of the chapter explains the meaning of his resurrection.

How we know what happened and what it meant: 'In accordance with the Scriptures'
The Bible is part of the gospel! For the Bible is God's description, promise, and explanation of the gospel. We short-change people when we keep from them the key to knowing the gospel. If we teach people the gospel and not the Bible, we make them rely on us, and make them vulnerable to anything they might hear in the future.

The phrase 'in accordance with the Scriptures' probably means 'as promised, predicted and interpreted in the Old Testament'. As Peter said: 'All the prophets testify about him that everyone who believes in him receives forgiveness of sins through his name' (Acts 10:43). For Christ's 'sufferings . . . and the subsequent glory' were the subject of Old Testament prophecy (1 Pet. 1:11).

It explains how we know the meaning and significance of Christ's promised death and resurrection. We know of Christ's death and resurrection, and the meaning of that death and resurrection, because these events were promised and explained in the Old Testament Scriptures, and described and explained again in the New Testament Scriptures. We know salvation history because it is recorded in the Bible. We know biblical theology because it is recorded in the Bible. The Bible is God's revelation about his Son. In the words of Jerome, 'Ignorance of Scripture is ignorance of Christ.'[22]

We are beneficiaries of those who have gone before us, the people of God throughout history. We have the enduring verbal revelation for the one people of God, that comes from the mind of God through the Holy Spirit, and serves God's gospel plan through the church, for the world, in Jesus Christ.[23] The Bible comprises God's words written for his people by his Spirit about his Son. And this gospel, this 'word of God' in the words of God, is not only able to bring people to faith in Christ and to salvation; it is powerful enough to plant churches, to bring believers to maturity in Christ, and to bring churches to that same maturity.

---

22. As quoted in Flannery, *Vatican Council*, p. 764.

23. I have developed these themes in Adam, *Speaking*, chapters 1 and 2; *Hearing*, chapter 4.

**'Every word of God proves true . . . Do not add to his words, or . . .
you will be found a liar' (Prov. 30:5–6): the completeness of Scripture**

The apostles and prophets of the early church received and passed on the
teaching that Jesus Christ promised would come through them by the work of
the Holy Spirit of truth, the 'other Advocate' or 'Comforter'. After they have
finished this ministry, there is no new universal revelation until the return of
Christ. As we will see in our study of John 14 – 16, many churches teach that
there will be more revelation, new truths, or greater truth. As we will find, the
promises of Christ about the ministry of the Holy Spirit were addressed to his
apostles for a particular time and ministry, and were not general teaching
addressed to all believers in every age.

The development of the doctrines about Christ (two natures, one person,
etc.), about the Trinity (three persons, one God), and about the Bible (including inspiration, authority, sufficiency, trustworthiness) were developments
about what the Bible taught, and not understood to be additional ideas or new
revelations.

Indeed, we cannot think of any new revelations since the end of the New
Testament which have made a positive contribution to Christianity. God
continues to reveal what he always revealed to us through the Scriptures since
the apostles, but has not added any substantial new revelations. We see
some things with new clarity, we learn from one another, we learn new things
because we bring new questions and issues to our study of the Scriptures. And
the Holy Spirit is always at work, opening our minds, and opening the
Scriptures to us. Praise God!

Until the return of Christ there are no new works of God (salvation
history), because there are no new words of God (biblical theology). Jesus
Christ was God's final work and word to us, and now we wait for his promised
return. The sufficiency of Christ is matched by the sufficiency of the Bible.

The work of the early church in clarifying doctrines of the person of Christ
and the Trinity was not an attempt to add to Scripture, but to interpret it rightly.
As T. F. Torrance wrote: 'The one, holy, catholic and apostolic Church is the
Church continuously occupied with the interpretation, exposition and application of Holy Scripture, for it is in that way that the Church opens its mind
and life to the direction and correction of the Word of God.'[24]

The words of the local prophets in New Testament churches were not preserved in the Bible, for they were of local interest only, and had to be tested

---

24. Torrance, *Faith*, p. 288.

before they were approved (Acts 21:7–14; 1 Cor. 14:26–33). They were not added to the word of God for the universal people of God in every age.

We will examine the issue of post-biblical verbal revelation in chapter 19, and Jesus' warning to the Pharisees about the danger of adding their traditions to the word of God in chapter 9.

Here are some affirmations by Christians of bygone ages about the sufficiency or completeness of Scripture. Tertullian: 'I adore the fullness of the Scriptures.' Basil: 'It is a proof of unbelief and a sign of pride either to weaken any of those things which are written or to introduce what is not written', and 'Let the divinely inspired Scriptures judge for us.' And Gregory of Nyssa: 'The inspired writing is the safe criterion of every doctrine.'[25]

We already have 'the faith that was once for all entrusted to the saints' (Jude 3), God's words written for his people by his Spirit about his Son.[26]

In this chapter we have seen that the Bible is about Jesus Christ, and that it is a self-interpreting book and its own 'Great Code'. We have learned that it warns of error as much as it shows what is true, and that the one gospel comes from the fact that there is one God with one gospel purpose through Christ. We studied Paul's summary of the gospel in 1 Corinthians 15, the relationship between Jesus the Word of God and the words of God in Scripture, and noticed that the sufficiency of Scripture derives from the unity of salvation history and biblical theology, the unity of the works and words of God.

---

25. As quoted in Turretin, *Theology*, 1, pp. 139, 162, 157.
26. See also Adam, 'The Preacher and the Sufficient Word'.

Part 2

RECEIVING GOD'S WORDS

5. GOD CAME DOWN TO SPEAK

EXODUS 19 – 25

We find a vivid and formative picture of the verbal self-revelation of God in the book of Exodus.

There are three places in the book of Exodus where God is described as 'coming down' to his people. The first is in Exodus 3:8, when God told Moses, 'I have observed the misery of my people . . . have heard their cry . . . and I have come down to deliver them' (3:7–8).

The second is in Exodus 19 – 20, where we read that God the Lord 'descended upon Mount Sinai . . . [he] summoned Moses . . . Then God spoke all these words . . .' (19:20; 20:1).

The third is in Exodus 24:16. Here we read of the instructions to Moses about building the tabernacle: 'Have them make me a sanctuary, so that I may dwell among them' (25:8); then in Exodus 40, when the tabernacle had been completed, 'the cloud covered the tent of meeting, and the glory of the LORD filled the tabernacle' (40:34). So God came down to deliver his people (Exod. 1 – 18), God came down to speak to his people (Exod. 19 – 24), and God came down to live among his people (Exod. 25 – 40).

Exodus records one of the defining moments in the history of God's people. Here God showed himself to be the God who kept his promises, delivered his people, spoke to his people, gave them his law and made a covenant with them, and came to live among them. The covenant words of the law form a pattern of words that are relevant for God's people at that time at Sinai, but which are also written and preserved for future generations. For Moses 'received living oracles' (Acts 7:38) to give to the people, and to us.

God came down to his people at Mount Sinai (19:16–25)

God came down to speak to his people. The Lord God, who brought the people out of Egypt, and to Mount Sinai, then 'came down' or 'descended' to meet them at the mountain. 'Now Mount Sinai was wrapped in smoke, because the LORD had descended upon it in fire' (19:18). God had summoned his people to Mount Sinai, and then he 'came down' to speak with them, to give them the law, to make a covenant with them, and to give them instructions about the building of the tabernacle. God's descent to the mountain is a sign of the future incarnation of Christ. For later, God in Christ 'descended into the lower parts of the earth' (Eph. 4:9).

God spoke all these words (20:1–3)

God's words are self-revealing, self-disclosing, self-introducing: 'Then God spoke all these words: I am the LORD your God, who brought you out of the land of Egypt, out of the house of slavery; you shall have no other gods before me' (20:1–3).

Here God introduced himself in terms of his name, 'the LORD ', the name by which he earlier revealed himself to Moses (3:13–15). He also revealed his relationship with them and their relationship with him: 'your God', and also by what he did for his covenant people: 'who brought you out of the land of Egypt'. God took the initiative in relating to his people. For 'the LORD your God' had been the God of this people since he chose them for himself.

Clearly, God's formal, self-introductory words stress his relationship with his people, as the first 'command' ('word') that the covenant-making God gives his people is 'You shall have no other gods before me' (20:3). The centrality of relationship is also found in chapter 24, in the making of the covenant of which these words are a part. For God's word is 'God's self performance',[1] as God revealed himself to his people.[2]

---

1. Bartow, *God's Speech*, p. 26.
2. See also Exod. 34:5 ff.

In fact, when the people saw and heard these things from around the mountain, they did not want to hear God's voice. '[They] said to Moses, "You speak to us, and we will listen; but do not let God speak to us, or we will die"' (20:19). However, God is still the God who speaks, and so he will speak his words to Moses, who will then pass on God's words to his people.

Moses wrote down God's words (24:3–4)

Moses passed on the words that God had spoken to him, acting as a true prophet of God. 'Moses came and told the people all the words of the LORD and all the ordinances; and all the people answered with one voice, and said, "All the words that the LORD has spoken we will do." And Moses wrote down all the words of the LORD ' (24:3–4).

It is easy to miss the significance of Moses' action here. Writing was a serious business at that time, and only words of great and long-term significance were written down. The people of God of that time did not need the words of God to be written down, because Moses had first spoken the words. These words were written down because they had great significance for God's people for the rest of their lives, and for all future generations. For the words were covenant words, words by which God promised his covenant constancy and faithfulness to his people, and words by which God also instructed his people how he wanted them to live and serve him. The two stone tablets of the words and the book of the covenant that Moses wrote were lost, but we still have the words that Moses wrote down for God's people.

For these covenant words of God were relevant for every generation of God's people in Old Testament times and beyond. These covenant words of the law of God remain relevant for the people of God in every age, even after the coming of Christ. For Jesus said, 'Do not think that I have come to abolish the law or the prophets; I have come not to abolish but to fulfil. For truly I tell you, until heaven and earth pass away, not one letter, not one stroke of a letter, will pass from the law until all is accomplished' (Matt. 5:17–18).

This law of God not only shows us that we are sinners; it also points to its fulfilment in Christ. Of course, the law is interpreted from a new-covenant perspective, but it is still relevant to Christian believers. Rightly understood in the light of Christ's coming, parts of this law also show us how we should live as God's people today.[3] So we find, for example, in Paul's instructions to

---

3. See Enns, *Inspiration*, pp. 115–116.

children in Ephesians, 'Children, obey your parents in the Lord, for this is right. "Honour your father and mother" – this is the first commandment with a promise: "so that it may be well with you and you may live long on the earth"' (6:1–3).

The essential role of the words of God in the relationship between God and his people is very clear in the event of the golden calf, when in the absence of Moses God's people made a calf and worshipped it. Moses went down to the people, carrying the two tablets of the covenant in his hands. When Moses saw what the people had done, their idolatry, 'he threw the tablets from his hands and broke them at the foot of the mountain' (Exod. 32:19). So the covenant between God and his people was broken, just as the words of that covenant were broken.

After the prayer and intercession of Moses, and the judgment of the people, God again made a covenant with his people, represented by the instruction to Moses: 'Cut two tablets of stone like the former ones, and I will write on the tablets the words that were on the former tablets, which you broke' (Exod. 34:1). When Moses had done this, and ascended the mountain, taking the two tablets of stone, 'The LORD descended in the cloud and stood with him there, and proclaimed the name, "The LORD"' (34:5). So the people were forgiven, the covenant restored, and the LORD revealed as 'the LORD, the LORD, a God merciful and gracious, slow to anger, and abounding in steadfast love and faithfulness' (34:6).

The covenant is made up of words, words of God's promise, God's plan, God's character, and God's requirements of his covenant people. Moses not only spoke God's words; he also wrote them down.[4]

God used the 'book of the covenant' and 'the blood of the covenant' to join himself to his covenant people (24:4–8)

We often think of what happened on Mount Sinai as 'God giving the law to his people'. Yet here we find that there is more going on than the giving of the law.

Moses . . . rose early in the morning, and built an altar at the foot of the mountain . . . He sent young men of the people of Israel, who offered burnt-offerings and sacrificed oxen as offerings of well-being to the LORD. Moses took half of the blood and put it in basins, and half of the blood he dashed against the altar. Then he took the book of

---

4. For Moses as writer, see also Exod. 17:14; Num. 33:2; Deut. 31:9–29; 32.

the covenant, and read it in the hearing of the people; and they said, 'All that the LORD has spoken we will do, and we will be obedient.' Moses took the blood and dashed it on the people, and said, 'See the blood of the covenant that the LORD has made with you in accordance with all these words.' (24:4–8)

What was the relationship between book and blood? The book contained the words of God, the content of the covenant. The covenant book reminded God's people who God is, and who they are, and also reminded them of the terms of the covenant, what God asks of them, and what God promises to do for them.[5]

The first function of the blood is that it is addressed to God, as Moses sprinkled half of the blood on the altar (24:6). It is by the offering of sacrifices that sin was atoned for as God's wrath and judgment were deflected onto the animal that had died. The sacrifices secured the promise of a restored relationship between God and his people. George Knight wrote: 'God . . . has placed in man's hands the means by which he will forgive sins, if only man wants to use those means.'[6] The covenant blood binds God. He promised later to keep his words: 'As for you, because of the blood of my covenant with you, I will set your prisoners free' (Zech. 9:11).

The second function of the blood is for the people. The forgiveness offered in this covenant sacrifice is not for any particular sin, but for the general and habitual sinfulness of the people. God's grace and forgiveness are crucial, because the sin of the people is habitual. For despite the repeated affirmation of the people that they will do what God has said (Exod. 24:3, 7), within forty days they will have broken their words by creating and worshipping the golden calf. Their potential for sinfulness in keeping their promises was implicit in Moses' offering burnt-offerings as well as offerings of well-being in Exodus 24. Offerings of well-being represent and express the fellowship between God and his people (Lev. 3). Burnt-offerings clearly imply that they will need the forgiveness of God in this relationship, for in Leviticus 1:4 we read that the burnt-offering 'shall be acceptable in your behalf as atonement for you'.

Words and blood go together, for it is by the blood of the new covenant that God will put his laws in their minds, and write them on their hearts (Heb. 8:10).

Covenant blood wins forgiveness for the failure of the people to obey the words of the covenant, and appeals to God to maintain the covenant, despite

---

5. These elements can be clearly seen in Exod. 23:23–32, and see Motyer, *Exodus*, p. 247.

6. Quoted in Tidball, *Leviticus*, p. 78.

the failure of the covenant people. The writer of Hebrews comments on
Exodus 24:

> Hence not even the first covenant was inaugurated without blood. For when every
> commandment had been told to all the people by Moses in accordance with the law,
> he took the blood of calves and goats, with water and scarlet wool and hyssop, and
> sprinkled both the scroll itself and all the people, saying, 'This is the blood of the
> covenant that God has ordained for you' . . . Indeed under the law almost everything
> is purified with blood, and without the shedding of blood there is no forgiveness of
> sins. (Heb. 9:18–22)

Not only is the new covenant promised in the Bible, but so too is Jesus' role
in the making of that new covenant. Our covenant relationship with God is
'covered with a warranty sealed in blood'.[7] The blood of Christ achieves and
seals the covenant, provides forgiveness of sins to God's covenant people, and
binds God and his people together. In Jesus' words: 'This is my blood of the
covenant, which is poured out for many for the forgiveness of sins' (Matt.
26:28).

No wonder we believers find such strength and comfort in Jesus, and in 'his
oath, his covenant and blood'. In the Bible we find the Lord Jesus Christ
clothed in his gospel promises, the covenant promises of our faithful God, and
find the new covenant sealed and guaranteed by the blood of Christ.

Clearly, the law was given so that God and his people can be joined
together in holy covenant, joined by the blood of the covenant and the book
of the covenant. Both blood and book link God and his people. The blood of
the covenant is dashed against the altar (representing God), and dashed on
the people, so linking the two; and the book of the covenant is read as God's
words to his people, binding both God and the people to their covenant
responsibilities.

In the later prophets this event was described as the marriage of God with
his people: 'I passed by you again and looked on you . . . I pledged myself to
you and entered into covenant with you, says the LORD God, and you became
mine' (Ezek. 16:8).

This marriage of God to his people on Mount Sinai was a foreshadowing
of the final marriage of Lamb to his bride, the church. 'Christ loved the church
and gave himself up for her, in order to make her holy by cleansing her with
the washing of water by the word, so as to present [her] to himself in splendour'

---

7. Hans Urs von Balthasar, as quoted in Work, *Living*, 103.

(Eph. 5:25–27). And again, 'I saw the holy city, the new Jerusalem, coming down out of heaven from God, prepared as a bride adorned for her husband' (Rev. 21:2).

The words of the law are the proposal of marriage, so the response of the people is a joyful acceptance of those words, that covenant, and their God: 'All that the LORD has spoken we will do, and we will be obedient' (24:7). The words of God and the words of the people are the means by which the marriage is established and expressed. Words are central to any marriage: they express the relationship, and are the covenant promise to maintain the relationship. Covenant book and covenant blood bind God and his people.

The covenant words of God were to be kept in the 'ark of the covenant', God's throne on earth (25:1–22)

God who has 'come down' to rescue and deliver his people, and who has 'come down' to speak to them and to make a covenant with them, is the God who will also 'come down' to live among his people, with 'the ark of the covenant' as his throne among them. Here we come to the climax of the book of Exodus. God's plan was to live among his covenant people.

In Exodus chapters 24 – 31 we read of the instructions that God gave to Moses to build the tabernacle (movable tent), and the ark of the covenant which was to be set in the most holy place within the tabernacle. God's purpose is clearly stated in 25:8: 'And have them make me a sanctuary, so that I may dwell among them.'

Then God gave Moses the instructions about the building of 'the ark of the covenant'.[8] 'They shall make an ark of acacia wood; it shall be two and a half cubits long, a cubit and a half wide, and a cubit and a half high . . . You shall put into the ark the covenant that I shall give you' (25:10, 16). The 'covenant' was to be put in this ark or box. This 'covenant' was the two stone blocks with the covenant words engraved on them. The 'ark' was God's throne on earth, so God's covenant relationship with his people was present within his throne, in the form of the words of the covenant. The words were there to remind God and remind the people of the details of their covenant relationship: 'You shall put the mercy-seat on the top of the ark; and in the ark you shall put the covenant that I shall give you. There I will meet you, and from above the

---

8. The 'ark of the covenant' was a rectangular box, with provision for rings and rods so that it could be carried.

mercy-seat, from between the two cherubim that are on the ark of the covenant, I will deliver to you all my commands for the Israelites' (25:21–22).

The 'mercy-seat' was the cover of the box, and God's seat or throne. It was the sign of God's mercy, and was the place described in the ritual of the Day of Atonement, when the cloud of incense covered this mercy-seat, and the high priest sprinkled blood from the sin offerings on the front of the mercy-seat and before it, to make atonement for himself, and then for the people (Lev. 16:11–16). The two cherubim placed at either end of the mercy-seat were there to show that God is present, seated on his throne, with the words of the law inside his throne. In Psalm 80 we read, 'You who are enthroned upon the cherubim, shine forth . . . Stir up you might, and come to save us!' (Ps. 80:1–2).

God's words were to be kept in perpetuity, as the sign of his covenant with his people.

These actions and words and works of God were not only preserved for future generations of Israel in the Old Testament, but are also preserved for believers of new-covenant times, who know that 'our paschal lamb, Christ, has been sacrificed', and that 'these things were written down to instruct us, on whom the ends of the ages have come' (1 Cor. 5:7; 10:11).

These words are the means of access that people of later generations have to the history and meaning of the works and words of God. The works of God are definitive for the people to whom they happen, but also for future generations of God's people. These acts of God must be remembered, and they can be remembered only if they are again recounted among God's people.

The climax of the book of Exodus is in chapter 40, when 'the cloud covered the tent of meeting, and the glory of the LORD filled the tabernacle' (40:34). Consider these words in their context within the whole of the book of Exodus. God has delivered his people from Egypt, and brought them to Mount Sinai. He has made his covenant with them, and given them his laws and instructions. He has told them to build a dwelling-place, a sanctuary, that he might live among them. They have been delivered, they have received his words, and they have built the tabernacle according to his instructions. (The words 'they did everything just as the LORD had commanded them' and their variants come eight times in these last chapters.) So the climax of the works and words of God is that God himself comes to live among his people, to be present and dwell among them. Furthermore, there is a visible public sign of God's presence, that is, the cloud during the day and the fire in the cloud at night (40:36–38).

In Judaism today, there is no temple, and no ark of the covenant to put in the temple. The ark of the covenant constructed by Moses was carried through the wilderness for forty years, and taken across the Jordan into the promised land. It was later placed in the temple built by Solomon, and then carried off into exile in Babylon. While some cups, plates and other vessels returned to Jerusalem (Ezra 1), the ark of the covenant itself was never returned, and was presumably lost and destroyed when Babylon itself was overthrown.[9] There was no ark of the covenant in the second temple, built after the return from the exile in Babylon, and so no ark in Herod's rebuilt temple of Jesus' day.

Yet in every synagogue, there is what is called 'the ark', where the sacred writings are kept, and from which they are taken to be read and preached. The name 'the ark' is a reminder of that 'ark of the covenant' that was the throne of God on earth. God is still present and speaking in his covenant words.

So three great themes come together in Exodus: the God who is present to act, to speak, and to live or dwell with his people. As so often, what we tend to separate, God puts together. There are groups of Christians who focus on 'the God who acts', and who have a weaker view of 'the God who speaks'. Others focus on 'the God who speaks', and have less interest in 'the God who acts'. Others focus on 'the God who is present', but do not want to be tied down to any specific works or words of God. What we separate, God puts together in Exodus. Of course, we find this revelation of God in Exodus in the words of the book.

We too, as the people of God, still treasure these words, for they tell us of God, and promise the Christ to come, and show us how to be God's people today.

So in Exodus we can see the pattern of God's relationship with his people. God kept his covenant promise to Abraham, rescued his people, spoke to them, gave them his law, and came to live among them. The covenant words of the Law are spoken to the people, but also written and preserved for future generations, including ourselves. Truly Moses 'received living oracles to give to us', and 'was faithful in all God's house as a servant, to testify to the things that would be spoken later' (Acts 7:38; Heb. 3:5).

Here in this chapter we have found that God's coming down to our level was partly expressed through the words that he spoke, as it was later expressed in bodily form in the incarnation. We discovered Moses, the writing prophet, who wrote down the words of God for all generations. We found that the blood of the covenant and the book of the covenant bound God and his people together, and that covenant words, preserved in the ark of the covenant, were a central focus of God's presence, and of the response of the people of God.

---

9. Jer. 3:16.

Jeremiah Burroughs, one of the great preachers of the seventeenth century, wrote a book called *Gospel Worship*, a series of sermons on how to relate to God. He taught that one of the most important things we do each week is to go to church, and there listen to the reading and preaching of the Bible. As you sit still to listen, he explained, 'you come to tender up your homage to God, to sit at God's feet and there to profess your submission to Him'.[10]

God 'comes down' to our human level to speak in human words. And, as we now see, those human words of God are powerful just as God is powerful.

---

10. Burroughs, *Worship*, p. 197.

6. THE POWER OF THE WORD OF THE LORD

ISAIAH 55

Just as Ezra and the other priests in Old Testament times taught the words of God to God's people, so too the prophets were called to bring God's words to his people. I have chosen Isaiah 55 because Isaiah was one of the major prophets of the Old Testament, but also because of the theme of this chapter, the power of God's word. It is often the case that evangelical discussions about the nature of the Bible focus on its truth and authority. However, these topics are not a major preoccupation of the Bible itself. When it describes or refers to itself, it is more often in terms of its power, trustworthiness, and reliability. God's words are powerful, because God is powerful; God's words are trustworthy, because God is faithful. This is not to deny the authority of the Bible, but it does mean that we should understand that authority in the context of the Bible's power and reliability.

Isaiah 55 is a celebration of the power of God's words. As we read it, we should remember that those powerful words include the very words of this chapter: these words exemplify their message, and convey God's power.

God is powerful, creative, and able to achieve his purposes, and the Bible uses a variety of graphic images to convey the significance of that power in action. The right hand of God wins victory, the mighty hand of God delivers his people, the eyes of God see all that happens throughout the world, and also the word of God achieves God's purposes.[1] God creates a new reality by the power of his speaking. God's words not only convey the meaning intended by God, but also create the response that God intends.

Sometimes things go wrong with words. We don't like having people misunderstand our words, or being misquoted. We all know that it is possible to mishear and misunderstand what someone else is saying, or to misread a Bible text. However, there is no need to make a necessity out of a common mistake. We have a moral duty to pay attention to the words of others, to try to enter their world of meaning rather than staying in our own, to discipline our hearing and concentration so as to listen for the meaning and significance of those words to the person who is speaking.[2]

To do this well takes concentration, imagination, patience, interest in the one who speaks, and the humility to admit when we have misheard or misunderstood. The longer we have known someone, and the more attentively we have listened to them in the past, and the more patience and love we have for them, the more likely we are to understand the meaning of their words to us.

However, when we think of our reading of the Bible, then it is not so much a matter of an individual reading an ancient document on his or her own, as of joining a community (the church), which has long experience in hearing these words and reflecting on their meaning. Of course, we may get it wrong; we may be deaf to what God says to us in the Scriptures; we may misconstrue God's meaning; but that does not mean that we can never understand. Attentive, patient, and humble hearing is a form of loving. Thank God that his words are powerful enough to break through our deafness and our misunderstandings, and powerful enough to create in us the positive response of receiving and obeying those words.

The powerful word of the Lord

We begin with words from Isaiah 55:

> For as the rain and the snow come down from heaven,
>   and do not return there until they have watered the earth,
> making it bring forth and sprout,

---

1. Some of the material in this chapter was first published in Adam, 'God's Powerful Words'.
2. Vanhoozer, *Meaning*.

giving seed to the sower and bread to the eater,
so shall my word be that goes out from my mouth;
  it shall not return to me empty,
but it shall accomplish that which I purpose,
  and succeed in the thing for which I sent it.

(55:10–11)

Here is an outline of this chapter:

An invitation, to come, buy and eat (1).
Advice to listen carefully to me (2–3).
The promise of an everlasting covenant (3–5).
(At the heart of the chapter) a command to seek the Lord, to call upon him,
  to forsake wickedness, and to return to a merciful and pardoning God
  (6–7).
The radical nature of the command: 'my thoughts are not your thoughts, nor
  are your ways my ways' (8–9).
The power of the word of God to effect repentance (10–11).
The cosmic effects of the covenant power of God (12–13).[3]

The power of the word of God is of central importance in this chapter. It is
not just a call to repent, to return to God, as if all that is needed is great
human effort. The call of God is an effective call. It is a call or invitation, that
is, it comes in the form of words (1–2). It is effective because it is based on
the hope of an everlasting covenant, based on that made to King David
(3–5). It is effective because God's word will not return empty, but will
accomplish and succeed in achieving God's purpose. God by his word will
bring his people to seek him, call upon him, forsake their wicked ways and
return to their merciful and pardoning God (11, 6–7). It is effective, even
though the minds and hearts of the people are so far away from God's mind
and heart (8–9).

The cosmic effects of God's words are reflected in the comparison between
rain, snow, and the word of God in verses 10–11. 'As the rain and snow come
down from heaven' (10), so does 'my word . . . that goes out from my mouth'
(11). As the rain and snow do not return until they have watered the earth (10),
so God's word does not return to him empty (11). Just as the rain and snow
not only water the earth, but do so purposefully and effectively, making it bring

---

3. Motyer, *Isaiah*, p. 452.

forth and sprout, giving seed to the sower and bread to the eater (10), so God's word achieves all that he intends: 'it shall accomplish that which I purpose, and succeed in the thing for which I sent it' (11).

So too, the results of the effective and powerful word of God are seen in the cosmic renewal of verses 12–13. There is a powerful parallel between God's gift of rain and snow producing fertility and plenty, and God's covenant word achieving fertility and plenty.

We should also note the comparison and contrast between verse 9 and verses 10–11. In verse 9, the theme is that of distance and contrast between heaven and earth, between God and his people:

> For as the heavens are higher than the earth,
> so are my ways higher than your ways
> and my thoughts than your thoughts.

This gap between God's ways and thoughts and the ways and thoughts of the people is not because the latter are merely human, but because they are wicked and unrighteous (7). The word of God bridges the gap between divine and human reality, between heaven and earth, as it goes out from God's mouth to achieve his saving purpose, similar to the rain and snow coming down from heaven (11, 10). God is near in his word, so his people should seek him while he may be found, and call upon him while he is near (6). As Alec Motyer commented: 'The second natural illustration turns on a different relationship between earth and heaven . . . The parallel between the life agency of rain and the effective word is exact . . . The word of God is the unfailing agent of the will of God.'[4]

There is a gap between God and his sinful people, but God bridges the gap by his powerful and effective word. This word will not only communicate present reality, that God's people are far distant from God, but will also effect and bring about a change in that reality, as God brings his people to repentance as they hear and obey his words of invitation and covenant promise. John Oswalt wrote: 'God has come *near* his people, not only in the work of the Servant that has been predicted, but also in the preaching of the prophet throughout the book',[5] and 'It is because *what* God says is the truth that the word *will* perform exactly what God intends.'[6]

---

4. Motyer, *Isaiah*, pp. 457–458.

5. Oswalt, *Isaiah*, pp. 442–443.

6. Ibid., p. 446 fn. 61.

Isaiah 55 in context

Isaiah 40–66

This message of Isaiah 55 is reinforced by its context in the whole book of Isaiah. Barry Webb shows how the theme of chapter 54 is that of 'every promise fulfilled', as we see that God's covenant promises through Abraham (54:1–3), at the exodus (54:4–8), and his covenant with the nations through Noah (54:9–17) will yet reach their complete fulfilment.[7] As their partial fulfilment gives the people hope in trusting God's present promises, so also God's present promises and powerful words will also mean the more complete fulfilment of those covenant promises from the past. Again, as Webb observes, 'the resounding affirmations of the power of God's word in 40:6–8 and 55:10–11 form a kind of bracket around the whole of chapters 40–55.'[8]

Again, we can see the power and efficacy of God's words in the theme of the fulfilment of prophecy in chapters 40 – 48. God's words have not only predicted the future deliverance from exile in Babylon, but have created it, as God's words achieve God's will. In contrast, the gods of the nations cannot predict, much less create, the future.

> Who declared it from the beginning, so that we might know,
>   and beforehand, so that we might say, 'He is right'?
> There was no one who declared it, none who proclaimed,
>   none who heard your words.
> I first have declared it to Zion,
>   and I give to Jerusalem a herald of good tidings.
> (41:26–27)[9]

It is not just that God knows the future, but that God creates the future. God's words create the future according to God's will.

As God's word is powerful, so too God values those who receive his word in humility, for they are his true house and resting-place:

> Thus says the LORD:
> Heaven is my throne

---

7. B. Webb, *Isaiah*, pp. 215–216.

8. Ibid., p. 218.

9. See also Isa. 43:8–13.

and the earth is my footstool;
what is the house that you would build for me,
    and what is my resting-place? . . .
But this is the one to whom I will look,
    to the humble and contrite in spirit,
    who trembles at my word.
  (Isa. 66:1–2)

Isaiah 40

The same theme of the power of the word of God is found in Isaiah 40. Here the theme and invitation are found in God's words 'comfort', 'speak', and 'cry' or proclaim (1–2). The words are addressed to God's people in exile in Babylon, just as they are also addressed to the prophet who will take these words to God's people ('What shall I cry?', verse 6).

What is the basis for a message of comfort to the people of God?

The answer is fourfold: they are God's people ('my people', 1); they have been forgiven ('her penalty is paid', 2); God himself will act to deliver them and bring them home ('in the wilderness prepare the way of the LORD, make straight in the desert a highway for our God', 3); and finally, they can trust God's word (though the 'people are grass . . . the word of our God will stand for ever', 6, 8).[10] All of these truths are communicated by means of words, the words of God and of the prophet. These words will stand for ever: they will achieve God's purpose, and accomplish his saving will.

Furthermore, we can see the clear distinction between the destructive force of the breath of the Lord in verse 7 and the enduring power of the word of our God in verse 8. In verses 6–7, the inconstant and ephemeral people are like grass that withers and fades, but this fragility also derives from the breath or wind of God, as when a hot wind devastates grassland. However, if the breath or wind of God means destruction in verse 7, the word of the Lord means hope in verse 8. For if the people are inconstant, God is constant; if the people are mortal, God is unchanging; if the people are ephemeral, God's word will stand for ever.

As we have seen, God's words are powerful, not only to achieve communication, but also to enable a response, and to create a new situation. God's words are powerfully effective, and powerfully fruitful. When God has spoken his powerful human words, how should we respond? Receive and believe God's gracious words written for us.

---

10. B. Webb, *Isaiah*, pp. 160–163.

EZRA 7; NEHEMIAH 8

Moses was the first great prophet of God to his people, and brought to God's people the covenant words of God in the law. That law was written down for us, as also for generations of God's people who lived before the coming of Christ. Moses was the first writing prophet, and his written words are still heard in our churches today. We read and hear them in the light of their fulfilment in Jesus Christ.

In Old Testament times, Moses' words came to the people of God in two ways. The priests had the duty and responsibility of teaching and applying those words to the people, and in this chapter we will see Ezra doing this ministry. The prophets also preached the law, and also applied it in new situations, and added to it all the persuasive power that God gave them. In this chapter we see Ezra, descendant of Moses' brother Aaron, the high priest, leading God's people by teaching them God's law.

The law of the Lord will be taught by Ezra, the priest

The books of Ezra and Nehemiah describe how three large groups of God's people returned from exile in Babylon to live in Jerusalem. The first group returned in Ezra 1 – 2, the second group in Ezra 7 – 8, and the third group in Nehemiah 1 – 7.

God's purpose was not only to bring his people back from captivity in Babylon and settle them in Jerusalem, but also to help the people to reshape their lives so that they could serve him truly and faithfully. He wanted them to stop that way of life that led to their exile, that strange mixture of idolatry and ignoring the words of God (2 Chr. 36). As they had previously ignored the law of Moses, so now they needed to learn it and do it.

God sent Ezra the priest, who not only helped to re-establish the temple, but also performed another priestly task: that of teaching, explaining, and applying the law of the Lord to the people.[1]

> After this, in the reign of King Artaxerxes of Persia . . . Ezra went up from Babylonia . . . Some of the people of Israel, and some of the priests and Levites, the singers and gatekeepers, and the temple servants also went up to Jerusalem, in the seventh year of King Artaxerxes. They came to Jerusalem in the fifth month, which was in the seventh year of the king. (Ezra 7:1, 6–8)

The date given was 458 BC, which was sixty years after the completion of the new temple recorded in Ezra 6. Artaxerxes I was described as the king of Persia, because his ancestor Cyrus, king of Persia, had captured Babylon, and had begun a policy of sending captured people back to their homelands.

Skilled in the law of Moses

What qualities did Ezra have? He was described as a 'scribe' (7:6). To be a 'scribe' meant to be a writer, preserver, and teacher of the law – in Hugh Williamson's description, 'a student and expositor of God's written word'.[2] He was also described as 'skilled in the law of Moses' and a 'scribe of the law of the God of heaven' (Ezra 7:6, 12).[3] He was ready and alert to remember relevant sections of

---

1. See Deut. 33:10a; Hag. 2:10–19; and Mal. 2:4–9.

2. Williamson, *Ezra, Nehemiah*, p. 92.

3. The same expression is used in Ezra 7:21. We see Ezra's successors in the scribes of New Testament times, though by then their Bible study seems to have gone rancid. See for example Jesus' warning in Matt. 23:2, 'The scribes and the Pharisees sit on Moses' seat; therefore, do whatever they teach you and follow it; but do not do as they do, for they do not practise what they teach.'

the Law, and ready and alert to explain the application of that Law. He knew his Bible, and was adept at finding the relevant verse or section.

The gracious hand of God was on the teacher of the Law

It was clear that God was directing his life and ministry: 'The king granted him all that he asked, for the hand of the LORD his God was upon him' (7:6).

God's hand was on him, both in the preparations for the journey, and also in its achievement. The 'gracious hand of his God' (7:9) was a way of saying that God was actively enabling and protecting Ezra's life and work; that his achievements could not be explained in merely human terms. Ezra was obviously aware of his constant dependence on the active protection and blessing of God, for in the words of personal praise that end this chapter, we read: 'I took courage, for the hand of the LORD my God was upon me, and I gathered leaders from Israel to go up with me' (7:28).

As God's 'right hand . . . glorious in power . . . shattered the enemy' (Exod. 15:6), and brought the people of Israel out of Egypt, so the gracious hand of God was on Ezra, protecting him, enabling him, and making his ministry productive.

We frequently read of 'the hand of God', or 'the gracious hand of God', in Ezra. In Ezra 8:18 we read again that 'the gracious hand of our God was upon us', in 8:22, 'that the hand of our God is gracious to all who seek him, but his power and his wrath are against all who forsake him', and in 8:31, 'the hand of our God was upon us, and he delivered us from the hand of the enemy and from ambushes along the way'.

The teacher of the law set his heart to study, practise, and teach that law

We find that Ezra's skill in Bible teaching was not a matter of a slick mind. It came from determined and disciplined long-term activities, those of study, practice, and teaching it to others. 'For Ezra had set his heart to study the law of the LORD, and to do it, and to teach the statutes and ordinances in Israel' (7:10).

What he learned, he put into practice, and what he learned and put into practice he also taught to others. Furthermore, the word 'study' could be better translated 'interpret'.[4] His study was an exercise not just in memory, but in

---

4. Ellis, *Old Testament*, p. 91. The word is *darash*, from which we get the word *midrash*.

interpretation and understanding. Not for him the self-indulgence of learning without doing, or learning without bothering to explain to others. Not for him that shallow teaching of others without a lifetime of learning and self-disciplined action. Not for him unthinking practice without serious learning, or that selfish practice that does not bother to encourage others to learn and do as well. Derek Kidner wrote of Ezra:

> He is a model reformer in that what he taught he had first lived, and what he lived he had first made sure of in the Scriptures. With *study, conduct and teaching* put deliberately in the right order, each of these was able to function properly at its best: study was saved from unreality, conduct from uncertainty, and teaching from insincerity and shallowness.[5]

The people of God wanted the law of God

Here is the great picture of Ezra's public ministry of bringing God's word to God's people that we find in Nehemiah 8 – 10. 'All the people gathered together into the square before the Water Gate. They told the scribe Ezra to bring the book of the law of Moses, which the LORD had given to Israel' (Neh. 8:1).

What an extraordinary moment, when the people of God beg to hear the word of God! What a contrast to that account in 2 Chronicles 36, where we read of God's people before the exile, that 'they kept mocking the messengers of God, despising his words, and scoffing at his prophets, until the wrath of the LORD against his people became so great that there was no remedy' (2 Chr. 36:16).

This is an encouraging sign of God's effective work in bringing reformation and renewal to his people. They now welcomed and received his words through the teacher he had sent.

The reading of the law

> Accordingly, the priest Ezra brought the law before the assembly, both men and women and all who could hear with understanding. This was on the first day of the seventh month. He read from it facing the square before the Water Gate from early morning until midday, in the presence of the men and the women and those who

---

5. Kidner, *Ezra and Nehemiah*, p. 62.

could understand; and the ears of all the people were attentive to the book of the law. The scribe Ezra stood on a wooden platform that had been made for the purpose. (Neh. 8:2–4)

The book of *2 Esdras*, not in our Bible, but a popular book within Judaism, described Ezra as a second Moses, bringing a new revelation to the people of God. However, the text of Ezra and Nehemiah repeats the point that Ezra was a scribe of the law of Moses, reading, teaching, explaining and applying that teaching, and not bringing a new teaching.

Here we have the public reading of the word of God, and also the first pulpit mentioned in the Bible, a pulpit large enough for fourteen people! Perhaps they took it in turns to read and explain, or perhaps Ezra wanted leaders of the people to identify publicly with this vital moment in the history of the reformation of God's people after their return from exile.

God was present in his words

And Ezra opened the book in the sight of all the people, for he was standing above all the people; and when he opened it, all the people stood up. Then Ezra blessed the LORD, the great God, and all the people answered, 'Amen, Amen', lifting up their hands. Then they bowed their heads and worshipped the LORD with their faces to the ground. (Neh. 8:5–6)

Notice the actions of the people. They stood up, as they welcomed God into their presence (verse 5). They lifted up their hands, as they yearned to hear the words of the Lord (6). They bowed their heads to the ground, and worshipped the Lord, who was present with them in his words (6). Here were the people of God as they were at Mount Sinai, not the people of God gathered around the word of God, but the people of God gathered around God, who was present and speaking to them through his words. As Derek Kidner wrote, 'What is strikingly apparent is the royal reception given to the Word of God.'[6]

This is not bibliolatry (the worship of a book or scroll), because the people are clearly worshipping the Lord.[7] Yet neither is it the dispassionate study of some words and ideas, even words and ideas of divine authority: the people

---

6. Kidner, *Ezra and Nehemiah*, pp. 105–106.
7. See Ward, 'Incarnation and Scripture', for an explanation of the difference between respecting Scripture and worshipping Christ.

not only listened, but they stood up, then raised their hands in prayer, then bowed their heads to the ground as they knew that God was present in his words. This a great example for us as we welcome the words of God among us.

The law of God read, explained, and understood

The law of God was not only read, but also explained, or translated and explained. The Levites had the job of moving through the crowd, possibly translating for those who understood Aramaic better than the Hebrew of the law of Moses, and certainly explaining the meaning and implications of what Ezra was reading. 'The Levites . . . helped the people to understand the law, while the people remained in their places. So they read from the book, from the law of God, with interpretation. They gave the sense, so that the people understood the reading' (Neh 8:7–8).[8]

Ezra and his colleagues were working hard so that the people could understand the law and its meaning. The reading was given in sections, for the text says, 'from the book, from the law of God'. This meant that the people had time to hear and understand, not least because the Levites also gave an explanation of each of the sections. The summary makes it clear that understanding is the result. We can hear resonances with Paul's words in 1 Corinthians, 'I would rather speak five words with my mind, in order to instruct others also, than ten thousand words in a tongue', and, 'Let all things be done for building up' (1 Cor. 14:19, 26), while making it clear that 'building up', or 'edification', occurs only when there is comprehensible explanation given in love (1 Cor. 13 – 14). Ignorance is not bliss, and uncomprehending submission is not enough.

Nehemiah 8 also foreshadowed the notable addition that the Lord Jesus made to the great command to 'love God'. For in the Old Testament, it read: 'You shall love the LORD your God with all your heart, and with all your soul, and with all your might' (Deut. 6:5). To this demanding requirement Jesus Christ added the words 'with all your mind', when he said: 'you shall love the Lord your God with all your heart, and with all your soul, and with all your mind, and with all your strength' (Mark 12:30). Mindless religion is not the goal of either the Old Testament or the New Testament. The people of God

---

8. The role of the Levites in the teaching of the Law is found in Deut. 33:10 and 2 Chr. 17:7–9.

should be a learning people, a people who want to be taught the words of God. The leaders of God's people must be teachers of the words of God, so that the people can understand, and respond in faith and obedience.

God's words bring grief and joy

Right understanding leads to an emotional response to the words and message of God. The people were rightly disturbed, because they had been hearing about the Feast of Tabernacles (Neh. 8:13–18), and they were upset because they had not been celebrating this festival. The people were instructed to keep the Feast of Tabernacles in Leviticus 23:39–43 and Deuteronomy 16:13–15. We read in Nehemiah 8:9–12:

> And Nehemiah, who was the governor, and Ezra the priest and scribe, and the Levites who taught the people said to all the people, 'This day is holy to the LORD your God; do not mourn or weep.' For all the people wept when they heard the words of the law. Then he said to them, 'Go your way, eat the fat and drink sweet wine and send portions of them to those for whom nothing is prepared, for this day is holy to our LORD; and do not be grieved, for the joy of the LORD is your strength.' So the Levites stilled all the people, saying, 'Be quiet, for this day is holy; do not be grieved.' And all the people went their way to eat and drink and to send portions and to make great rejoicing, because they had understood the words that were declared to them.

Notice the healthy mixture of clear understanding and powerful emotion, and of both grief and joy. No artificial distinction of head and heart in Nehemiah 8!

See, too, that Nehemiah the governor and Ezra the priest not only manage the reading and teaching of the law but also the people's emotional responses of grief and joy. Lots of emotional intelligence and awareness among the leaders of God's people in Nehemiah 8!

Joyful obedience to the words of God

The Bible studies begun in Nehemiah 8:1 go on for seven days. On the second day the people kept the Feast of Tabernacles or Booths, in which they lived in huts made of branches, to remember their wilderness wanderings after the exodus. We read the extraordinary words in Nehemiah 8:17: 'From the days of Jeshua son of Nun to that day the people had not done so.' This probably means that although this festival had been celebrated (1 Kgs 8:2; Ezra 3:4), they may have focused on thanksgiving for harvest, and have neglected living in booths as a reminder of the exodus. Now the people do what God has told them to do, and celebrate the festival with great joy: 'And there was very great rejoicing' (Neh. 8:17).

Ezra's ministry was that of a teacher of God's written word. He did not add to that word. He studied it, lived it, taught it, read it to the people, explained it, applied it, and showed the people how to respond to it. It is a great delight to see the words of God having their full effect, as God's people received them, understood them, and obeyed them. And what a delight to see the leadership of Ezra and Nehemiah, as they encouraged God's people in response to God's words! God provided not only his words though his servant Moses, but also a faithful and effective teacher of those words in his servant Ezra.[9]

Ezra provides a great model for teachers of God's word in later times. Whereas Ezra taught the law given through Moses, we have the whole Bible to teach to God's people. We need more leaders like Ezra today, to teach and reform God's people with God's powerful words. Pray that God will raise up leaders like Ezra for God's people in every nation.

We have seen in this chapter what it meant in practice for God's people to receive and respond to God's words written so many generations before. We have seen the ongoing significance of God's written words, and the vital role of the faithful teacher of God's word, who studied God's words, put them into practice, and taught them to God's people.

In Part 2 of this book we have studied the first foundation of a theology of the Bible, that is, the conviction that God has spoken, using human words, that God's words are crucial to God's covenant relationship with his people, and that God's words are powerful from his mouth. We have seen the important role of the teachers and prophets of God's words. We have seen that great joy is found in receiving those words with faith and obedience.

We now turn in Part 3 to the second foundation doctrine of a biblical theology of the nature of the Scriptures: that of the one people of God in history, whom God has addressed with his cumulative words in Scripture.

---

9. See also Lawson, 'Pattern', for a study of Ezra's preaching.

RECEIVING GOD'S WORDS WRITTEN FOR HIS PEOPLE

In this Part we see that God's words were not only spoken but also written down, and that God's provision for his people included the accumulation of writings that recorded and matched salvation history and expressed biblical theology. The Holy Scriptures of the Old and New Testaments were produced because, in Kenneth Cragg's words, 'Unless one is to betray the future one must ensure that the past abides.'[1]

---

1. Cragg, *Credentials*, p. 109.

8. LOVING THE LAW OF THE LORD

PSALM 1

Many of the great Bible themes come together in the book of Psalms. The Psalms celebrate God's creation and his great acts of deliverance. They express joy, sorrow, frustration, lament, and praise of God. In the Psalms we sing to God as God's people, call the nations to know God, and express deep personal faith in him. We celebrate God's works in the past, and pray for him to act again and deliver his people. We also find that meditation on the law of the Lord which was so strong a part of the life of the people of God in the Old Testament.[1] Significantly, the book of Psalms begins with such a psalm, one that shows a keen awareness of the ubiquity of wickedness and the attractive renewing power of meditating on the words of God.

> [Blessed] are those
>> who do not follow the advice of the wicked,
> or take the path that sinners tread,
>> or sit in the seat of scoffers;

---

1. Adam, *Hearing*, pp. 60–67.

> but their delight is in the law of the LORD,
>
> and on his law they meditate day and night.
>
> (Ps.1:1–2)

We use the phrase 'Two ways to live' in challenging those who do not believe in Christ to repent of their self-centred idolatry and turn to serve the one true and living God. However, in Psalm 1, we find a description of two groups within the people of God. The strong contrast between the two groups is found in the first and last words of the psalm, 'blessed' (NRSV 'happy') in verse 1, and 'perish', the last word of verse 6. The purpose of the psalm is to warn us of the danger of perishing, and encourage us to delight in the law of the Lord and to meditate on it day and night (verse 2).

The subject of this delight and meditation is 'the law of the LORD'. When we read the word 'law', we naturally think of commands and instructions. These are certainly present in the Law, those five books from Genesis to Deuteronomy. However, 'law' here means 'instruction' or 'teaching', and 'the law of the LORD' is a reference to all the instruction and teaching in the first five books of the Bible. There is much more to the law than instructions and commands. We can see this if we ask the question, 'What kind of God do we meet in the law?'

Here is a brief answer to that question.

In Genesis we meet the mighty Creator, who formed the universe and made humanity in his image. God related closely to humanity, and judges those who sin against him. However, that is not the end of the story, for despite the judgments of Eden, the flood, and the tower of Babel, God's plan was still to bring blessing to all nations, and this plan he began to put into effect when he called Abram, and promised that through his descendant, all the nations of the earth would be blessed.

In Exodus, God came down to rescue his chosen people, the children of Abraham, from Egypt. He saved them by using his servant Moses, and brought them to Mount Sinai. Here God came down to speak with his people, to make a covenant with them, to instruct them how to live as his people. Here too God came down to live among his people, with the tabernacle as his courtyard, and the ark of the covenant as his throne on earth among his people.

In Leviticus, God showed Moses and his people the system of sacrifices, priests, and worship that they must follow. For how can a holy God live among his unholy people and not destroy them? The answer is that God provided priests and sacrifices, for by these sin can be atoned, the people forgiven, and fellowship and peace celebrated. At the same time, God also showed his people how to be holy: 'You shall be holy, for I the LORD your God am holy' (Lev. 19:2), and this holiness should be shown in every part of their lives.

In Numbers, we meet the God who did all that he had promised. As his people travelled through the wilderness for forty years on their way to the promised land, God did indeed live among them, protect them, discipline them, comfort them, provide for them, and bless them. What God had promised in Genesis–Leviticus, he did in Numbers.

In Deuteronomy, we find the people of God on the edge of the promised land, about to enter, it, and being given their last instructions and reminders from the mouth of Moses. It is a reminder of the saving actions of God, of his covenant faithfulness, of his provision for all their needs, and of his warning judgments of them. It is a call to covenant faithfulness as God's people enter the land, an invitation to receive and live in God's blessings, and also a warning to obey God, lest they receive his curses. It concludes with the promise that even if they disobey, and are judged and scattered, God will one day gather them and forgive them, and achieve his covenant purpose through them. When God made himself known in the books of the Law, then we have what Charles Bartow calls 'God's self-figuration of God in Holy Writ'.[2]

The blessing given by God

The word 'blessed' in Psalm 1:1, reminds us that God's purpose is to bless humanity, to enrich our lives, and to make us secure, strong, and fruitful. God's great purpose is to bring blessings: 'If you fully obey the LORD your God and carefully follow all his commands I give you today . . . all these blessings will come upon you and accompany you if you obey the LORD your God' (Deut. 28:1–2 [my trans.]).

The blessing of God given to those who keep rubbish out of their minds

This reflects the complementary theme of cursing in Deuteronomy 28:15: 'However, if you do not obey the LORD your God and do not carefully follow all his commands and decrees I am giving you today, all these curses will come upon you and overtake you' (my trans.).

Notice that the blessing is given to those who do not do the actions of verse 1, in order that they may do the actions of verse 2. For our minds are vacuums,

---

2. Bartow, *God's Speech*, 34.

and if we do not fill them with the words of God, then we will fill them with
the destructive words of the wicked, the sinners, and the scoffers (1).

See too the destructive downward spiral conveyed in verse 1, where there are
three features in a worsening sequence: 'follow . . . advice . . . wicked; take . . .
path . . . sinners; sit . . . seat . . . scoffers'. If it is bad to follow the advice of the
wicked, it is worse to take the path of sinners, and worst of all to sit in the seat
of scoffers. It is a kind of 'rake's progress' into habitual and vicious sin, with
the ultimate state being that of sitting in the seat of mockers: that is, setting
your mind to mock God and associating yourself with those who do the same.

Furthermore, it is most likely that the 'wicked, sinners, and scoffers' are
those who are within the people of God, not outside, and that is the point of
the warning of verse 5: 'sinners [will not stand] in the congregation of the
righteous'.

Who are those who receive God's blessing?

The answer is given in verse 2, and it is in terms of 'delighting in' and 'meditating on'. The person who turns away from the rubbish described in verse 1
is able to receive the blessings of verse 2. If we turn away from the influence,
advice, lifestyle and pressure of ungodly people, we will be able to pay attention to the words of God, and not just receive them and obey them, but delight
in them and meditate upon them.

The law of the LORD is fundamental to the biblical revelation. In it we
find the stories, events, and promises that are the key to every part of the
Bible. The rest of the Bible is like a commentary on and development of the
Law. The prophets call the people of God back to the covenant recorded in
the Law, the writers of wisdom express the living out of the Law in daily life,
and the historical books show how God's blessings and God's curses work out
in the life of God's people. Jesus often took people back to the teaching of the
Law, in answering questions about divorce (Matt. 19:1–12), in his sermon on
the mount (Matt. 5:17–48), in his teaching about the resurrection (Matt.
22:23–33), and in his explanation of his own life and ministry (Luke 24:27, 44).
Paul loved the Law: 'in my inner being I delight in God's law' (Rom. 7:22 [my
trans.]), even though he found himself unable to achieve its demands. For he
found himself cursed by it, and without hope except for the promise of life in
Christ Jesus, received by faith, and not by works of the law: 'For through the
law I died to the law, so that I might live to God' (Gal. 2:19). Paul taught that
through Christ the 'righteous requirements of the law might be fully met in us,
who do not live according to the flesh but according to the Spirit' (Rom. 8:4

[my trans.]), and James taught the ongoing value of 'the perfect law that gives freedom' (Jas 1:25 [my trans.]).

The theme of meditating on the law of the LORD is found within the Law itself. In Deuteronomy 6 we read: 'Hear, O Israel: The LORD is our God, the LORD alone. You shall love the LORD your God with all your heart, and with all your soul, and with all your might' (6:4–5). How then are we to love God? The answer is given in the next few verses:

> Keep these words that I am commanding you today in your heart. Recite them to your children and talk about them when you are at home and when you are away, when you lie down and when you rise. Bind them as a sign on your hand, fix them as an emblem on your forehead, and write them on the doorposts of your house and on your gates. (Deut. 6:6–9)

What is it like to meditate on the law of the LORD?

We find answers to this question in many different ways in the book of Psalms.

Psalm 8 is a celebration of God the creator as found in Genesis 1: 'O LORD, our [Lord], how majestic is your name in all the earth!' (Ps. 8:1).

Psalm 12 is a prayer for God to protect those who obey him from those who do not obey him.

Psalm 44 is a celebration of God's deeds long ago:

> We have heard with our ears, O God,
>   our ancestors have told us,
> what deeds you performed in their days,
>   in the days of old:
> you with your own hand drove out the nations,
>   but them you planted;
> you afflicted the peoples,
>   but them you set free;
> for not by their own sword did they win the land,
>   nor did their own arm give them victory;
> but your right hand, and your arm,
>   and the light of your countenance,
>   for you delighted in them.
> (44:1–3)

Psalm 51 is a meditation on the approach of a sinner to a holy God.

Psalms 68, 95, 105, 106, 107, 108, 114, etc., show what meditating in the law of the Lord looks like, as the writers of the psalms rehearse God's mighty acts and meditate on the lessons to be learned and the hopes to be maintained. They are a meditation on the words and works of God in the exodus and in the wilderness wanderings, as recorded in Exodus, Leviticus, Numbers, and Deuteronomy.

In Psalm 1 the blessing is given to the people of whom it can be said, 'but their delight is in the law of the LORD, and on his law they meditate day and night' (verse 2). The point is not that the person reads the Bible; it is that he or she delights in the law, and so meditates on it all the time. We need to be deeply and constantly shaped and formed by God's powerful words, so that we are fundamentally transformed, and our deepest thoughts, motivations, and desires come to reflect God's perfect will for our lives.

What are the motivations for this delight and this mediation?

There are two motivations, one positive, and one negative. The positive motivation is not an argument, but a picture of a flourishing tree: 'They are like trees planted by streams of water, which yield their fruit in its season, and their leaves do not wither. In all that they do, they prosper' (Ps. 1:3).

The tree is well planted, with a plentiful supply of water, and so is constantly fruitful and never drought-stricken. This is a picture of the kind of blessings that God promised through Moses in Deuteronomy 28 and Leviticus 26. God's plan is to bring blessing to all the nations, and his blessings rest on his own people when they delight in, meditate on, and obey his teaching and trust his promises.

The negative motivation is even more vivid. It is introduced with the powerful phrase, 'The wicked are not so', or literally, 'Not so the wicked' (verse 4). Unlike a strong and fruitful tree, they are like chaff, the husks of grain that has been thrown into the air so that the grains will fall to the ground and be collected, while the husks, the chaff, will be blown away by the wind into the desert. This picture is explained in verse 5: 'Therefore the wicked will not stand in the judgment, nor sinners in the congregation of the righteous.'

Finally, the two ways to live are brought together and explained in verse 6: 'for the LORD watches over the way of the righteous, but the way of the wicked will perish'.

So Psalm 1 shows us why we should meditate on the words of God, as it describes the attractive and renewing power of the law of the Lord. The writer of this psalm wants us to make good use of the written words of God given to the people of God.

Stephen Charnock wrote about the danger of what he called 'practical atheism': that is, living as if God does not exist. He showed that this way of living is found among God's saints, who, at times, live as foolishly as people who say in their heart, 'There is no God.' Here is part of his description of those who twist or interpret the Scripture to their own meaning:

> It is evidenced, in suiting interpretations of Scripture to their own minds and humours. Like the Lacedæmonians, that dressed the images of their gods according to the fashion of their own country, we would wring Scripture to serve our own designs, and judge the law of God by the law of sin, and make the serpentine seed within us to be the interpreter of divine oracles . . . As God is the author of his law and word, so he is the best interpreter of it . . . but when, in our inquiries into the word, we inquire not of God, but consult flesh and blood, the temper of the times wherein we live, or the satisfaction of a part we side withal . . . it is to put laws upon God, and make self the rule of him. He that interprets the law to bolster up some eager appetite against the rule of the lawgiver, ascribes to himself as great an authority as he that enacted it.[3]

More positively, here are words from the twentieth-century martyr Dietrich Bonhoeffer on the delights of meditating on the Bible: 'Every day in which I do not penetrate more deeply into the knowledge of God's Word in Scripture is a lost day for me. I can only move forward with certainty upon the firm ground of the Word of God, and, as a Christian, I learn to know the Holy Scripture in no other way than by hearing the Word preached and by prayerful meditation.'[4]

We have seen in this chapter the benefit found in meditating on the written words of God. We have been warned that we need to make room to receive God's words by resisting the powerful words of godless people around us. We have been encouraged by the promise of God's blessing on those who delight in and meditate on his words, and have been warned of the destruction that awaits those who do not. Psalm 1 is a positive invitation to meditate on God's written words.

---

3. Charnock, *Discourses*, p. 77.
4. Bonhoeffer, *Meditating*, p. 22.

9. UNDERSTANDING GOD'S WORDS

MATTHEW 22; MARK 7

Followers of Christ should follow his teaching, not least his teaching about the Bible. In this chapter we find Jesus in debate with the Sadducees and Pharisees about the Old Testament.

There was a variety of interpretations of the Old Testament in Jesus' day. In the New Testament we meet the Pharisees, the disciples of John the Baptist, the Sadducees, and the Samaritans. We also know of the Essenes, and of some Jews who tried to make the Old Testament more like Greek culture.[1] The main features of being a Jew were race and nationality, monotheism, and Old Testament moral standards. Orthodox theology was not a major issue. Indeed, it was no great crime to claim to be the Messiah.

However, Christ was a controversialist, and his public teaching often took the form of disputes about the true interpretation of the 'Holy Scriptures' (what we now call the Old Testament). Jesus debated and argued about the true meaning of the word of God, because false interpretations meant that people

---

1. The Essenes were a group of Jews who withdrew from public life in order to follow their religion more strictly. The Dead Sea Scroll community may have been Essene. Philo was an example of Jewish accommodation to Greek ideas.

did not turn to him in repentance and faith, practised vain worship, and lived without hope. It is encouraging to meet exceptions, like Simeon and Anna, who were in the temple when Mary and Joseph brought Jesus to be circumcised, and who saw in him the fulfilment of God's promises in the Old Testament (Luke 2:21–38).

Jesus often asked the question, 'Have you not read . . .?' in order to challenge people to rethink what they had indeed read, and read it again to find the right interpretation.

I well remember, when I was a young Christian, reading John Stott's splendid book *Christ the Controversialist*. This book had three profound effects on me. I realized that I should expect that the teaching of Jesus would be relevant to issues in my life; I understood that Jesus was not a passive ecclesiastic who never disagreed with people, but cared so much for people that he engaged in public controversy; and I realized that I needed to study the Scriptures very carefully, to find out their meaning, lest I be open to the rebuke, 'Have you not read . . .?'

While a right reading of the Old Testament is only a start, and by itself is not enough, for Jesus it was of fundamental importance, and the key to knowing him and to knowing and serving God. Orthopraxy (right living) and *orthokardia* (right emotions)[2] spring out of orthodoxy (right opinions and ideas), and orthodoxy springs out of *ortho-anagnōsis* (right reading and understanding of the Holy Scriptures). Jesus obviously regarded the careful and right reading and understanding of the (Old Testament) Scriptures as of crucial importance. He also taught that rightly understanding his own words was of the same importance. This surely challenges us to find the right understanding of the Holy Scriptures. These include the Scriptures that Jesus used (the Old Testament), the words that he spoke to his disciples when he was on earth, and also the words he caused to be written by sending the Spirit of truth on his apostles (the New Testament).

We now turn to two Gospel narratives in which Jesus challenged people to pay attention to the Old Testament.

The Sadducees (Matt. 22)

The question
This story began when the Sadducees asked Jesus a question that ridiculed the idea of resurrection. (The Sadducees did not believe in the resurrection, or any

---

2. See Cole, 'Heart of Spirituality'.

form of life after death.[3]) A woman was married to seven brothers one after the other. This followed Moses' instructions about a widow who had no children marrying her dead husband's brother.[4] It is most likely that this story was made up in order to ridicule the resurrection.

> The same day some Sadducees came to him, saying there is no resurrection; and they asked him a question, saying, 'Teacher, Moses said, "If a man dies childless, his brother shall marry the widow, and raise up children for his brother." Now there were seven brothers among us; the first married, and died childless, leaving the widow to his brother. The second did the same, so also the third, down to the seventh. Last of all, the woman herself died. In the resurrection, then, whose wife of the seven will she be? For all of them had married her.' (Matt. 22:23–28)

The reply

Jesus' reply is very instructive, because he not only told the Sadducees that they were wrong, but also told them the two sources of their error: 'You are wrong because you know neither the scriptures nor the power of God' (verse 29). They were wrong for two reasons: they did not really know and understand the Scriptures (even though they knew them well enough to ask the question), and they did not know the power of God.

Then Jesus tackled the two sources of their error, beginning with their ignorance of the power of God. 'For in the resurrection they neither marry nor are given in marriage, but are like angels in heaven' (30). God will transform humanity in the resurrection by his power.

He then tackled the other source of their error, their ignorance of the Scriptures. 'And as for the resurrection of the dead, have you not read what was said to you by God, "I am the God of Abraham, the God of Isaac, and the God of Jacob"? He is God not of the dead, but of the living' (31–32).

Jesus' response was extraordinary. He asked them the question, 'Have you not read . . .?' No doubt they had read the book of Exodus, but they must realize that they had missed its meaning. When he asked them, 'Have you not read . . .?' he asked it with this significant addition, 'Have you not read *what God said to you?*' These words indicate not only that the Sadducees should have read the book of Exodus more carefully, but that what was written in Exodus is

---

3. In Acts 23 the Sanhedrin included both Sadducees and Pharisees, and Paul effectively divided them when he claimed that he was on trial because of his belief in the resurrection (Acts 23:6–8).

4. This was known as levirate marriage. See Deut. 25:5–10.

what God has said to them: they are addressed by the words of God spoken to Moses, and recorded in this part of 'Holy Scripture'. The relevance of the quotation from Exodus is that it implies that Abraham, Isaac, and Jacob were living, not dead, when God spoke to Moses. They had died their normal human deaths, but they were still alive to God.

We can then see that the two errors of the Sadducees were connected. If they had truly known the Scriptures, they would have known what the power of God was able to achieve, that is, to sustain human life beyond death.

Jesus showed that right understanding came from right reading, and that ignorance of the Scriptures was the cause of great confusion. This story challenges us to careful reading of the Bible. For Jesus sent the Sadducees back to Bible school, because although they had read the Holy Scriptures many times, they had not yet understood them. Here is a great warning for us today, to have the humility to turn again to well-known scriptures to study them and learn from them, and also have the humility to trust Jesus as our interpreter of the words of God.

We should be like those Beroeans described in Acts: 'They welcomed the message very eagerly and examined the scriptures every day to see whether these things were so' (Acts 17:11).

I sometimes ask ministers at preaching conferences, 'How long is it since you have learned something new from the Bible?' We can always learn new truths from old texts.

The Pharisees (Mark 7)

Although Mark's Gospel is famous for its account of the constant activities of Jesus, it also contains significant blocks of teaching: for example the parables of chapter 4, Jesus' prediction of his death and resurrection in chapter 8, and the parables and teaching in chapters 12 and 13. Mark. 7:1–23 is another significant section of teaching, and takes the form of a dispute with some Pharisees, and then Jesus' teaching of his disciples that follows that dispute.

The complaint
The dispute begins with some of the Pharisees and teachers of the law criticizing Jesus' disciples as they asked:

Now when the Pharisees and some of the scribes who had come from Jerusalem gathered around him, they noticed that some of his disciples were eating with defiled hands, that is, without washing them . . . So the Pharisees and the scribes asked him,

'Why do your disciples not live according to the tradition of the elders, but eat with defiled hands?' (Mark 7:1–2, 5)

Jesus gave them two replies about these two issues, firstly that of 'the tradition of the elders' (verses 6–13), and secondly about what really makes people 'unclean' (14–15). Then Jesus discussed with his disciples the second issue, namely, what makes people unclean (17–23).

Your tradition

In his comments about 'the tradition of the elders' (5), or 'your tradition' (9, 13), Jesus contrasted that tradition with the commands or word of God. Clearly this distinction is of vital importance, and commitment to the former means that the latter is effectively lost. Jesus distinguished between two sets of instructions, to show that they are incompatible, and that merely human ideas must be discarded and God's instructions followed. Let us see how Jesus described the situation.

In verses 6–8 Jesus showed that Isaiah prophesied the actions of these leaders:

Isaiah prophesied rightly about you hypocrites, as it is written,

> 'This people honours me with their lips,
>   but their hearts are far from me;
> in vain do they worship me,
>   teaching human precepts as doctrines.'

Jesus used the very word of God that he is defending to explain what the leaders are doing in terms of their hypocrisy. Their hearts are wrong. Their worship of God is in vain, because their teachings are just human rules. Jesus will return to the problem of the heart later in his words to the disciples.

Jesus then showed the implications of following merely human teachings, with the first of three summary statements: 'You abandon the commandment of God and hold to human tradition' (8). In verses 9–13 we find Jesus' second and third summary statement: 'You have a fine way of rejecting the commandment of God in order to keep your tradition!' (9), and '. . . thus making void the word of God through your tradition that you have handed on' (13).

Whereas in the previous section he used a quotation from the prophet Isaiah to show the nature of their mistake, he now uses teaching from Moses to show how their practice resulted in nullifying God's word. We should notice that Jesus equates what Moses said with 'the word of God', showing his commitment to both its divine origin and the human means:

For Moses said, 'Honour your father and your mother'; and, 'Whoever speaks evil of father or mother must surely die.' But you say that if anyone tells father or mother, 'Whatever support you might have had from me is Corban' (that is, an offering to God) – then you no longer permit doing anything for a father or mother. (10–12)

Then he claimed that this was not an isolated event, but a habit and tendency of life: 'And you do many things like this' (13).

What really defiles

Jesus then continued the discussion of what it means to be 'unclean' in his address to the crowd. 'Then he called the crowd again and said to them, "Listen to me, all of you, and understand: there is nothing outside a person that by going in can defile, but the things that come out are what defile"' (14–15).

In his words to the leaders he pointed to the fundamental error that caused their mistake, that of giving up the word of God in order to follow human traditions. Here he points to the problem and origin of uncleanness.

When he was alone with his disciples, Jesus then answered their question about the meaning of the parable. It is not what goes into a person that makes them unclean, but what comes out of the heart.

'Then do you also fail to understand? Do you not see that whatever goes into a person from outside cannot defile, since it enters, not the heart but the stomach, and goes out into the sewer?' (Thus he declared all foods clean.) And he said, 'It is what comes out of a person that defiles. For it is from within, from the human heart, that evil intentions come: fornication, theft, murder, adultery, avarice, wickedness, deceit, licentiousness, envy, slander, pride, folly. All these evil things come from within, and they defile a person.' (18–23)

Notice that though Jesus condemned the Jewish leaders for setting aside and nullifying the word of God in the Old Testament, the implication of his teaching is that he declared all foods clean. So Jesus had the authority to reinterpret and adjust the teaching of the word of God, even as he had the authority to correct others for their misinterpretation.[5]

This teaching was followed by a miracle in which Jesus showed his authority and power to expel an 'unclean' spirit. So Jesus had the power to change people from uncleanness to cleanness (24–30).

---

5. The same happens in Mark 2 and 3, where Jesus claimed the divine power to forgive sins and to be Lord of the sabbath.

The problem of universal and complete human uncleanness is left unre-solved at the conclusion of this teaching and miracle. It will finally be over-come by Jesus' death and resurrection. For it is Jesus' atoning and saving death that can make people clean; 'his blood can make the foulest clean'.[6] It is also his death that will break down the barrier between Jew and Gentile that was expressed through the food laws of the Old Testament.

In summary, we can see three important insights here into Jesus' attitude to the word of God in the Old Testament.

1. Jesus explained the situation of human sin that was before him by showing that Isaiah prophesied it.
2. Jesus condemned the practice of following human traditions, 'your traditions', and so letting go, setting aside, and nullifying the commands and word of God in the law of the Lord.
3. Jesus pointed to a radical revision of the laws of uncleanness of the Old Testament that he brought about by his coming.

Mark 7 is a key chapter in understanding that Jesus pointed to the continu-ing relevance of the Old Testament, and also had the authority to show how the new covenant transformed its meaning. He also showed the danger of adding to the words of God.

Let's think of some contemporary examples of ordinary Christians making additions to the word of God. In each case, I suspect, we think that we are filling out the implications of the word of God, and providing helpful ways of putting it into practice. Yet we should heed Jesus' warning about how danger-ous it is to follow merely human ideas, how this may mean that we let go, set aside, and nullify the commands and word of God. Doing this may distort our Christian life, and lead us to honour God with our lips when our hearts are far from him, and so to worship God in vain. Here are some examples of adding to the word of God:

- The Roman Catholic church accepts the Bible, and then adds to it the traditions of the church to form one word of God.
- Some conservative evangelical Christians tend to add the middle-class culture and attitudes of the 1920s to the Bible without noticing what they are doing.

---

6. I am grateful to Dave Spencer for explaining this point most powerfully in his sermon in the Ridley College Chapel in July 2005.

- Some Pentecostal churches accept the Bible and add to it some recent words from the Spirit.
- Legalistic evangelicals expand the Bible by adding some useful rules about how we should behave.
- Many denominations hold to their cherished denominational traditions even more firmly than they hold to the Bible.
- Liberal Christians hold on to recent insights from current thought even when they contradict the Bible.
- Many congregations hold to their cherished traditions even more firmly than they hold to the Bible.
- Many Christian subcultures unconsciously add to the Bible their own assumptions and prejudices.

Our traditions make good servants but bad masters. When they serve our doing of the word of God they are helpful. When they hinder our doing of the word of God they are destructive. They are especially dangerous when we use them to condemn others; this is exactly what is happening in Mark 7, where some of the Pharisees and teachers of the law are using their traditions to condemn Jesus' disciples, and so to criticize Jesus.

Finally, we should note the peculiar patterns of theological arithmetic. You might think that if people add their the traditions to the Bible, then this means they will do all that the Bible teaches and more as well. However, as Jesus shows us in Mark 7, adding to the word of God actually means that in fact we let go, set aside, and nullify that word of God. 'Addition is subtraction', as everything we add takes our attention away from what God has said, and interprets and reinterprets what God has said.

If we set aside God's words by our own ideas or traditions, we make it of no effect, and our worship and service of God is in vain. How easy it is to see others making this mistake; how difficult it is to see when we do it ourselves! Let us take notice of Jesus' teaching. We must relativize merely human traditions in order to serve God with the traditions he has given us.

In this chapter we have learned from Jesus' debates with Sadducees and Pharisees about the right interpretation and use of Scripture. From his debate with the Sadducees we learned that the Scriptures needed careful attention lest their message be missed, and that the Scriptures, although written many years before, were also God's contemporary words. We discovered that because the Sadducees misread the Scriptures, they did not know that God's power would create a new kind of existence in the resurrection. We learned from Jesus' debate with the Pharisees that they should not have added to the word of God, and that adding to God's word reduces it. This supports the claim for the completeness and sufficiency of God's written word. We also saw that Jesus supported the validity and authority of the Old Testament, but also used his power to change its application in the light of his own significance and ministry.

10. WRITTEN DOWN FOR US

1 CORINTHIANS 10; ROMANS 15

This chapter show us how Paul the apostle continued to use the Old Testament as relevant material for learning how to live the Christian life, and that his assumption was shared by the churches to which he wrote. This shows the enduring relevance of the Scriptures in the life of the people of God, and that God can speak in the present by using words from the past. There is one people of God, and God's accumulated words still remain significant for God's people in every age.

Paul is of particular relevance, because he was the apostle to the Gentiles, and so part of his responsibility was to determine what aspects of Old Testament faith and practice should be required of non-Jewish converts to Christ.[1] It was significant that he retained the Old Testament Scriptures for non-Jewish Christianity, and did so because he recognized that the Gentiles were 'fellow-heirs, members of the same body, and sharers in the promise in Christ Jesus' (Eph. 3:6).

---

1. Rosner, 'Written for Us'.

An example written down for us (1 Cor. 10:1–14)

Our ancestors

Paul had many issues to tackle in 1 Corinthians. This was a lively church. It showed all the signs of experimental adolescence, not mid-life lethargy. The members of the church were enthusiastically religious, even if their enthusiasm was not always well expressed. Their sins included idolatry and sexual immorality.

How did Paul tackle this issue here in 1 Corinthians? It is an unexpected method that he uses. It is that of family history, which is why he began by writing about 'our ancestors'.

> I do not want you to be unaware, brothers and sisters, that our ancestors were all under the cloud, and all passed through the sea, and all were baptized into Moses in the cloud and in the sea, and all ate the same spiritual food, and all drank the same spiritual drink. For they drank from the spiritual rock that followed them, and the rock was Christ. (1 Cor. 10:1–4)

He argued that the church at Corinth should learn a lesson from their family history about the danger of idolatry, and that God did not allow our ancestors to serve God and also serve other gods.

This argument depended on the believers at Corinth recognizing that they were indeed part of the one family of God across the ages, that even those who had not been born Jews had been adopted into the one family of God, and so the message of the Old Testament was profoundly relevant to their daily lives. It is extraordinary that Paul did not need to argue this case: he assumed not only that they believed this, but also that an argument based on this idea would be effective in changing them, and stopping their idolatry.

As we have seen earlier, the idea that all believers in all ages are part of the one family and people of God is fundamental to understanding the nature of the Bible. Here we find Paul using this principle, and applying it to his readers.

In fact, Paul went even further than this, and assumed so much similarity between the people of God in the Old Testament and the people of God in Corinth that he claimed that when the people of God in Moses' day drank water from the rock, they were also drinking spiritually from Christ (Exod. 16 – 17). Just as the Corinthian believers 'shared in the blood of Christ' in the Lord's Supper by faith (1 Cor. 10:16), so the Old Testament believers drank of the Christ to come by faith. So they are not only in the same family (in different generations), but have the same experience of Christ, although in a different way, and, of course, with very different levels of understanding. By receiving supernatural gifts of God's grace, they received the promise of the Christ to come.

The point of all of this is that though the people of God in Moses' day received the rich blessings that God gave them, including the promise of the Christ still to come, they still fell into danger and sin.

Examples for us

> Nevertheless, God was not pleased with most of them, and they were struck down in the wilderness.
>
> Now these things occurred as examples for us, so that we might not desire evil as they did. (1 Cor. 10:5–6)

Greater blessing brings greater responsibility, and greater responsibility brings greater judgment. The people of God in the Old Testament had just been delivered from captivity and slavery in Egypt by the mighty hand of God in the Passover.[2] How could they so quickly lose their focus, and be distracted from their single-minded service of God? And how could their descendants, who had been rescued by the sacrifice of Christ, 'our paschal lamb' (5:7), imagine that they would escape God's judgment if they turned against him?

What were the sins of the people of God in Moses' day, fresh from the rescue from Egypt? Idolatry, sexual immorality, putting God to the test (that is, seeing what they could get away with), and complaining or murmuring against God (10:7–10).[3] This was a practical and relevant warning to the church at Corinth, and is a practical and relevant warning to churches and believers today!

God not only dealt with the people of God who came out of Egypt, but used them as an example for subsequent generations of his people. How would subsequent generations know of these God-provided examples? These stories were 'written down', not just for subsequent generations in the Old Testament, but also for Christian believers, those living in the last days.

Written down to instruct us

'These things happened to them to serve as an example, and they were written down to instruct us, on whom the ends of the ages have come' (10:11).

Suddenly all of the Old Testament is shown to be relevant to us, because it is the history of our family, and was written for us. For we who believe in Jesus

2. Exod. 12.

3. Num. 11, 14, 21, 24, 25, and Exod. 32.

Christ are adopted into the family of God, the people of God. We join not only our Lord and God, but the people of God; and not just the people of God alive today, but also the universal people of God in every age. And it is always useful to know your family history, not least because you can see instructive patterns of behaviour, as well as seeing the patience and success of God in persisting with his people.

The people of Moses' day did not need these things to be written down: they were in the middle of them! We needed them to be written down, so that we could learn the lessons of history (even if one of the lessons of history is that people don't often learn the lessons of history).

Paul then applied his message:

> So if you think you are standing, watch out that you do not fall. No testing has overtaken you that is not common to everyone. God is faithful, and he will not let you be tested beyond your strength, but with the testing he will also provide the way out so that you may be able to endure it.
>
> Therefore, my dear friends, flee from the worship of idols. (10:12–14)

Be alert, and not overconfident. We can fall as easily when we think we are safe. God won't push us too far, so there is no excuse for not proving trustworthy. So run as fast as you can from idolatry. We can but hope that many of the people of Corinth took Paul's advice.

We find the same themes and ideas in Paul's letter to the church at Rome.

Written for our instruction (Rom. 15:1–7)

There were many similarities between 1 Corinthians and Romans. They both dealt with the issue of the 'strong in faith' and the 'weak in faith', and in both Paul pointed to the value of the Old Testament for understanding Christ, and for teaching us how to live.

Here in Romans Paul tried to encourage those who were 'strong in faith' and those who were 'weak in faith' to accept and welcome one another, and not to judge one another. Here is a remarkable application of justification by grace: it should form not only the way we view ourselves, but also the way we treat fellow believers with whom we differ. The 'strong in faith', who knew that they could eat any kind of food, including what was 'unclean' under the Old Testament rules, had also given up Old Testament holy days. The 'weak in faith' were still following old food laws, and still keeping old holy days.

Christ did not please himself, as it is written

Paul pointed to the example of Christ, and challenged the 'strong in faith' to be patient and to please others, not themselves. One ingredient of being strong in faith and being critical of others may be that of pleasing ourselves. 'We who are strong ought to put up with the failings of the weak, and not to please ourselves. Each of us must please our neighbour for the good purpose of building up the neighbour. For Christ did not please himself; but, as it is written, "The insults of those who insult you have fallen on me"' (15:1–3).

What an insight into human behaviour that Paul must add 'not pleasing ourselves' in order for us to 'put up with the failings of others'! We have to die to sin in order to live to righteousness.

Notice too that in giving Christ's example, Paul did not use a story or saying from his incarnate life, but words from Psalm 69:9. The God of the Old Testament is later rightly understood as being Father, Son, and Spirit, so that the words of the Psalms can rightly be heard as coming from the mouth of Christ. The example of Christ that Paul used is that of Christ taking on himself the anger of humanity that was directed at God. On the cross he acted as a lightning-rod for God, and took into himself those reproaches: he did not please himself. And this was characteristic of his life, as well as his death.

Written for our instruction – encouraging Scriptures

Then Paul explained his use of the Old Testament: it was written for us. 'For whatever was written in former days was written for our instruction, so that by steadfastness and by the encouragement of the scriptures we might have hope' (15:4).

John Stott, with his customary clarity, noted five lessons about the Old Testament that we can learn from this comment:

1. The Old Testament, *written in former days* had contemporary intention: it was *written for our instruction.*
2. It has inclusive value, because *whatever was written*, not just this one verse, was written for us.
3. It is about Jesus Christ, as Psalm 69 is understood to refer to him.
4. It also has a practical purpose, as it brings us *steadfastness* and *encouragement.*
5. It is God's message (and God works through it), as both *steadfastness* and *encouragement* come through the Scriptures, and from God (verses 4–5).[4]

---

4. Stott, *Romans*, p. 370.

These are remarkable insights into Paul's use of the Old Testament.

Paul then prayed that God would do for the Christians at Rome what he had promised: 'May the God of steadfastness and encouragement grant you to live in harmony with one another, in accordance with Christ Jesus, so that together you may with one voice glorify the God and Father of our Lord Jesus Christ' (15:5–6).

The steadfastness and encouragement of the Scriptures come from the fact that God is the God of steadfastness and encouragement. The Scriptures reflect the character of God their author, and achieve his purposes. This is how Paul put into practice the living use of the Old Testament as instruction for Christian living.

As we conclude Part 3, here are two excerpts from Thomas Cranmer's sermon on Scripture:

> For the Scripture of God is the heavenly meat of our souls: the hearing and keeping of it makes us blessed, sanctifies us, and makes us holy: it turns our souls; it is a light to our feet: it is a sure, steadfast and everlasting instrument of salvation: it gives wisdom to the humble and lowly-hearted: it comforts, makes glad, cheers, and cherishes our consciences.

Again:

> The words of Holy Scripture are called the words of everlasting life; for they are God's instruments, ordained for the same purpose. They have power to convert through God's promise, and they are effectual through God's assistance; and being received in a faithful heart, they have a heavenly spiritual working in them.[5]

In this chapter we found that the Old Testament naturally applies to the Gentiles, as we are all part of the one family of God. The Old Testament was intended to be used by later generations of God's people. It is part of our accumulated Scriptures, the Bible. We have seen the doctrine of receiving God's verbal revelation ('Receiving God's words'), and a doctrine of the people of God, or ecclesiology ('written for his people').

We now turn to a doctrine of the Holy Spirit, or pneumatology ('by his Spirit').

---

5. Cranmer, *Sermons*, pp. 3–4, modernized.

Part 4

RECEIVING GOD'S WORDS
WRITTEN FOR HIS PEOPLE
BY HIS SPIRIT

11. THE SCRIPTURES: HOLY, INSPIRED, USEFUL, AND EFFECTIVE

2 TIMOTHY 3 – 4

The second letter to Timothy gives an insight into what ministry would be like after the apostles. For Timothy was among those being trained to lead churches in the absence of Paul, and his pattern of ministry would become a model for church leaders after the period of the biblical revelation.

In 2 Timothy Paul challenged Timothy with the commitments that are required for vital ministry and encouraged him to persist in that ministry.

From this perspective, chapters 1 – 3 include various commitments, including five convictions about Scripture in 3:15–17, before Paul gives six instructions about ministry in 4:1–2.

Timothy was Paul's representative in Ephesus, and seems to have been fighting a lone battle within the church for the apostolic gospel. The others in the pastoral team in the church in Ephesus appear to have abandoned Paul's gospel and the ministry that flows from that gospel. Paul's comment in 2 Timothy 1:15 that 'all who are in Asia have deserted me, including Phygelus and Hermogenes', may mean that all the leaders of the churches in Asia Minor (including the capital of the province, Ephesus) have turned away from Paul's gospel and pattern of ministry.[1]

---

1. Possibilities include all the leaders in the province of Asia, a particular group of

Furthermore, in addition to those named in chapters 1 and 2, there seems to have been a larger group, described in vivid terms in 3:1–8: 'People will be lovers of themselves, lovers of money . . . lovers of pleasure rather than lovers of God, holding to the outward form of godliness but denying its power . . . among them are those who make their way into households . . . these people . . . oppose the truth.'

This declension from the truth was to be found not only among its leaders, but also among its members: 'For the time is coming when people will not put up with sound doctrine, but having itching ears, they will accumulate for themselves teachers to suit their own desires, and will turn away from listening to the truth and wander away to myths' (4:3–4).

What then were the commitments that Timothy needed to have in place? Here they are, summarized from 2 Timothy chapters 1 – 2.

Timothy must 'rekindle the gift of God that is within you' (1:6); 'join with me in suffering for the gospel' (1:8); 'guard the good treasure entrusted to you' (i.e., guard the gospel, 1:14). He must 'be strong in the grace that is in Christ Jesus' (2:1); so that what he has heard from Paul he will be able to 'entrust to faithful people who will be able to teach others as well' (2:2).

This will call for careful preparation: 'Do your best to present yourself to God as one approved by him, a worker who has no need to be ashamed, rightly explaining the word of truth' (2:15); and 'shun youthful passions and pursue righteousness, faith, love, and peace' (2:22).

These commitments were personal ('rekindle the gift of God', 'join in suffering', 'be strong in the grace of Christ'), theological ('guard the good treasure', 'rightly explain the word of truth'), moral ('shun youthful passions, and pursue righteousness', etc.), and educational ('what you have heard from me . . . entrust to faithful people who will be able to teach others as well').

We now turn to five convictions about Scripture that Paul required of Timothy.

Five convictions about Scripture

2 Timothy 3:14–17 includes five convictions about the Scriptures that Timothy needs to have in place before he hears the challenge of 4:1–2.

(Footnote 1 *continued*)

    leaders, or leaders from Asia who were in Rome with Paul. This last option contrasts the actions of those leaders in 1:15 with the actions of Onesiphorus in 1:16–18. See Knight, *Epistles*, pp. 382–383.

The sacred writings (15) and the scripture (16) include books of the Old and New Testaments

Here 'scripture' means firstly the Old Testament, for the 'sacred writings' of verse 15 are those which Timothy has known 'from childhood'.

The word 'scripture' in verse 16 includes a wider range of writings in addition to the Old Testament, namely some of what we now call 'New Testament' writings. In 1 Timothy 5:18 Paul introduces two quotations with the words 'the Scripture says'. The first quotation ('you shall not muzzle an ox . . .') is from the Old Testament, the second ('the labourer deserves to be paid') appears in Luke 10:7. Paul referred to a saying of Jesus as 'Scripture' in the same way he described the Old Testament as 'Scripture'. In 2 Peter 3:15, 16, Peter also described Paul's letters as 'Scripture'. Here are the first signs that the early Christians were beginning to add new 'Scriptures' to those of the Old Testament.

The Old Testament has the power to 'instruct you for salvation through faith in Christ Jesus' (3:15)

Note how this is worded: the emphasis is on the ability of the Old Testament to instruct us. The Old Testament Scriptures have the power (*ta dynamena*) to teach us. We also see here how Paul viewed the Old Testament as teaching us the message of the gospel, that is, 'salvation through faith in Christ Jesus'.

I wonder how many Christians today, if asked to summarize the message of the Old Testament, would reply, 'Salvation through faith in Christ Jesus'. Yet Paul made the same point that Jesus made in Luke 24, when he summarized the Old Testament in these words: ' "Was it not necessary that the Messiah should suffer these things and then enter into his glory?" Then beginning with Moses and all the prophets, he interpreted to them the things about himself in all the scriptures' (Luke 24:26–27).

The message of the Bible is one message, so the message of the Old Testament and New Testament alike is that of salvation through faith in Christ.

'All scripture is inspired by God' (3:16)

This verse is frequently quoted in support of the idea of the inspiration of Scripture, though in fact the main point that it is making is that the Scriptures are 'useful', as we shall see.

What then of 'inspiration'? The word is *theopneustos*, or 'God-breathed'. This does not mean that humans were not consciously involved in the writing of Scripture, but it preserves God's initiative in the creation of Scripture of both the Old and the New Testaments. The biblical doctrine of inspiration included both inspired writings and also inspired people (2 Pet. 1:21). It meant that God was the originator of these writings through these people. Aquinas commented:

> The authority of these words arises from this, that they are not the products of human invention, but of the Holy Spirit . . . He adduces the words of the Old Testament for the New, lest it be thought that their reference is only to the Old Testament, and to a former time, instead of also to the New. And they are words of the Holy Spirit because, as declared in 2 Peter 1:21, 'no prophecy ever came by the impulse of men, but men moved by the Holy Spirit spoke from God.' For David himself says, in 2 Kings 23:2, of himself: ' The Spirit of the Lord spoke through me.' This therefore demonstrates the genuineness of the authority, because it derives from the Holy Spirit.[2]

Here, as we have seen, he used 'Scripture' which included books of the New Testament. We do not know how many New Testament books were written at this time, but Paul had more Scriptures in mind than those of the Old Testament. We see in 2 Peter that the Old Testament prophets were moved by the Holy Spirit. So both the people and their words were inspired. God did not inspire the words without inspiring those who spoke or wrote them, nor did he inspire the people but leave them to do their best with the words. People and words were inspired.

'All scripture . . . is useful for teaching, for reproof, for correction, and for training in righteousness' (3:16)

Here Paul taught the value of Scripture for education, coaching and information. As William Mounce explained, 'teaching' means that the Bible is useful to instruct us in what to believe, 'reproof' to teach us what we should not believe, 'correction' to show us how we should not live, and 'righteousness' to show us how we should live.[3]

It is important to see that Paul did assert this educative and moral use of Scripture (Old and New Testaments), as earlier in 3:15 he asserted the theological use of Scripture, namely to point to the gospel of Christ. We do not have to choose between these two uses. The Bible not only instructs us

---

2. Aquinas, *Super Epistolam ad Hebraeos Lectura*, as quoted in Hughes, *Hebrews*, pp. 141–142.
3. Mounce, *Epistles*, p. 570.

for salvation through faith in Christ, it also teaches and trains us in believing and living. It is easy for preachers to specialize in one use or the other, just as it is easy for Bible readers to focus on the Bible as the gospel of God's grace in Christ, or on the Bible as coaching for living. What we separate, Paul here puts together. We see in Hebrews both these uses of the Old Testament.[4]

All Scripture has the power to ensure that believers (or more exactly, leaders[5]), are 'proficient, equipped for every good work' (3:17)

Here Paul pointed out that Scripture provides a comprehensive training manual, so that we are trained not only in how to live, but also in how to do ministry. God uses Scripture to prepare, coach, train and equip us for 'every good work'. It is the usefulness, the power, of Scripture to achieve human transformation which is the main focus of these verses. 'All scripture is inspired by God and is useful for teaching, for reproof, for correction, and for training in righteousness, so that everyone who belongs to God may be proficient, equipped for every good work' (2 Tim. 3:16–17).

These five convictions, then, are the basis for Paul's encouragement and instructions to Timothy in 4:2, 'Preach the word' (my trans.), or 'Proclaim the message'. If Timothy did not have these five convictions, he would not be able to sustain the demanding ministry of 'preaching the word'.

If Timothy did have these five convictions about the Bible, then he would be ready to hear the instructions of 4:1–2.

Preach the word: six instructions

> In the presence of God and of Christ Jesus, who is to judge the living and the dead, and in view of his appearing and his kingdom, I solemnly urge you: proclaim the message; be persistent whether the time is favourable or unfavourable; convince, rebuke, and encourage, with the utmost patience in teaching. (2 Tim. 4:1–2)

---

4. See for example the use of Moses in Hebrews as both a figure in salvation history (Heb. 3:1–6) and an example for us to follow (Heb. 11:24–28), as we will see in chapter 19.

5. Literally, 'the man of God', an Old Testament expression meaning the leader of God's people, God's representative.

Before God

It is a challenge for which Timothy is answerable not just to Paul, 'an apostle of Christ Jesus by the will of God' (2 Tim. 1:1), but to God, and to Christ who is judge of all, who will appear and bring his kingdom (4:1). No wonder Paul wrote, 'I solemnly urge you' (4:1)!

Preach the word

Timothy is to be proactive and take every opportunity to proclaim, hand on, declare, 'the gospel' (1:8, 10, 11), the 'standard of sound teaching' (1:13), the 'good treasure' (1:14), 'what you heard from me through many witnesses' (2:2), or 'the word of truth' (2:15). Paul has reminded Timothy of the content and source of this message or gospel in 3:15: 'the sacred writings . . . are able to instruct you for salvation through faith in Christ Jesus'. Timothy is to preach the message or word, from the words of God, the inspired and useful Holy Scriptures.

Be persistent

Timothy is to be persistent whether the time is favourable or unfavourable (4:2). This means that Timothy is to persist when people want to hear his message, and also when they do not. Paul warned of reluctant hearers in 4:3–4, when he wrote of a time when people would not put up with sound doctrine.[6]

Convince, rebuke, encourage

The words 'convince, rebuke, encourage' (4:2) expand what it will mean to preach the word. It will always be a purposeful message, an applied message. As Timothy preaches the word, he will work to convince, to rebuke, to encourage. Timothy is to do more than 'teach the Bible'. He is to proclaim the message of the Bible, the gospel from the Bible. And as he does so, it will always be related to the people to whom he speaks and their situation. In Calvin's words:

> Therefore he that will be a good and faithful teacher, must frame his style of preaching wholly to the rule that was given him by God . . . seeing there is not just a bare declaring of the law of God in the Holy Scriptures, but also an earnestness to rebuke, warn and threaten, let us note that is it not enough for a man to say in a sermon, 'This is what God teaches us', but he must also spur his hearers to respond.[7]

---

6. Mounce, *Epistles*, p. 573.

7. Calvin, *Timothy*, p. 958, modernized.

Scripture is the means

He will work hard to 'convince, rebuke, encourage'. These three words reflect what Paul has written about the Scriptures in 3:16, that they are 'useful for teaching, for reproof, for correction, and for training in righteousness'. If proclaiming the message is the aim, then Scripture is the means that Timothy is to use.[8]

'Utmost patience' and 'all teaching'

Timothy is to do all this 'with the utmost patience' (4:2). How difficult it is to combine great convictions and urgent strategy with the patience required to help people to learn, to repent, to change and to grow, as they find that the Scriptures teach salvation through faith in Christ Jesus, as they are taught, reproved, corrected, and trained in righteousness! Slow learners need patient teachers: Timothy must not let the seriousness or urgency of his ministry make him impatient or angry. For 'the Lord's servant must not be quarrelsome but kindly to everyone, an apt teacher, patient, correcting opponents with gentleness' (2:24–25).

Calvin commented: 'Yet must we be armed with patience, for otherwise we should be at the point every day to renounce the office that God has committed to us.'[9]

This ministry must also be done with ' in' or 'with teaching' (4:2). So there must be no challenge to respond without information, no invitation without the opportunity to learn first. Doctrine or teaching is the groundwork, and exhortations and rebukes are the building.[10] Timothy's ministry of 'proclaiming the message' must have patient teaching as its means, and this teaching, as we have seen, is teaching of the Scriptures, which are able to instruct in salvation through faith in Christ Jesus, and are also useful for 'teaching, for reproof, for correction, and for training in righteousness' (3:16). Just as Timothy will need utmost patience, so he will need to do lots of teaching. Teaching by itself is not enough, and patience by itself is not enough: we need teaching which is patient, and patience which is expressed in teaching. 'The task is difficult, and will require the greatest amount of patience.'[11]

---

8. Mounce, *Epistles*, p. 573: 'The four main imperatives (Preach! Confront! Rebuke! Exhort!) loosely parallel the four . . . phrases in 3:16 (profitable for teaching, reproof . . . correcting . . . training in righteousness).'

9. Calvin, *Timothy*, p. 962, modernized.

10. Ibid., p. 948.

11. Knight, *Epistles*, p. 454.

The task is to proclaim the message, and the necessary ingredients are persistence, the ability to convince, rebuke and encourage, the Holy Scriptures, lots of patience, and lots of teaching.

We see in these verses that Paul challenges Timothy to apply the Bible to his hearers. He must decide to convince, rebuke, encourage with both patience and teaching.

Let me here include some general comments on the application of Scripture.

Ten keys to the useful application of the Bible

The Bible was written 'to them, for them, and for us'

It is a mistake to move immediately to the question, 'What does this mean for us?' without first asking the question, 'What did this mean for them?' We must take account of the first audience of the books of the Bible, and so respect God's purpose in placing them in their particular context within God's providential care, his works of salvation history and his verbal revelation that forms biblical theology. They are not timeless truths, but time-expressed truths. And in the case of historical narratives, we must ask not only, 'What did this mean for the people described in the narrative?' (Jacob, the people of Israel, Isaiah, the disciples, etc.), but also, 'What did this mean for the first readers of this narrative?' The meaning of the text will not be exactly the same for us as for them, as we will see. However, if we do not take this step, we will miss the historical particularity of the text, and may read it inappropriately, wrenching it out of its original context, or reading our questions and answers into the text, or missing the fact that we are at a different stage in salvation history from the first readers or hearers.

Biblical theology

We will make many mistakes if we do not use biblical theology, which helps us to understand the shape of the gradual and cumulative revelation of God in the Bible. Without remembering the progression in revelation from Israel in the Old Testament to the people of God in the New Testament, we might find ourselves living in the Holy Land, trying to find a temple in which to offer sacrifices, and still observing the food laws. We have to take into account the fact that the Old Testament was written for God's people before the coming of Christ, and so what we have in the Old Testament cannot apply to us directly, or not without recognizing that difference. We cannot rightly understand any part without understanding the whole. We will misuse a part of the

Bible if we read it out of its big context, which is the big theme of the Bible. We have already seen the language Paul used in Acts 20 to describe this big theme: 'the message' (verse 20), 'repentance toward God and faith towards our Lord Jesus' (21), 'the good news [gospel] of God's grace' (24), 'the kingdom' (25), 'the whole purpose of God' (27), 'the truth' (30), and finally 'the message of his grace' (32).

Midner: text without context is a con.

Text in immediate context
We need to work on the immediate context of a verse in the Bible to find its meaning. We know that 'a text without a context is a pretext'. We know that we cannot remove a few words or a sentence from a story, an argument, a parable, or a song and apply them in isolation. 'Do quickly what you are going to do' (John 13:27) could be applied to many situations, but is liable to be misused if we do not take the original context into account. This focus will also help us to avoid preaching the same biblical-theology message from every text.

The message of the particular book of the Bible
One context that is often overlooked is that of the book of the Bible in which the verse or chapter is found. The Bible comes to us in the form of sixty-six units of revelation. If we do not know the meaning, purpose, and main themes of the book of the Bible which we are reading, then we are more likely to mis-understand any part of it. A book of the Bible is like a sentence: to understand it we need to know what each part means, and also what the whole sentence means. One good way to do this is to find the verse or collection of verses that forms the heart of the Bible book. Focusing on the particularities of the book of the Bible from which we preaching will also help us to avoid preaching the same biblical theology from every verse in the Bible.

Pastoral intelligence or awareness[12]
Even within the same period of salvation history and biblical theology, preach-ers and speakers of the Word have still needed pastoral intelligence to know when to apply which word of God. The classic example of the lack of pas-toral awareness was Job's friends. They accused Job of secret sins. That would have been appropriate in 99% of cases, but was drastically wrong for Job.

---

12. Pastoral intelligence requires biblical understanding, theological awareness, a loving understanding of people, and a good perception of how different people hear, change, and are motivated.

Despite their best intentions, despite their time-consuming ministry, they were wrong. As God said: 'My wrath is kindled against you and against your two friends; for you have not spoken of me what is right' (Job 42:7).[13]

We see good examples of pastoral intelligence or awareness in Jesus' varied responses to individuals, when he recognized that some needed direct challenge, some gentle rebuke, some consolation, some deep understanding. We find it too in Paul. He encouraged, rebuked, informed, reminded, instructed or commanded, according to the state of the people to whom he was writing. The great challenge of pastoral ministry is to have the pastoral awareness to know what parts of the Bible this person needs now, what part of the Bible this church needs now. Pastoral intelligence includes psychological and cultural awareness, understanding of how communities function, and lots of 'quick-eyed love'.

Educative intelligence

The quest for relevance may blind us to information or formation or deep issues that we need to consider. Not every part of the Bible can be reduced to 'a practical action for me today'. The Bible's message in this text need not be of obvious immediate application.

It may be something that I need to know in order to shape my long-term learning about God. It may be a corrective that I do not need now, but which will keep me from error in the future. It may not be relevant for me, but may be something that God wants me to pass on to a fellow believer in a few weeks' time, or an answer to a question that an enquirer will ask me tomorrow. It may be something that God is teaching our church at this time, and which we all need to learn together. Relevance is not limited to immediate and recognized relevance. God has a long-term educative purpose, to bring his people to maturity in Christ, and this Bible passage may be intended to serve that purpose.

Corporate application

Most books of the Bible are addressed to the people of God, rather than to individuals. Even books like 1 and 2 Timothy are addressed to the church as well as to the leader, and although Luke and Acts were written for Theophilus, this was a practice of the time, and did not mean that Luke had only one reader in mind. It is so striking that as Moses addressed his words in the book of Deuteronomy to God's people, so Paul addressed most of his letters to

---

13. Adam, *Hearing*, pp. 56–60.

churches, not to their leaders. One difficulty we have in applying the Scriptures is that we try to apply to the individual what God caused to be written to churches. It is obvious in the Bible that God spends more time addressing the health of the people of God than he does addressing the health of individual believers. We should ask, 'What is God saying to us?' as least as often as we ask, 'What is God saying to me?' The former question will make us more useful members of our churches, and better able to help our brothers and sisters. It will help us to that corporate maturity that is God's will for his people.

Variety of styles of writing and variety of motivations

Many preachers fall into the trap of preaching every text as if it were part of a propositional argument, or a parable, or a story. We must be alert to the varied styles of writing in the Bible, and adapt our interpretation to that style.

Many of us also use the same motivation: 'Do this, because God has told us to do it in the Bible.' We should avoid reading our favourite motivation into every part of the Bible, especially when the Bible text itself uses so many different motivations.[14] We saw some of these in our study of Psalm 1 above.

What are these words doing? What did God want to result from these words?

I was brought up to ask, 'What do these words mean? What does this word mean?' This is a useful start, but we need to go on to the questions, 'What are these words doing? What did God want to result from these words?' For words and sentences and chapters and books and the Bible as a whole are trying to achieve a result, are given for a purpose. Our reading of the Bible and our teaching of the Bible to others will be more productive if we pay attention to the purpose of Scripture. 'These are written so that . . .' (John 20:31) is a key to the Gospel of John, just as it is a key to the application of every part of the Bible.

Understand different kinds of 'application'

To 'apply' the Scriptures means to use those Scriptures to 'preach the word' and 'convince, rebuke, and encourage'. For, as we have seen, Paul instructed Timothy to 'apply' the Scriptures in 2 Timothy 4:2, in these words: 'convince, rebuke, and encourage, with the utmost patience in teaching'.

We need to think carefully about the range of what 'application' means in practice.

---

14. Adam, *Hearing*, pp. 67–73.

As we have already seen, relevance is not limited to immediate and recognized relevance. God has a long-term educative purpose, to bring his people to maturity in Christ, and this Bible passage may be intended to serve that purpose.

We also need pastoral wisdom to know that this part of the Bible does *not* apply in this present situation (see above). Presumably churches in the first century needed the same skills of discerning how they should apply the Old Testament, and also how to apply other New Testament books that were not written directly to them, but which they still received. So the church at Ephesus will have needed to think carefully how the letter to the Romans applied to them. Similarly, they would have realized that while Ephesians applied directly to them when they first received it, they had a more complicated task in thinking how it applied twenty years later.

As we have seen, not every part of the Bible can be reduced to 'a practical action for me today'. We need to be aware of different kinds of 'application'.

We have here in 2 Timothy clear instructions about the nature of Christian ministry, and especially the ministry of church leaders. May God raise up, train, prepare, equip, and strengthen many for this ministry of leadership for churches throughout the world until the return of the Lord Jesus.

In this chapter we have seen that the verse which supports the idea of the inspiration of Scripture puts that notion in the broader context of the need to be equipped for ministry with personal, theological, moral, and educational commitments. It is connected with the conviction that the message of the Old Testament is that of 'salvation through faith in Christ Jesus', and with the belief that the inspiration of the Scriptures means that they are useful and powerful to train people for ministry. We have also seen the expected output of those who have been trained in this way: that they will preach the word, use the Bible to do it, convince, rebuke, and encourage, and do this with great patience and lots of teaching. The doctrine of the inspiration of Scripture enables a vigorous model of ministry.

In 2 Timothy we have the doctrine of the inspiration of the Scriptures. In 2 Peter we find the complementary doctrine of the inspiration of the human authors of the Scriptures.

12. MOVED BY THE HOLY SPIRIT, THEY SPOKE FROM GOD

2 PETER 1 – 2

2 Peter 1 – 2 shows us the importance of the historic witness of the disciples and apostles of Christ as eyewitnesses and 'earwitnesses' of Christ's majesty, who spoke of what they had seen and heard, and the way in which God used the Old Testament in his witness to Christ. It also teaches the work of the Spirit in the writers of the Old Testament, and that we must resist false prophets and receive the words of true prophets. We also find here that the Old Testament and the apostolic witness combine to provide certainty for faith in Jesus Christ.

Furthermore, just as in 2 Timothy we found reference to the inspiration of Scripture, here we find reference to the inspiration of the human authors of Scripture. So a biblical doctrine of inspiration includes the inspiration of both the authors and the writings: the inspiration of the authors is the means by which the writings themselves are inspired.

As so often in the Bible, here we find that the truth is more clearly articulated because of an attack made upon it by false teachers, those who teach another gospel. It may be that we can discern the providential hand of God in this process: God allowed false apostles and false teachers in the time of the apostles so that the apostolic defence of the gospel would result in great understanding of the gospel of truth.

There was no expectation that the time of the apostles or the time after the apostles would be heresy-free. Jesus himself warned that 'false messiahs and false prophets will appear and produce signs and omens, to lead astray, if possible, the elect' (Mark 13:22). Paul warned the Ephesian elders that 'savage wolves will come in among you, not sparing the flock. Some even from your own group will come distorting the truth in order to entice the disciples to follow them' (Acts 20:29–30).

Here is a double warning, of those who invade to destroy, and also of members of the church who know the truth but distort it to attract followers. However, in the light of the Old Testament, we should not be surprised to find teachers of falsehood or false prophets among the people of God. Having seen Jesus' own ministry of defending the right interpretation of the Old Testament against other false interpretations, we should not be surprised at the presence of false teachers in apostolic churches, or, for that matter, in our own churches today.

No wonder, then, that the requirements and gifts needed for the elder/overseer include these: 'He must have a firm grasp of the word that is trustworthy in accordance with the teaching, so that he may be able both to preach with sound doctrine and to refute those who contradict it' (Titus 1:9).

Here is a double responsibility: to teach what is true, and to refute what is false. And of course the refutation of false teaching will help people to see the truth with greater clarity. 'The pastor ought to have two voices: one for gathering the sheep; and another, for warding off and driving away wolves and thieves. The Scripture provides him with the means of doing both; for he who is deeply skilled in it will be able both to govern those who are teachable, and to refute the enemies of the truth.'[1]

What was the false teaching that Peter wrote this letter to refute? It is helpful to see that it had three elements.

1. The main point of the false teaching was the denial of the return of Christ (2 Pet. 3:3–4). This explains Peter's teaching about Christ's return in 3:1–10, and his statements about Christ's divinity and glory in 1:2, 11; 3:18.
2. The false teaching also included the basis for this denial, which was the claim that Old Testament prophets' words did not come from God, and that New Testament apostles had no basis for teaching the glorious return of Christ (1:12–21; 3:1–2, 15–18).

---

1. Calvin, *Commentaries*, 21, p. 296, on Titus 1:9.

3. The false teaching also included the application of the denial of the return of Christ, which was adultery, greed, and corruption (2:1–21). Hence Peter's teaching about the need of godliness and holiness (1:1–11; 3:11–13, 18).

As a wise teacher, Peter needed to refute these three elements, namely the main point of their teaching, the basis for their teaching, and the implications of their teaching. For if he did not refute the basis of their teaching, the danger would still be present, and would emerge in the assertion of some other falsehood. The claim of the false teachers was that the words of Old Testament prophets did not come from God, and that New Testament apostles had no basis for teaching the glorious return of Christ. If he critiqued only the implications of the teaching, that is, licentious behaviour, then he would not be able to show the seriousness of their error, or the basis for leading a new life.

Furthermore, Peter not only needed to refute these three elements, he also needed to assert what were the three elements of the truth, so that his readers could both repent of what was wrong, and also do what was right.

In summary, there are no fewer than six elements in Peter's letter. Three are negative: his analysis of the ideas of the false teachers, and three are positive: his statement of the truth (see Table 2). This provides a very useful template for our warning about error and false teaching, and our teaching of gospel truth and life.

Table 2

	False teachers	**2 Peter**
The main idea	1. Return of Christ	4. Christ will return
The basis for this idea	2. Prophets and NT apostles wrong	5. Taught by Old Testament Prophets and New Testament apostles
The practical implications of this idea	3. Various forms of licentiousness	6. Godliness and holiness

So we turn to 2 Peter 1:12 – 2:3. In this section Peter reminded his readers of the gospel truth they had learned (1:12–15), and then reminded them of the basis of believing in the full glory of Christ, especially in his return or coming, namely, the apostles' teaching (1:16–18), and the teaching of the Old Testament prophets (1:19–21). He then pointed to the false prophets of the Old Testament and false teachers of his day, by way of contrast with true prophets and apostles (2:1–3).

Established in the truth, reminding you of the truth (1:12–15)

> Therefore I intend to keep on reminding you of these things, though you know them already and are established in the truth that has come to you. (1:12)

Peter was not ashamed to remind his readers of the content of the Christian faith. It is so easily forgotten: how else could the false teachers win converts from among believers to their fanciful ideas? As the old saying puts it: 'It goes without saying so it needs to be said.' What 'goes without saying' is soon lost and forgotten.

That is why it is so important to ask prospective preachers, ministers, and lecturers not only, 'What do you believe?' but also, 'What will you teach?' For it is not much use someone believing everything that is true if they do not teach it! And so much damage is done when we focus in our teaching on secondary issues, and neglect to teach the content of the faith.

Peter made it plain that by reminding them of these things, he was not implying that he thought that they did not know them. On the contrary, he knew that 'you know them already and are established in the truth that has come to you' (1:12).

What are 'these things'? Of course, they are what he has just written: 'faith ... through the righteousness of our God and Saviour Jesus Christ' (1:1); '[Christ's] divine power' that 'has given us everything needed for life and godliness' (1:3); Christ's 'precious and very great promises', given 'so that through them you may escape from the corruption that is in the world because of lust, and may become participants in the divine nature' (1:4).

They also included the expected response of believers: not a passive acceptance of God's grace, or their own natural sinfulness, but rather making 'every effort to support . . . faith with goodness, and goodness with knowledge, and knowledge with self-control, and self-control with endurance, and endurance with godliness, and godliness with mutual affection, and mutual affection with love' (1:5–7). For if 'these things' are present and increasing in their lives, they will not be 'ineffective and unfruitful in the knowledge of our Lord Jesus Christ' (1:8).

So 'these things' are both the active and personal grace of our God and Saviour Jesus Christ, and also our duty to confirm both call and election (1:10), and so to receive the rich provision of 'entry into the eternal kingdom of our Lord and Saviour Jesus Christ' (1:11).

'These things' (1:8–9, 12) are the same as 'the truth that has come to you' (1:12). Of course 'truth' is 'a widespread and frequent designation for the gospel from an early period'.[2] And Peter also described this truth as 'the way of truth' (2:2), and 'the way of righteousness' (2:21). So it is gospel truth that must be lived, for it is a way: when it is lived, it will be lived in righteousness.

They not only know the truth of the gospel, they are 'established in the truth' (1:12). Jesus told Peter to 'establish your brothers' (Luke 22:32 [my trans.]), and Peter acknowledged that his readers were established in gospel truth.

Why did Peter write this letter? He wanted to 'remind' them, as he also 'reminded' them in 1:13, 15, and 3:1–2. 'He intends the letter to be a permanent reminder of his teaching . . . to be available at all times . . . a permanent reminder of the apostle's definitive teaching.'[3] Peter wrote to remind them of what they already knew, so he wrote 'to refresh your memory' (1:13), and especially as he faced imminent death.[4] For what would happen when the eyewitnesses and apostles died out? Without written records of their teaching, their irreplaceable teaching would be lost. Peter's plan was that 'after my departure you may be able at any time to recall these things' (1:15).[5]

After Peter reminded them that they were indeed established in the truth, because they already knew the basics of the gospel, he then began his statement of the basis for believing the truth, namely the teaching of the apostles, and the teaching of the Old Testament prophets. For, as we have seen, the attack of the false teachers is not only on the doctrine of the glorious coming of Christ, but also on the basis for that doctrine provided by apostles and prophets.

Eyewitnesses and 'earwitnesses' of his majesty: apostolic witness

What we saw

> For we did not follow cleverly devised myths when we made known to you the power and coming of our Lord Jesus Christ, but we had been eyewitnesses of his majesty. (1:16)

It is likely that the false teachers were claiming that stories like that of Christ's transfiguration, and promises of his coming return, were only myths, and

---

2. Bauckham, *2 Peter*, p. 198.
3. Bauckham, *2 Peter*, pp. 195–196.
4. Possibly in the light of John 21:18–19.
5. Lucas and Green, *2 Peter*, p. 65.

should not be taken literally.[6] They may have accepted the spiritual meaning of these stories, but not their historical reality. Peter claimed that 'we' – that is, the apostles – were eyewitnesses of Christ's majesty. Of course, only Peter, James, and John were on the mountain when Christ was transfigured: 'Though to some extent all the apostles were eyewitnesses, they were not all eyewitnesses of every important event in the ministry of Jesus, and so their common message was in part based on the eyewitness testimony of only some of their number.'[7]

The words 'power and coming of our Lord Jesus Christ' need careful attention. The phrase 'power and coming' is a reference to what we commonly call the return of Christ, and means 'the powerful coming' or 'coming in power'. While we assume that the 'coming' of Christ naturally refers to his first coming, and then also speak of his 'second coming', in the New Testament, the 'coming', the *parousia*, refers to his return, what we call his 'second coming'.[8]

So Peter here referred to the apostolic teaching about the future coming in power of Christ. How is this relevant to the transfiguration? How does the event of the transfiguration support the idea of the powerful coming of Christ? Both describe the glory and power of Christ, but it is more than that, for, in the words of Richard Bauckham, 'The Transfiguration is the basis for the Parousia expectation because it is God's appointment of Jesus to a rôle which he has not yet exercised but will exercise at his coming in glory.'[9]

This idea is supported by the fact that in the three Gospel accounts of the transfiguration, the event is preceded by a reference by Jesus to his coming again in glory. So, for example, in Luke 9, just before the account of the transfiguration, we find Jesus' words, 'Those who are ashamed of me and of my words, of them the Son of Man will be ashamed when he comes in his glory and the glory of the Father and of the holy angels' (Luke 9:26).[10]

So we should expect the coming of Christ because of what happened at the transfiguration: we should recognize the teaching authority of the apostles because Jesus invited them to see and hear this great event: 'we had been eye-witnesses of his majesty'.

---

6. Bauckham, *2 Peter*, pp. 213–214.

7. Ibid., p. 214.

8. As in 2 Pet. 3:4, 12, and as in Matt. 24:3, 27, 37, 39; Mark 13:26; 1 Cor. 15:23; 1 Thess. 3:13; 4:15; Jas 5:5–7; and 1 John 2:28. In 1 Pet., instead of *parousia*, we find *apokalypsis*, 'revelation'.

9. Bauckham, *2 Peter*, p. 220.

10. See also Matt. 16:27 and Mark 8:38.

Not only did the presence of the apostles make it easier for their hearers to believe in the future majestic and powerful coming of the Lord Jesus, but by their account of what they saw and heard, we too can be helped to hope for his return. For we know that glory and majestic power are not alien to Christ, but are aspects of his true status and dignity. Peter drew attention to the divine dignity of Jesus Christ several times in this letter. In 1:1 he wrote of 'the righteousness of our God and Saviour Jesus Christ'. At the end of his letter, he attributed 'glory both now and to the day of eternity' to 'our Lord and Saviour Jesus Christ' (3:18). This is very unusual, as when letters end with an attribution of glory, it is usually glory to God. It is very significant that Peter attributes 'glory' to Jesus Christ. Majestic Christology indeed.

Peter claimed that he and the other apostles were 'eyewitnesses of his majesty'.[11] In the accounts of the transfiguration in the Gospels[12] the disciples were encouraged to see the cross as the destiny of Christ, and to recognize that his divine mission would be accomplished through suffering and death. The transfiguration had another purpose as well: to bring assurance of the future glorious coming again of the Lord Jesus. It showed how God planned to honour his Son.

Peter's claim to have been among those who were 'eyewitnesses of his majesty' reminds us of the importance of eyewitnesses in the early church. It was essential for the apostles to bridge the gap between Jesus' earthly ministry and his death and resurrection. For those two revelations could not be separated: it was important to know that the risen Christ was not a ghost, but the Jesus whom they knew, now raised from the dead. And only eyewitnesses and 'earwitnesses' could say that they had seen how Old Testament prophecies and promises were fulfilled in Jesus. Witnesses are those who will speak of what they have seen and heard. So Jesus said to his disciples, 'You are witnesses of these things' (Luke 24:48). So too when Judas was to be replaced, Peter said, 'One of the men who have accompanied us throughout the time that the Lord Jesus went in and out among us, beginning from the baptism of John until the day when he was taken up from us – one of these must become a witness with us to his resurrection' (Acts 1:21–22).

---

11. As I have made good use of Richard Bauckham's commentary, I should note that he does not think that Peter wrote 2 Peter, but claims that it was written after his death by an associate of Peter, who wanted to apply Peter's teaching authority in a new situation. See Bauckham, 2 Peter, pp. 158–162. For a defence of Peter's authorship, see Green, 2 Peter, Jude, pp. 13–38, and Lucas and Green, 2 Peter, pp. 21–22.

12. Matt. 17:1–8; Mark 9:2–8; and Luke 9:28–36.

This idea of the definitive generation whose witness is needed by all subsequent generations is also reflected in John 1:14, 'And the Word became flesh and lived among us, and we have seen this glory', and in 1 Cor. 15:3, 'For I handed on to you as of first importance what I in turn had received.' Richard Bauckham has argued that we should understand the Gospels as the record of 'eyewitness testimony' of Jesus Christ.[13]

Of course, 'witness' and 'testify' in this context refer to an eyewitness, that is, one who gives an account of historical reality and events, and not, as we commonly use the term, one who 'witnesses' to their internal convictions.[14]

This is not the same as Karl Barth's idea that the Scriptures are a witness to a revelation which may occur independently of them or may use them.[15] Peter claims that the apostles were witnesses of the objective and public reality of God's actions and words, and that he has recorded those events here in his letter.

What we heard (1:17–18)

Eyewitnesses were also 'earwitnesses'! For Peter now recounted what they heard. 'For he received honour and glory from God the Father when that voice was conveyed to him by the Majestic Glory, saying, "This is my Son, my Beloved, with whom I am well pleased." We ourselves heard this voice come from heaven, while we were with him on the holy mountain' (1:17–18).

Here Peter explained the meaning of the event: 'For he received honour and glory from God the Father.' As Henry Alford observed, 'He received honour in the voice that spoke to him, and glory in the light that shone from him.'[16] Peter told of hearing the voice of God, and what God said 'when that voice was conveyed to him by the Majestic Glory, saying, "This is my Son, my Beloved, with whom I am well pleased"' (1:17). As many have pointed out, revelation in the Bible comprises event and interpretation, God's work and God's word.[17] Significantly, Richard Bauckham has shown that the idea of

---

13. See Bauckham, *Eyewitnesses*.

14. Though Bauckham does not believe that Peter wrote this letter, he still asserts that this account of the transfiguration reflects the experience of Peter, and that it was faithfully communicated in this letter by Peter's follower, who wrote the letter.

15. Wolterstorff, *Discourse*, pp. 63–74. Luther accused Zwingli of holding the same view, see Adam, *Hearing*, pp. 198–199.

16. From Alford's commentary, as quoted in Green, *2 Peter*, 94.

17. Or, as David Jackman expresses it, Event + Explanation = Revelation. Jackman, *I Believe*, p. 24.

'eyewitness' or 'testimony' includes both history and theology, both, of course given by God in the original context.[18]

Peter then reminded his readers that the apostles not only saw what happened, but also heard what happened: 'We ourselves heard this voice come from heaven, while we were with him on the holy mountain' (1:18). Just as in 1:16 he claimed that 'we' were 'eyewitnesses', so here in 1:18 he emphasizes that 'we ourselves heard' God's words to his Son.

Let us look more closely at what God said, at what they heard from that voice from heaven. The words 'This is my Son' are based on Psalm 2:7 'You are my son; today I have begotten you.' This psalm may also be reflected in the words 'holy mountain', as Psalm 2:6 reads, 'I have set my king on Zion, my holy hill.' Of course, the transfiguration did not happen on Mount Zion in Jerusalem, but the wording of the psalm has influenced Peter's language.

The words 'my Beloved' may come from Isaiah 42:1, 'my chosen', and/or from Genesis 22:12, 'my only one'.[19] 'The Beloved' as a title for Christ is also used in Ephesians 1:6, 'grace that he freely bestowed on us in the Beloved'.

The words 'with whom I am well pleased' mean that God has chosen Christ and favoured him,[20] and imply that God will honour him. God honoured Christ when he raised him from among the dead, and he will honour him when Christ returns, at his coming again. What are we to make of these words from the voice from heaven?

We should notice that there are varied accounts of what God said in the three Gospel accounts and here in 2 Peter. This is no surprise, as in most accounts of someone saying something in the Bible, what we have is a reduced summary of what was said. This is true of Jesus' teaching, of the sermons in Acts, and of Old Testament speeches. Each author presents the version of the words that best suits his purpose. Here in 2 Peter, for example, Peter did not include God's words 'Listen to him!' recorded in Matthew, Mark, and Luke. He did not include them because they were not relevant to his purpose in writing this letter. For the point of referring to the transfiguration here is not the authority of Jesus' words and teaching, but the fact that God will honour and glorify him. The words are recorded in the Gospels, because the words had particular relevance when Jesus had just been explaining about his coming suffering, death and resurrection. There it was relevant that he was the prophet promised in Deuteronomy 18:15. Here the point is that Jesus is king and judge.

---

18. Baukham, *Eyewitnesses*, pp. 505–508.

19. Bauckham, *2 Peter*, p. 220.

20. Ibid. p. 220.

We should also notice that God used quotations from the Old Testament to tell the disciples of Jesus' honour and glory. Why did God do this?

We can only surmise the answer to this question. God need not have used language from the Old Testament, but he did so. Presumably it was because he wanted to affirm the significance of the Old Testament as the source of the right interpretation of Jesus Christ, and to affirm that the Old Testament pointed to Christ. If this is the case, then God was not only revealing the nature of Christ, but also educating the disciples in biblical theology, showing how the Holy Scriptures revealed Christ, and showing the value of his prophets. It was an educational exercise in the interpretation or internal hermeneutics of the Bible. This was relevant for our author, for, in the next verses (1:19–21), he claimed the God-given inspiration of the writers of the Old Testament. He did this in order to correct the false teachers, and to state the truth.

This also means that we should not think of these quotations from the Old Testament as being used as rhetorical flourishes with no theological significance. Each quotation brings with it the theological themes of its original context. 'This is my Son', from Psalm 2, brings with it the themes of the rebellion of the nations against 'the LORD and his anointed', and the Lord's determination to set his king on Zion's holy hill. The decree of the Lord, 'You are my son; today I have begotten you', contains the promise that this son will rule the nations, and the call for the rulers of the earth to submit to God (Ps. 2:2, 6, 7, 8, 10). All of these themes are of great relevance to the whole message of 2 Peter.

God's words 'my Beloved' may come from Isaiah 42:1, in which case they introduce the theme of the Servant of the Lord from these chapters of Isaiah, including the suffering Servant, with his atoning death, in chapters 52 and 53. The words might also have reference to the story of Abraham and Isaac in Genesis 22, in which Isaac is described as Abraham's 'only son . . . whom you love' (Gen. 22:2). Here too is a mountain, here is a father willing to sacrifice his only and beloved son, and here too is a substitute sacrifice, when the ram, and not Isaac, is made the burnt offering.

The words 'with whom I am well pleased', also from Isaiah 42:1, mean that God has chosen and appointed Jesus to his role, and is publicly identifying Jesus, as he did at his baptism, as his chosen one, Servant, Messiah, Son of Man, and Son.[21]

Peter's account in these verses of what they saw and what they heard mirrors the words of Peter and John in Acts 4, when their reply to the

---

21. See Lucas and Green, *2 Peter*, pp. 75–79, for an excellent exposition of these verses.

Jerusalem council's attempt to silence them was: 'We cannot keep from speaking about what we have *seen* and *heard*' (Acts 4:20). It is important to realize that Peter is here claiming to have been a witness to both the historical event and to God's interpretation of that event. For the revelation that God gave to the apostles on the mount of transfiguration was both event and interpretation: what the apostles saw, and what they heard.

God did not give them an event and leave them to work out the interpretation. Nor did God give them an interpretation with no historical event behind it. They did not need to invent the interpretation, for God had given it. They did not need to construct or create an event to support or fill out the God-given interpretation. God did both. The task of a witness is not to invent or create, but to give a truthful account of what he or she saw and heard. God chose the apostles, Peter among them, for this crucial role. For just as God decided that his revelation was to be given in history, so we need authenticated God-given witnesses, who provide us with an authorized account of what they saw and heard. Otherwise both salvation history and biblical theology are lost. The scandal of particularity of the historical revelation in word and deed requires faithful witnesses for the benefit of subsequent generations. Otherwise, there can be no universal witness to God and his saving plan in his Son and our Saviour.

Peter has learned a lot since Caesarea Philippi and the mount of transfiguration. Remember the conversation between Jesus and Peter, when Jesus began to teach them that the Son of Man must undergo suffering, death, and resurrection. There Peter began to rebuke him for these ideas, but Jesus rebuked Peter and said, 'Get behind me, Satan! For you are setting your mind not on divine things but on human things' (Mark 8:33). Then when Jesus was transfigured, Peter said, 'Rabbi, it is good for us to be here; let us make three dwellings, one for you, one for Moses, and one for Elijah.' Mark commented, 'He did not know what to say, for they were terrified' (Mark 9:5–6). Peter has learned a lot since those days.

The more fully confirmed prophetic message: Old Testament prophecy

'So we have the prophetic message more fully confirmed' (2 Pet. 1:19). The false teachers rejected the authority of both the apostles and the Old Testament. So Peter, having defended the role of the apostles in 1:16–18, then defended the authority of the Old Testament. The 'prophetic message' or 'prophetic word' clearly means the Old Testament, perhaps with special reference to those parts of it that point to the full glory, power, and majesty of Christ at his (second) coming, when he will raise the dead and judge the nations.[22]

The New Testament writers refer to the Old Testament in a variety of ways. Sometimes it is 'the law of Moses, the prophets and the psalms' (Luke 24:44), sometimes 'the law and the prophets' (Rom. 3:21), sometimes 'the prophets' (Rom. 1:2; Acts 10:43; 26:27; Eph. 2:20; Heb. 1:1), and often 'the scripture(s)', or the 'holy scriptures' (Matt. 22:29; 26:54; John 5:39; Rom. 1:2; 2 Tim. 3:16). Here it is 'the prophetic message'.

Peter wanted to assert the value of the true Old Testament prophets, as in 2:1 he will refer to the false prophets whose ministry is also recorded in the Old Testament.

What did he mean by saying that we have the prophetic message of the Old Testament 'more fully confirmed'? He is connecting the verbal witness of the apostles and the Old Testament. What is the connection?

Some suggest that he meant that the witness of the apostles gives a firmer confirmation of the prophetic message of the Old Testament, because that witness fulfils the Old Testament.[23] Others suggest that the fact of the Old Testament prophetic message gives greater confirmation to the witness of the apostles.[24] However, no comparison may be intended between the value or authority of the Old Testament and the apostles. Richard Bauckham wrote that 'more fully confirmed' may mean 'very firm', and added, 'No comparison need be intended.'[25]

The point is that each supports the other. We can value the Old Testament prophetic message because it was in part fulfilled in the transfiguration (and the transfiguration also pointed to the greater glories of Christ still to come), and we can also value the apostles' witness to the transfiguration events because we can see that they were foreshadowed and promised in the Old Testament. Each part of God's verbal revelation supports the other.

Furthermore, the two are closely linked in that what the apostles hear from the voice of God at the transfiguration is part of the prophetic message itself, as the words God speaks on the mountain come from that prophetic message, namely, Psalm 2, Isaiah, and Genesis.

---

22. Bauckham, *2 Peter*, p. 24: 'The prophetic word . . . is virtually synonymous with "Scripture".'

23. For example, Lucas and Green, *2 Peter*, p. 80.

24. For example, Green, *2 Peter*, pp. 97–98.

25. Bauckham, *2 Peter*, p. 223.

So the transfiguration which they had seen and heard, and the inspired Old Testament prophetic word, both point to the glory of Christ's second coming as judge and saviour.

Peter also brought together the mutually supportive authority of both the Old Testament and Christ's apostles later in 2 Peter, in this instruction: 'You should remember the words spoken in the past by the holy prophets, and the commandment of the Lord and Saviour spoken through your apostles' (3:2).

So these are not 'cleverly devised myths' (1:16), for the words of God spoken to the apostles on the mountain and the words of God spoken through the prophets both point to the future glory of Christ.

A shining lamp till the dawning day

'You will do well to be attentive to this as to a lamp shining in a dark place, until the day dawns and the morning star rises in your hearts' (1:19). Just as Peter has focused their attention on the sights and sounds of the transfiguration, so he now urges them to focus their attention on the Old Testament, this 'prophetic word'. He likened the Old Testament to a light or lamp shining in a dark place, implying that without the Scriptures, people will be ignorant, whereas with them, they can find some truth. 'Into this darkness the prophetic Scripture casts a ray of light by awakening hope.'[26]

The light that shines from the Old Testament is itself prophetic of the future, because it anticipates the great light of the coming of Christ, when 'the day of eternity' (3:18) dawns. Peter then described the coming of the Lord Jesus as the day, and likened his arrival to the morning star. Peter and his contemporaries read the prophecy of Balaam in Numbers 24:17 as a prophecy of Christ: 'a star shall come out of Jacob, and a sceptre shall rise out of Israel'. (This an example of the prophetic word.) And Christ described himself as the morning star in Revelation: 'I am the root and the descendant of David, the bright morning star' (Rev. 22:16). When Peter wrote of the time when 'the morning star rises in your hearts' (1:19), he referred to the fact that although the Scriptures do bring light to us, a far greater light will be ours at the coming of Christ, our 'morning star'.

This is a very helpful way of thinking about the relationship between the illumination that comes to us from Scriptures now, and the great outpouring of light that Christ will bring at his return. We have enough light now from the

---

26. Bauckham, 2 Peter, p. 225.

Scriptures to be 'established in the truth' (1:12) and 'fully confirmed' (1:19), for the Scriptures are like 'a lamp shining in a dark place'. However, we wait for the coming of Christ, when the 'day of eternity' dawns, and Christ, 'the morning star', will rise in our hearts (1:19).

No Scripture is a matter of one's own interpretation

'First of all you must understand this, that no prophecy of Scripture is a matter of one's own interpretation' (1:20). Like the good teacher he was, Peter first clarified and corrected the error of the false teachers, before he stated the truth. Their error is that of not understanding the true origin of the words of the writers of the Old Testament.

The issue is not whether anyone can read anything into the text of the Old Testament, as in the claim, 'It's all a matter of interpretation.' The issue was whether the theology of the Old Testament came from God or not. The false teachers may have thought that everything in the Old Testament was only the product of human imagination. Or they may have thought that God gave visions and signs, but that the interpretation of those visions and signs came from the writers, and not from God. No wonder Peter later accused them of twisting the Scriptures to their own destruction (3:16).

For example, in Jeremiah 24, Jeremiah was given a vision of two baskets of figs, one with very good figs, and the other with bad figs, so bad that they could not be eaten (Jer. 24:1–3). Presumably the false teachers thought that God give the vision to Jeremiah, but not the explanation of the vision. However, if God did not give an explanation of the vision, then Jeremiah would still not know what God wanted to communicate through the vision. However, God did give the explanation – that the good figs where those taken into exile and the bad figs were those who had stayed in Jerusalem (Jer. 24:4–10).

So the connection between 2 Peter 1:20 and 1:21 is obvious. In the words of Martyn Lloyd-Jones, 'No prophecy of Scripture arises or originates in the prophet's own understanding of things, for the prophecy came in the old time not by the will of man: but holy men of God spake as they were moved by the Holy Ghost.'[27]

In the New Testament, we are told that Jesus died and rose again, but we are also told the significance of his death and resurrection. In the book of

---

27. Lloyd-Jones, 2 Peter, p. 95.

Revelation, John's 'visions' include not only what he saw, but also what he heard. It is often the case that what he heard explains what he saw, or that what he saw explains what he heard. For example, in Revelation 5, he *heard of* 'the Lion of the tribe of Judah' (5:5); then he *saw* 'a Lamb standing as if it had been slaughtered' (5:6). The Lion is the Lamb.

We find similar views today to those of the false teachers, views that limit the extent or mode of God's revelation. Some limit the revelation of God to the deeds or acts of God, value the Bible for the record of those deeds or acts, but then assume that the interpretation of those deeds or acts in the Bible is just the Bible writers' attempts to make sense of what God had done. Then the assumption is that we have as much right to create our own interpretations and explanations of God's mighty deeds or acts. Or others see the Bible writers as being merely examples of the people of God doing their best to understand God in their own terms: that this was valid for their day, and that we in our turn must follow their example and do the same for our day.

This is why it is important to see that Peter refuted the theological method-ology of the false teachers, not just the products of their false teaching. For God did act in history, and did saving acts. However, those acts were not ambiguous, nor were they given without interpretation. God *spoke* as well as *acted*, and God's *words* explained *his works*.

In the Old Testament, the explanation or interpretation of a vision 'is not the prophet's own interpretation of his vision, but an inspired, God-given interpretation'.[28]

Having clarified the error, Peter then clarified the truth.

Moved by the Spirit, they spoke from God

The origin of the words of the prophetic message, the prophetic word, the Old Testament, was divine, not human. The origin of the message was God, and the Holy Spirit moved the writers, so that they spoke from God. God was the origin, and the Holy Spirit moved or carried along the human authors: 'because no prophecy ever came by human will, but men and women moved by the Holy Spirit spoke from God' (1:21).

While the prophets saw the acts of God, and received signs and dreams and visions, their prophecies were not merely their own interpretations of these God-given events. The Holy Spirit of God inspired not only the prophets'

28. Bauckham, *2 Peter*, p. 231.

dreams and visions, but also their interpretation of them, and interpreted the acts or deeds of God, so that when they wrote Scripture, they spoke 'from God'.

The point is made even clearer when we notice that the word that Peter has used for 'moved' or 'carried along', here in verse 21, is the same word he used in verse 17, when he wrote that God's voice had 'come' or 'was conveyed' from heaven.[29] For as the words spoken at the transfiguration came from God, so too the words of the Old Testament came from God.

Furthermore, Peter pointed to the strongest contrast between the value of the prophetic message that has come from 'men and women moved by the Holy Spirit [who] spoke from God' (1:21), and the false teachers, who, like the false prophets of the Old Testament, bring only 'destructive opinions' (2:1).

Here the claim is that the Old Testament came from people 'moved by the Holy Spirit', so that they 'spoke from God'. We have in 2 Timothy 3:16 the idea that the writings were 'inspired'; here it is people who are 'moved by the Holy Spirit'. So both the people and their words were inspired. It was not the case that the people were inspired, and then they did their best with the words that they spoke or wrote. Nor was it the case that God bypassed the people in causing inspired words to be spoken or written. The Holy Spirit was active in people and in their words. 'He says they were moved, not because they were bereaved of mind (as the Gentiles imagined their prophets to have been) . . . but because they dared not to announce anything of their own, and obediently followed the Spirit as their guide, who ruled in their mouth as in his own sanctuary.'[30]

In 1 Peter, as we have seen, we find a complementary impression of the relationship between the Holy Spirit and the prophets of the Old Testament: 'The prophets who prophesied of the grace that was to be yours made careful search and inquiry, inquiring about the person or time that the Spirit of Christ within them indicated, when it testified in advance to the sufferings destined for Christ and the subsequent glory' (1:10–11).

Here Peter wrote of the careful searching and inquiring undertaken by the prophets themselves. They 'applied their minds to the revelation of the Spirit'.[31] Robert Leighton described this hard work of Old Testament prophets in these words:

---

29. From the verb *phero* we have *enechtheisan* in verse 17 and *pheromenoi* in verse 21.

30. Calvin, *Commentaries*, 22, p. 91, on 2 Pet. 1:21.

31. Ibid., p. 39, on 1 Pet. 1:11.

Again, it is no mean thing that such men as were of unquestioned eminency in wisdom and holiness, did so much study and search after, and having found it out, were not only to publish it in their own times, but to record it for posterity; and this not by the private motion of their own spirits, but by the acting and guidance of the Spirit of God; which likewise sets the truth of their testimony above all doubtfulness and uncertainty.[32]

He then adds a warning to those who study, read, and teach those inspired words with insufficient energy and attention: 'Were the prophets not exempted from the pains of search and enquiry, who had the Spirit of God not only in a high measure, but after a singular manner? How unbeseeming, then, are slothfulness and idleness in us!'[33]

So Peter has defended both the witness of the apostles and that of the writers of the Old Testament. God spoke to both, and God spoke through both. God spoke through the prophets, as God spoke on the mountain. Peter defended the truth in which the church had been established against the errors of the false teachers of his day. Then he turned to them, and to their malicious influence on the people of God.

False prophets, false teachers

There is the strongest contrast between the God-given, Spirit-moved writers of the Old Testament, and the false prophets whose words and actions are recorded in that same Old Testament. And there is a frightening parallel between the false prophets of the Old Testament and the false teachers who were corrupting the churches in Peter's day.

But false prophets also arose among the people, just as there will be false teachers among you, who will secretly bring in destructive opinions. They will even deny the Master who bought them – bringing swift destruction on themselves. Even so, many will follow their licentious ways, and because of these teachers the way of truth will be maligned. (2 Pet. 2:1–2)

False prophets and false teachers are false in three ways: God has not appointed them, they do not speak the truth, and they encourage 'false' ways

---

32. Leighton, *1 Peter*, 1, p. 62.
33. Ibid., pp. 67–68.

162 WRITTEN FOR US

of life among God's people.[34] In the Old Testament, the false prophets did not speak with God's commission or authority, their messages came from their own imaginations, and their messages often promised false security in continued sin. They were in the strongest opposition to God's true prophets, and they were ultimately repudiated or punished by God. All these characteristics were found in the false teachers of Peter's day.[35]

Their fundamental mistake was to turn away from Jesus Christ who died for them and redeemed them: 'They will even deny the Master who bought them.' To turn away from Christ, to deny him, must bring death and destruction: they 'will secretly bring in destructive opinions' (2:1), and, because the ideas bring destruction, they are actually 'bringing swift destruction on themselves' (2:1).

They bring with them two great dangers: some will follow them and their destructive ideas and theology, and the message of the gospel is brought into disrepute: 'Many will follow their licentious ways, and because of these teachers the way of truth will be maligned' (2:2). So the false teachers will bring destruction to people, and dishonour to God. When people follow their destructive teaching, they will think that there will be no return or coming of Christ, and therefore no judgment, and so all moral restraint will be lost, and so all moral transformation will be lost. These themes are worked out in the remainder of 2 Peter.

Here we conclude our study of 2 Peter as we note the term Peter used to describe the gospel, that is, 'the way of truth' (2:2). The gospel was described as 'the Way' (Acts 9:2; 19:9; 22:4; 24:14, 22), as 'the Way of the Lord' (Acts 18:25), and as the 'way of salvation' (Acts 16:17). Here it is 'the way of truth', because Peter is faced with grievous error, and the only remedy for error is truth. The great danger of these false teachers is that they will bring dishonour on this 'way of truth', that is, this truth about the Lord Jesus.

As Dietrich Bonhoeffer wrote:

The essence of the church is not to practise theology but to *believe* and *obey* the word of God. But because it has pleased God to make himself known in the *spoken human word* and because this word is subject to distortion and dilution by human ideas and opinions, the community needs clarity about what constitutes true and false preaching – it needs theology not as an end in itself but as a means to help keep its

---

34. God did send a lying spirit in the mouth of many prophets for his purpose of judgment of King Ahab in 1 Kgs 22.
35. See, for example, Deut. 13:1–5; 1 Kgs 22:5–28; Jer. 5:30–31; 23; Ezek. 13; Mic. 3:1–8; Mark 13:21–22; 1 John 4:1–6; and Rev. 2:18–29; 13 – 17.

proclamation authentic and combat false preaching. In times of testing and temptation the church is called in a special way to such maturity.[36]

We found the inspiration and power of the holy writings described in 2 Timothy 3; and we found in 2 Peter that the reason the writings were inspired was that the human authors of those writings were moved or carried along by the Holy Spirit.

This chapter has shown us the importance of the historic witness of the disciples and apostles of Christ as eyewitnesses and 'earwitnesses' of Christ's majesty, and God's use of the Old Testament in his witness to Christ. It has also shown us the work of the Spirit in the writers of the Old Testament. We saw too that Old Testament and apostolic witness combine to provide certainty for faith in Jesus Christ.

---

36. Bonhoeffer, *Reflections*, p. 89.

1 CORINTHIANS 1 – 2

This section of 1 Corinthians gives us vivid insights into the gospel message of Christ crucified, and the role of the Holy Spirit in revealing that gospel to the apostles. Here is the work of the Spirit of truth promised and enabled by Jesus Christ, that work of teaching the depths of God, the gospel of Christ, to the people of God through the apostle Paul. We see that the truth of the gospel does not arise from the church at Corinth, but comes from God in words taught by the Spirit through the apostle Paul. We see the identity of the message of Christ crucified with the deepest verbal revelation of the Spirit of God. Here again God speaks to his people by his Spirit about his Son.

God's wisdom and power: Christ crucified

God's wisdom, the power of God
For Paul, there is the strongest contrast between the wisdom of God and the wisdom of the world. As he wrote in 1:18–20:

> For the message about the cross is foolishness to those who are perishing, but to us who are being saved it is the power of God. For it is written,

'I will destroy the wisdom of the wise,
    and the discernment of the discerning I will thwart.'

. . . Has not God made foolish the wisdom of the world? For since, in the wisdom of God, the world did not know God through wisdom, God decided, through the foolishness of our proclamation, to save those who believe.

So, because human wisdom was not able to perceive God, he decided to demonstrate the futility of human wisdom, to destroy it and thwart it. He did so through the message about the cross. This message sounds like foolishness, but it is a message that saves those who believe, for it is the power of God. The message of the cross is God's wise power, God's powerful wisdom.

God's wisdom, Christ crucified

The world's wisdom is both practical and theoretical. Paul characterized his fellow Jews as those who look for signs, and he characterized Greeks as those who look for intellectual wisdom. Christ crucified is the power of God and the wisdom of God, and this power and wisdom look like folly and weakness. The message of Christ crucified rebukes both:

For Jews demand signs and Greeks desire wisdom, but we proclaim Christ crucified, a stumbling-block to Jews and foolishness to Gentiles, but to those who are the called, both Jews and Greeks, Christ the power of God and the wisdom of God. For God's foolishness is wiser than human wisdom, and God's weakness is stronger than human strength. (1:22–25)

God's wisdom in the church

The pattern of Christ crucified is reflected in the composition of the church, for God works the same pattern and so rebukes human wisdom and expectations.

Consider your own call, brothers and sisters: not many of you were wise by human standards, not many were powerful, not many were of noble birth. But God chose what is foolish in the world to shame the wise; God chose what is weak in the world to shame the strong; God chose what is low and despised in the world, things that are not, to reduce to nothing things that are, so that no one might boast in the presence of God. (1:26–29)

God's pattern of wisdom is found in the composition of the church, so 'Let the one who boasts, boast in the Lord' (1:31).

God's wisdom in Paul's ministry

As is the message, so is the ministry. 'Christ crucified' is reflected and expressed in the experience of ministry. How could lofty words or human wisdom communicate the gospel of a crucified Messiah?

> When I came to you, brothers and sisters, I did not come proclaiming the mystery of God to you in lofty words or wisdom. For I decided to know nothing among you except Jesus Christ, and him crucified. And I came to you in weakness and in fear and in much trembling. My speech and my proclamation were not with plausible words of wisdom, but with a demonstration of the Spirit and of power, so that your faith might rest not on human wisdom but on the power of God. (2:1–5)

Paul's weakness and fear and trembling did not mean that Christ crucified was a failure, but pointed to the unexpected power and wisdom of God in the foolish and weakness of the cross. And if Christ is wisdom and power, then the proclamation of Christ crucified is the power of God, with power to save (1:18–21). The power of the Spirit was present in Paul's proclamation, and so their faith rests on the wisdom and power of God.

God's wisdom and power: Christ crucified, and the Spirit's revelation

God's secret and hidden wisdom

Just as God's wisdom and power were shown in the message of Christ crucified, so those who do not receive this message show that God's wisdom is beyond their understanding. For God's wisdom was secret and hidden, because it is revealed only in that most unpromising of messages, Christ and him crucified: 'Yet among the mature we do speak wisdom, though it is not a wisdom of this age or of the rulers of this age, who are doomed to perish. But we speak God's wisdom, secret and hidden, which God decreed before the ages for our glory. None of the rulers of this age understood this; for if they had, they would not have crucified the Lord of glory' (2:6–8).

To miss Christ is to miss all. The rulers of this age (the Jewish and Roman leaders in Jerusalem) showed with blinding clarity their distance from God's wisdom. Rather than welcoming and believing in the Lord Jesus, they crucified him. Their rejection of Christ demonstrated God's hidden and secret wisdom. To miss the cross is to miss all.

Yet for some, Christ crucified is God's power and wisdom. They are those whom Paul describes as the mature, that is, mature in God's wisdom.[1]

Chronologically, the gospel was, comparatively speaking, a mystery until its full revelation in the preaching by Christ and his apostles. In practice, the gospel remains a hidden mystery until people turn from the wisdom of the world, and receive God's wisdom in Christ crucified, as revealed by the Spirit.

Jesus Christ also taught God's bias in favour of those who are weak and humble:

> At that time Jesus said, 'I thank you, Father, Lord of heaven and earth, because you have hidden these things from the wise and the intelligent and have revealed them to infants; yes, Father, for such was your gracious will. All things have been handed over to me by my Father; and no one knows the Son except the Father, and no one knows the Father except the Son and anyone to whom the Son chooses to reveal him.'
> (Matt. 11:25–27)

God's wisdom: The Spirit reveals

God's wisdom was expressed in the death of Christ. How was the meaning of that event communicated to humanity? By the Spirit: 'But, as it is written, "What no eye has seen, nor ear heard, nor the human heart conceived, what God has prepared for those who love him" – these things God has revealed to us through the Spirit' (1 Cor. 2:9–10).

Paul wanted to show the great gap between human expectation and the gift of salvation. When he used the word 'prepared', he was not writing about future experience, but referring to what God prepared for all believers in the gospel of Christ. We could never have imagined the gospel.

When Paul wrote, 'as it is written', we expect a quotation from the Old Testament to follow. The words are not a direct quotation, but seem to be an amalgamation of Isaiah 64:4 and 65:16. There were many such amalgamations of Old Testament texts in Judaism, and these words also occur in a document called the *Ascension of Isaiah*. We could reposition the quotation marks that show the extent of the quotation, so that the text would read: 'But, as it is written, "What no eye has seen, nor ear heard, nor the human heart conceived", what God has prepared for those who love him – these things God has revealed to us through the Spirit.'[2]

---

1. See also Rom. 16:25–27.
2. Charles Hodge suggested that we could understand 'as it is written' to mean 'to use the language of Scripture'. Hodge, *1 Corinthians*, p. 38.

What should we make of this use of the Old Testament? Here are three comments:

1. We should not be surprised that Paul's quotations from the Old Testament came from a variety of translations, or in the form of a quotation from a text of a hymn based on the Old Testament. He followed the customs of his age and culture, and God did not remove him from his historical context. As Richard Longenecker wrote, 'It is hardly surprising to find that the exegesis of the New Testament (of the Old Testament) is heavily dependent upon Jewish procedural precedents, for, theoretically, one would expect a divine redemption that is worked out in the categories of a particular history – which is exactly what the Christian gospel claims to be – to express itself . . . in terms of the concepts and methods of that particular people and day'.[3]

   The Bible writers used all the literary conventions of their day, and this reflects God's ability to use human beings in their historical contexts and still achieve his revelatory purpose.

2. We also practise a wide variety of uses of the Bible. These include exact quotation, selecting a translation that expresses our desired emphasis, and quotations from Christian sources which use Bible words or link texts. We also use allusions, where we use Bible words without necessarily implying their exact meaning in their original context. We do this instinctively, and recognize that the most exact scientific standards are not required in this context.

3. We can combine a theology of verbal inspiration with confidence that God's words can survive a variety of uses and still retain their power. We believe that God's words achieve God's purposes, even in unpromising circumstances. It is often the case that we misunderstand Bible verses when we read the truths of other verses into the verse we are reading. Our reading is technically incorrect, but we may not be led into great error. However, we should try to listen and read carefully, and understand what each part of the Bible means. There is no reason to think that God likes being misunderstood, misinterpreted, or misquoted.

The Spirit searches the depths of God
Paul added, 'These things God has revealed to us through the Spirit; for the Spirit searches everything, even the depths of God' (2:10).

---

3. Longenecker, *Exegesis*, p. 207.

What does it mean to say that the Spirit searches the depths of God? We are used to the language of 'depth' in Scripture. Paul wrote in Romans 11:33, 'O the depth of the riches and wisdom and knowledge of God! How unsearchable are his judgements and how inscrutable his ways!' Or again, notice the subtle paradoxes of Paul's prayer in Ephesians: 'I pray that you may have the power to comprehend, with all the saints, what is the breadth and length and height and depth, and to know the love of Christ that surpasses knowledge, so that you may be filled with all the fullness of God' (3:18–19).

Here Paul prayed that they might have 'power to comprehend', that is, to understand; and he wants them to know that love of Christ that 'surpasses knowledge'!

Well, are we able to know the depths of God or not? Paul's answer in 1 Corinthians 2:10 is 'Yes'. We can know the depths of God, because the Spirit of God searches those depths, and reveals them to us: 'He even searches the deep things of God: nothing is excluded from his searching.'[4] God the Holy Spirit searches the depths of God, to reveal them to us.

These words are of great importance in thinking about the self-revelation of God. It is sometimes claimed that God is a mystery, and that we cannot in any sense know that mystery. Here Paul used the word 'depths' for the deepest realities of God. He told us that the Spirit searched out these realities, and revealed them, and he will soon tell us that the Spirit revealed these realities in particular words, not just in general ideas. We can know the depths of God through the ministry of the Spirit.

Of course, this does not mean that we know God as well as God knows God, for our knowledge is finite, and God's knowledge is infinite. It does not mean that we can know more than God has revealed. It does, however, mean that we can know truly, even if we do not know completely. And it does mean that we can know what is essential and basic in God, the 'depths of God'. Love, faithfulness, holiness, justice, grace, and mercy are fundamental to God. Even if we do not know their full expression in God, we believe that nothing else in God will undermine or remove these fundamentals.

Of course, this is a common experience in human life. A wife or husband believes and risks her or his life in believing the words, 'I love you'. Neither wife nor husband knows the full meaning of those words at the beginning of marriage. 'God is light' and 'God is love' (1 John 1:5; 4:16), even if we do not know the full meaning of those words, or even the reality that God intended those words to communicate. To say that those words are true is to say that

---

4. Grosheide, *1 Corinthians*, p. 68.

nothing in God's nature or character will contradict those realities, but it is not to claim that we know the full meaning of them.

Charles Hodge wrote:

> Thus God is said to search the hearts of the children of men, to intimate that there is nothing in man that escapes his notice. Rom. 8, 27, Rev. 2, 23. So there is nothing in God unknown to the Spirit . . . This passage proves at once the personality and divinity of the Holy Ghost. His personality, because intelligent activity is ascribed to him; he *searches*; his divinity, because omniscience is ascribed to him; he knows all that God knows. [5]

What did Paul mean here by the words 'the depths of God'? C. K. Barrett gives the answer: 'For him (Paul) there is no profounder truth than the truth of the cross.'[6] For the 'depths of God' is the same as 'the wisdom of God', and 'the wisdom of God' is the message of 'Christ crucified'. That 'secret and hidden' wisdom of God (2:7), not known by those who crucified the Lord of glory (2:8), has been revealed to us by the Spirit, who searches the depths of God (2:10).

The Spirit of God gave understanding

None but the Spirit of God knows what God is like. Paul likened the Holy Spirit to the spirit of a person, to their self-understanding. Of course, it is not an exact likeness, for the 'spirit of a person' is a way of talking about self-awareness, whereas the Spirit of God is one of the persons of the Trinity.[7] 'For what human being knows what is truly human except the human spirit that is within? So also no one comprehends what is truly God's except the Spirit of God. Now we have received not the spirit of the world, but the Spirit that is from God, so that we may understand the gifts bestowed on us by God' (2:11–12).

So the Spirit of God knows 'what is truly God's', and we have received the Spirit of God, so that we may understand the gifts God has given us. God not only gives us gifts, that is, the gifts of salvation, but also gives us the Spirit, so that we may 'understand' those gifts. We not only receive salvation, but also 'understanding' of that salvation.

---

5. Hodge, *1 Corinthians*, p. 39.

6. Barrett, *1 Corinthians*, p. 74.

7. Fee writes, 'This sentence is not trying to make a definitive anthropological statement, nor is it suggesting that the analogy of the Trinity fits human personality.' Fee, *1 Corinthians*, p. 112.

These verses teach two vital points, which complement each other. The first is the negative point, that we cannot know God, because we are not God. The second is the positive point, that the Holy Spirit of God, who is God, does know God, and if we have received the Spirit's revelation, then we too can know the gifts that God has given us.

The Spirit of God teaches the apostles what words to use

'And we speak of these things in words not taught by human wisdom but taught by the Spirit, interpreting spiritual things to those who are spiritual' (2:13). The Spirit searches the depths of God, and reveals to us those salvation gifts we have received, so that we can understand them. The Spirit not only reveals these gifts, but also taught the apostles the words to use to interpret them. The very words are God's wisdom, which the Holy Spirit teaches. They are not human wisdom, but divine wisdom, 'words . . . taught by the Spirit'. The Spirit's revelation was *verbal* revelation, for the Spirit not only gave the revelation of the depths of God, but also gave the words to talk about that revelation. The Spirit of God bridged the gap between the depths of God and human language about God.

Paul developed the use of Spirit-given words elsewhere in 1 Corinthians. Here it is the Spirit-given words received by Paul as an apostle of Christ. Elsewhere it is teaching and prophecy based on these words that 'builds up', or 'edifies', the church. So those who minister should build 'with care' on the gospel foundation of Jesus Christ (1 Cor. 3:10–11). Paul's statement that 'knowledge puffs up, but love builds up' (1 Cor. 8:1) points to the danger of wisdom or knowledge. They may serve only to give the person who has them pride, conceit, and a false superiority. It also points to the fact that speaking the right words without the right motive is not enough: truth and wisdom demand love and patience. No wonder Paul develops the theme of love in 1 Corinthians 13, as a blunt warning of the dangers of the self-centred use of gifts. He also wrote that it is intelligible speech that builds up the church (14:1–12). The Spirit uses understanding, and so should we.

So we have the mind of God, the mind of Christ

Those who are unspiritual do not receive the gifts of God's Spirit, for they are foolishness to them, and they are unable to understand them because they are discerned spiritually. Those who are spiritual discern all things, and they are themselves subject to no one else's scrutiny.

'For who has known the mind of the Lord
   so as to instruct him?'

But we have the mind of Christ. (2:14–16)

The 'unspiritual' here are not inferior Christians who lack some special higher knowledge, but are those who do not know the gospel of Christ crucified, the wisdom of God. Those who are 'spiritual' are those who are believers, who have discerned God's wisdom and power in the death of Christ, those who have received the revelation of the Spirit about the nature and salvation plan of God. For by ourselves, we could never know 'the mind of the Lord'. However, by the revealing work of the Spirit, 'we have the mind of Christ'.

To say that 'we have the mind of Christ' sounds absurdly presumptuous. It is in fact a statement of humility, for it recognizes and acknowledges what the wisdom of God achieved through Christ's death, and through the verbal revelation of the Spirit of God that we may have Christ's mind. And because Christ has 'the mind of the Lord', and we have 'the mind of Christ', then we too have 'the mind of the Lord', as we think God's thoughts after him. Christ has shown us the mind and heart of God, and the Holy Spirit of God has searched God, and revealed the gospel of Christ to us through the apostles. If we read and receive what the apostles have written, then we too have the mind of Christ and of God.

There is one common theme in this section of 1 Corinthians. To put it simply, the message about 'the cross' (1:18) is the same as 'Christ crucified' (1:23), 'the power of God and the wisdom of God' (1:24), God's 'secret and hidden' wisdom (2:7), 'what God has prepared for those who love him' (2:9), 'these things . . . revealed . . . through the Spirit' (2:10), 'the depths of God' (2:10), 'what is truly God's' (2:11), 'words . . . taught by the Spirit' (2:13), 'the gifts of God's Spirit' (2:14), 'the mind of the Lord' (2:16), and 'the mind of Christ' (2:16).

God's powerful wisdom was achieved in the history of salvation by the crucifixion and death of the incarnate Christ: the meaning of that event was conveyed by the Spirit's ministry of revelation. The revelation of the Spirit is the gospel of Christ crucified. In Don Carson's words, 'We must recognize that what it means to be wise, what it means to be spiritual, is to embrace, by the help of God's Spirit, the message of the crucified Messiah.'[8]

It is highly significant that Paul speaks of the power of God not only in describing *Christ* the power of God and the wisdom of God (1:24), but also when he describes the *word* or *message* of Christ crucified: For 'the message about the cross

---

8. Carson, *Cross and Ministry*, p. 64.

is . . . the power of God' (1:18). The power of God is in both cross and message, for the powerful wisdom of the death of Christ was conveyed by the power of the Spirit's revelation. What God achieved so powerfully in history, he also conveyed powerfully by means of the Spirit's words in 'the word of the cross'.

If we focus on the power of God in the death of Christ without taking into account the power of God in the revelation of the Spirit, we may lose confidence in the effective power of the gospel message. If we focus on the power of the gospel message without grounding that power in the death of Christ, we individualize and 'psychologize' the message, and lose the historical reality of the death of Christ on the cross. Praise God that his powerful wisdom not only worked in history but also in people through the Spirit to communicate the message of the cross!

Here Paul showed us what it meant for the promised Spirit of truth to guide him into all the truth (John 14 – 16). This is not new truth, for it is truth about the meaning of Christ's death and resurrection. The Spirit does not teach a new gospel, but the gospel of Christ in greater clarity. It is, however, greater truth, as the implications of the gospel in life and ministry are made clear. It is truth revealed in words, and truth that came from the Spirit who searches the depths of God and reveals that truth in human words. We also see here the crucial role of the apostle, as one who knows the mind of Christ and of God, and who preaches and defends the gospel of Christ and him crucified. The Spirit led Paul to the same gospel that we have found in the Old Testament and in Jesus' teaching alike. God has spoken to his people through his Spirit about his Son. As Gordon Fee wrote, 'The Spirit [is] the key to the proper understanding of the gospel itself . . . and in this context, as always, the gospel, God's wisdom, is the message of salvation through the crucified one.'[9]

It is, as Fee also comments, a tragedy that these verses have often been used by Christians who have wanted to claim a superior knowledge of God, taught by the Spirit, and have claimed that they are truly 'spiritual' while other inferior Christians are carnal. He wrote:

Almost every from of spiritual elitism, 'deeper life' movement, and 'second blessing' doctrine has appealed to this text. To receive the Spirit according to their special expressions paves the way to know 'deeper truths' about God . . . one special brand of this elitism . . . make[s] a 'special revelation' from the Spirit their final court of appeal . . . What is painful about so much of this is that . . . so often it is accompanied by a toning down of the cross.[10]

---

9. Fee, *1 Corinthians*, pp. 102–110.
10. Ibid., p. 120.

He continued: 'Being spiritual does not lead to elitism; it leads to a deeper understanding of God's powerful mystery – redemption through a crucified Messiah.'[11]

We have learned from 1 Corinthians that the message of Christ crucified reveals God's strategy to combat human pride, and was itself revealed by the Holy Spirit. Here is the Trinitarian shape of the gospel: God's plan, achieved through Christ crucified, and revealed through the Spirit. This is a small version of the big shape of the Bible: God's plan, achieved through Christ, and revealed by the Spirit.

The section of 1 Corinthians that we have studied in this chapter has given us a vivid insight into the gospel message of Christ crucified, and the role of the Holy Spirit in revealing that gospel to the apostles and their associates.[12]

Here is the work of the Spirit of truth promised and enabled by Jesus Christ, that work of teaching the depths of God, the gospel of Christ, to the people of God through the apostle Paul. We see that the truth of the gospel does not arise from the church at Corinth, but comes from God, Father, Son, and Spirit in words taught by the Spirit through the apostle Paul. We see the identity of the message of Christ crucified with the deepest verbal revelation of the Spirit of God.

The theology of the Bible that we are building in this book depends on a doctrine of receiving God's gifts, including his words ('receiving God's words'), a doctrine of the people of God, or ecclesiology ('for his people'), and a doctrine of the Holy Spirit, or pneumatology ('by his Spirit').

In this Part we have seen the centrality of the idea that the Holy Spirit uses human words, that the Scriptures are holy because they come from the Holy Spirit, and that the Spirit of God is able to use human speakers and writers without bypassing their humanity, and still achieve effective verbal revelation. The writings themselves were inspired (and so are powerful and effective), and they were inspired because their human authors were driven or moved by the Holy Spirit. Just as the cross is the power of God for salvation, so too the message of the cross is powerful and effective through the Spirit's work of verbal revelation.

We now turn to Part 5, where we see that that the message of the Bible is that of receiving God's words about his Son.

---

11. Ibid.

12. Foord, *Weakest Link*, p. 11.

RECEIVING GOD'S WORDS WRITTEN
FOR HIS PEOPLE BY HIS SPIRIT
ABOUT HIS SON

God's words written for his people by his Spirit are also 'about his Son'. Jesus Christ is at the heart of the Scriptures.[1] Just as Christ was the exegesis or explanation of the Father (John 1:18), so the Spirit through the Scriptures gave the articulation of that exegesis. For, as John Owen observed, Christ and Scripture have the same formal content, that is, the saving will of God.[2] Our joy is to receive God's words written for his people by his Spirit about his Son.

---

1. The summary phrase is not exhaustive. We could also say that 'God and Christ', or that 'God the Trinity', or 'God and his people' is at the heart of the Scriptures.

2. Trueman, *Claims*, pp. 70–75.

14. EVERYTHING WRITTEN ABOUT CHRIST MUST BE FULFILLED

LUKE 24

Luke 24 is a most important chapter in understanding the gospel both in the Old Testament and in Jesus' own teaching. It is also a key to interpreting Luke's Gospel and the Acts of the Apostles.

Luke 24 contains three narrative appearances of the Christ on the day of his resurrection. These three narratives have a common pattern and a cumulative message. The first narrative is of the women who came to the tomb of Jesus, and met the two men in shining clothes (verses 1–12). The second narrative is of the two disciples on the road to Emmaus, who met Jesus (13–35). The third is of all the disciples, when Jesus came and revealed himself to them (36–53).

The common pattern is that in each case the evidence for believing in the resurrection of Christ is that this resurrection has been foretold, in the teaching of Jesus, or in the Old Testament, or in both. There is a cumulative message. The predictions found in Jesus' teaching in the first narrative, and in the Old Testament in the second narrative, are brought together with double force in the third narrative: both the Old Testament and Jesus' teaching predicted his death and resurrection.

Let us look at these three narratives in more detail.[1]

Remember what he told you

> But on the first day of the week, at early dawn, they came to the tomb, taking
> the spices that they had prepared. They found the stone rolled away from the
> tomb, but when they went in, they did not find the body. While they were
> perplexed about this, suddenly two men in dazzling clothes stood beside them.
> (24:1–4)

The women came to the tomb. Notice that the sight of the empty
tomb did not convince them of Jesus' resurrection, but only led to perplexity.

> The women were terrified and bowed their faces to the ground, but the men said to
> them, 'Why do you look for the living among the dead? He is not here, but has
> risen. Remember how he told you, while he was still in Galilee, that the Son of Man
> must be handed over to sinners, and be crucified, and on the third day rise again.'
> (24:5–7)

The message of the two men was clear. The women should have
remembered what Jesus had told them while he was still in Galilee. If they
had remembered that he had told them, then they would not have been
looking for one who was alive among those who were dead. In case they
had already forgotten what Jesus taught them in Galilee, the two men
reminded them of that gospel message: 'that the Son of Man must be handed
over to sinners, and be crucified, and on the third day rise again' (24:7).

If they had only believed what Jesus had told them, they would not have
needed to come to the tomb to believe in his resurrection. They would have
believed that he would rise from the dead, without seeing the empty tomb, and
without the words of the two men. In the words of Earle Ellis, 'Each episode
[narrative] sets forth the witness of prophecy as the sufficient and only persuasive evidence for the resurrection. The prophecies of Jesus in this regard
are equated with those from Scripture.'[2]

---

1. I also use Luke 24 in *Hearing*, pp. 81–86, for what it shows us about biblical
   spirituality. Again I express my gratitude to the Revd R. C. Lucas for his
   memorable sermon on Luke 24.
2. Ellis, *Luke*, p. 271.

All the prophets have declared

In the second narrative two disciples were on their way to Emmaus. While they talked together, Jesus himself came and joined them, but their eyes were kept from recognizing him. Jesus asked them what they were talking about, and they explained to him all the events of the last few days, which they described in these terms: 'The things about Jesus of Nazareth, who was a prophet mighty in deed and word before God and all the people, and how our chief priests and leaders handed him over to be condemned to death and crucified him. But we had hoped that he was the one to redeem Israel' (24:19–21).

See how Jesus then answered their questions and addressed their hopes. He rebuked their foolishness, which he described as slowness to believe what the prophets have declared: 'Then he said to them, "Oh, how foolish you are, and how slow of heart to believe all that the prophets have declared! Was it not necessary that the Messiah should suffer these things and then enter into his glory?"' (24:25–26).

In the first narrative the two men reminded the women of what Jesus had told them in Galilee: here in the second narrative Jesus reminded the two disciples of what God had told them in the Old Testament. 'Then beginning with Moses and all the prophets, he interpreted to them the things about himself in all the scriptures' (24:27).

Jesus did not just repeat the Scriptures; he interpreted them – that is, he explained their significance and reference to himself.[3] We find that 'what has happened with Jesus can be understood only in the light of Scriptures, yet the Scriptures themselves can be understood only in the light of what has happened with Jesus'.[4]

Jesus then joined them for a meal, during which 'their eyes were opened, and they recognized him; and he vanished from their sight' (24:31).[5] The two then returned to Jerusalem, where they joined all the disciples, and told them what had happened. This set the scene for the third narrative.

---

3. Thanks to Andrew Malone for this point. He also suggested that 'all the scriptures' does not mean every scripture. We find Christ promised in all parts of Scripture, but not in every verse. He also suggested that 'the things about himself' (verse 27) are specifically Christ's suffering and glory (26).

4. J. B. Green, *Luke*, p. 844.

5. I discuss the meaning of the meal in *Hearing*, pp. 83–84.

'These are my words . . . everything written about me . . . must be fulfilled'

In this third narrative, Jesus himself came and stood among the disciples. Even when he appeared before them, they were not convinced that he was indeed risen from the dead. Neither the empty tomb nor the presence of the risen Christ brought people to faith. Instead, they 'were startled and terrified, and thought that they were seeing a ghost' (24:37).

Jesus tried to convince them that he was not a ghost (that is, a disembodied or merely spiritual presence). He did so by showing them his hands and his feet (presumably with the nail wounds still visible), and then ate a piece of fish. Then he gave them the conclusive evidence, which, as a matter of fact, did not depend on his presence with them: 'Then he said to them, "These are my words that I spoke to you while I was still with you – that everything written about me in the law of Moses, the prophets, and the psalms must be fulfilled"' (24:44).

See how this brings together the first and second narratives: the first, in which the women have been reminded of Jesus' teaching, and the second, in which Jesus has reminded the two disciples of the message of the Old Testament.

Furthermore, not only did Jesus give a summary of his own teaching, and of the Old Testament, but he also stated his message: 'Everything written about me in the law of Moses, the prophets, and the psalms must be fulfilled.' Not only did Jesus' teaching and the Old Testament have the same message, but his teaching had also clearly linked the two.

Here too we find that 'not even incontrovertible evidence of Jesus' embodied existence is capable of producing faith; resolution will come only when scriptural illumination is added to material data'.[6]

This contrasts with the view that the resurrection experience came first, and then people described it in words, and then found Old Testament teaching to support it. C. K. Barrett wrote: 'Resurrection experience and faith came first; then the conviction that the resurrection must have been foretold.'[7] Oddly enough, Luke 24 has the opposite message!

'Thus it is written'

Then, in case they had already forgotten what was the message of the Old

---

6. J. B. Green, *Luke*, p. 855.
7. Barrett, *1 Corinthians*, p. 340.

Testament, and what he had told them, he reminded them: 'Thus it is written, that the Messiah is to suffer and to rise from the dead on the third day, and that repentance and forgiveness of sins is to be proclaimed in his name to all nations, beginning from Jerusalem' (24:46–47).

This was a key summary, not only of the Old Testament, but also of Jesus' own teaching. It included the prediction of events, and those events included both what was to happen to the Messiah (he would 'suffer and . . . rise from the dead on the third day'), and what was the meaning of the Messiah's death and resurrection ('repentance and forgiveness of sins').

It included not only what had already been fulfilled (he will 'suffer and . . . rise from the dead on the third day'), but also what was still to happen ('that repentance and forgiveness of sins is to be proclaimed in his name to all nations, beginning from Jerusalem'). It was not only a summary of the teaching of the Old Testament, but also a summary of both Luke and Acts.

'You are witnesses of these things'

The role and function of Jesus' disciples are summed up in the words 'You are witnesses of these things' (24:48).

That is, they were witnesses that what had been predicted in the Old Testament and in Jesus' teaching had in fact been fulfilled. Because they were already passive witnesses of these things, because they had seen what God had done in Christ, they would now be active witnesses of these things, 'clothed with power from on high' when the Spirit came at Pentecost (24:49), and then 'bearing witness' by speaking of the gospel.

We often use the word 'witness' to mean a person who tells someone that he or she is a Christian. However, in the Bible a 'witness' is an eyewitness and 'earwitness' who can give an account of something that happened. This is like being a witness in a court of law. The question is not 'What do you feel about this possibility?' but 'Were you there?' 'What did you see?' 'What did you hear?' Witnesses in the Bible have a role that you or I could never have, because we were born too late. We should ask people to look at the witness of people in the Bible who truly were witnesses of God's acts in Jesus Christ in history, and whose verbal witness is preserved for us in the Bible. Richard Bauckham has shown us that the Gospels are the products of the eyewitness experience of the disciples and apostles.[8]

---

8. See Bauckham, *Eyewitnesses*.

Christ opened the Scriptures, and opened their minds

Just as Jesus taught in Galilee before his death and resurrection, so he also taught on the day of his resurrection. It was a twofold ministry of opening the Scriptures, and opening their minds. There would have been no point in opening the Scriptures if their minds were closed, and no point in opening their minds if he did not open the Scriptures.

So the two disciples said, 'Were not our hearts burning within us while he was talking to us on the road, while he was opening the scriptures to us?' (24:32). As Jesus began his final Bible study in Luke's Gospel, we read, 'Then he opened their minds to understand the scriptures' (24:45).[9] Jesus continued this ministry for the next forty days, as we read in Acts 1:3: he was 'appearing to them over the course of forty days and speaking about the kingdom of God'.

Luke also linked teaching about the kingdom of God and opening the Scriptures in his account of Paul's ministry at the end of Acts. Here Luke equated 'testifying to the kingdom of God' with 'trying to convince them about Jesus both from the law of Moses and from the prophets' (Acts 28:23), and 'proclaiming the kingdom of God' with 'teaching about the Lord Jesus Christ' (Acts 28:31).[10] For Acts ended with Paul finally in Rome.

> From morning until evening he explained the matter to them, testifying to the kingdom of God and trying to convince them about Jesus both from the law of Moses and from the prophets . . . He . . . welcomed all who came to him, proclaiming the kingdom of God and teaching about the Lord Jesus Christ with all boldness and without hindrance. (Acts 28:23, 30–31)

It is striking that both Luke and Acts end with Bible studies, with Jesus teaching the disciples in Jerusalem in Luke, and Paul teaching all who came to him in Rome in Acts. It is also significant that both Jesus and Paul have the same message, and that both Jesus and Paul have the same text: 'the law of Moses and . . . the prophets' (Acts 28:23; cf. Luke 24:27, 44).

---

9. In Acts 16 we read of Lydia that the Lord 'opened her heart' to listen to Paul's message.

10. See D. S. McComiskey, *Lukan Theology*, pp. 60–67, for a description of how the themes of Luke 24 are reflected in Acts.

All the Scriptures and the death and resurrection of Christ?

What were all those Scriptures? And did they really promise the death and resurrection of Christ? This claim was so common in the New Testament that it
is worth investigating, especially as many today find it less than convincing.
Here are some comments that may clarify the subject.

1. It is a common claim in the New Testament. 'Moses said, "The Lord
   your God will raise up for you from your own people a prophet like me.
   You must listen to whatever he tells you. And it will be that everyone
   who does not listen to that prophet will be utterly rooted out from the
   people"' (Peter, in Acts 3:22–23; see Deut. 18:15–19).
2. It is implied even when it is not articulated. 'You know that you were
   ransomed from the futile ways inherited from your ancestors, not with
   perishable things like silver or gold, but with the precious blood of
   Christ, like that of a lamb without defect or blemish' (1 Pet. 1:18–19; see
   Exod. 12).
3. It was a claim that Jesus made and that he used in debates and
   arguments. See John 5:39–47.
4. We can assume that the list included the Old Testament references
   that Jesus applied to himself, e.g. Matthew 21:4–5, 42. We can assume
   that Jesus taught at least some of the other references used by the
   early preachers because of Luke's account of Jesus' teaching to the
   disciples in Acts 1:3. It is instructive to look at other examples in Acts.[11]
5. What were 'predictions' like? They included:
   - Events in the history of God's people that foreshadowed what would
     happen to Christ, like the exodus from Egypt: 'This was to fulfil what
     had been spoken by the Lord through the prophet, "Out of Egypt I
     have called my son"' (Matt. 2:15, from Hos. 11:1).
   - Rituals and sacrifices that would be fulfilled in Christ, like the Passover
     sacrifice or the Day of Atonement rituals: 'For Christ did not enter a
     sanctuary made by human hands, a mere copy of the true one, but he
     entered into heaven itself, now to appear in the presence of God on
     our behalf' (Heb. 9:24; see Lev. 16).

---

11. Acts 2:16–21 (Joel 2:28–32); 2:25–28 (Ps. 16:8–11); 2:34–35 (Ps. 110:1);
    4:11 (Ps. 118:22); 4:25–26 (Ps. 2:1–2); 8:32–33 (Isa. 53:7–8); 13:33 (Ps. 2:7); and
    13:34 (Isa. 55:3). See also France, *Jesus*, chapters 1–4; Longenecker, *Exegesis*; Carson
    and Beale, *Commentary*; and Adam, *Hearing*, chapter 4.

- Buildings and objects, like the tabernacle, that would be fulfilled in Christ: 'They offer worship in a sanctuary that is a sketch and shadow of the heavenly one' (Heb. 8:5).
- People whose lives foreshadowed what would happen to Christ: 'For just as Jonah was for three days and three nights in the belly of the sea monster, so for three days and three nights the Son of Man will be in the heart of the earth' (Matt. 12:40; see Jon. 2).
- Prophecies that were fulfilled in Christ: 'Then Jesus said to them, "You will all become deserters because of me this night; for it is written, 'I will strike the shepherd, and the sheep of the flock will be scattered'"' (Matt. 26:31, from Zech. 13:7).
- Statements and promises that remained unclear or unfulfilled until Christ came, or that were fulfilled in part, but still promised a greater fulfilment. For example, 'All this took place to fulfil what had been spoken by the Lord through the prophet: "Look, the virgin shall conceive and bear a son, and they shall name him Emmanuel", which means, "God is with us"' (Matt. 1:22–23, from Isa. 7:14).

Luke 24 showed us the centrality of the gospel message of Jesus' death and resurrection, resulting in the preaching of repentance and forgiveness of sins in Jesus' name being proclaimed to all nations. It showed us that this message was central to the Old Testament, and to Jesus' own teaching, and so it also showed us the unity of the Old Testament and Jesus' teaching. The fulfilment of written verbal prophecy is the basis for confidence in God and in Christ.

In one of P. D. James's books a famous actress described her rendition of Lady Macbeth in these words: 'I wasn't the usual kind of Lady Macbeth, tall, domineering, ruthless. I played her like a sex kitten but a kitten with hidden claws . . . But was it true to the text? Oh, my dear, who cares about the text? I don't mean that exactly, but Shakespeare's like the Bible: you can make it mean anything.'[12]

However attractive that idea might be, we have found that Jesus was committed to teaching the right interpretation of the Old Testament and of his own teaching. We should follow him in believing and teaching his interpretation of the message of the Bible.

---

12. James, *Skull*, p. 140.

15. THE GOOD NEWS PROMISED TO OUR ANCESTORS AND NOW FULFILLED IN CHRIST

ACTS 13

There was a great explosion of the preaching and teaching of the words of God in Acts, as we would expect immediately after the death and resurrection of Christ and the coming of the Holy Spirit at Pentecost. In Acts we see not only Jews converted to Christ, but also the conversion of many Gentiles, non-Jews. We see God's mission to the world in obedience to the command of Christ. We also see that when the gospel was preached to Gentiles, the Old Testament was not left behind, but continued to serve as the Scriptures of the post-Pentecost church.

Hearing the word

'The next sabbath almost the whole city gathered to hear the word of the Lord' (Acts 13:44). We pick up the story of the book of Acts in chapter 13, which began with the strategic event of the church at Antioch setting aside Barnabas and Saul for the work to which they had been called by the Holy Spirit (13:2). Antioch in Syria replaced Jerusalem as the city which sent out missionaries, for the gospel ministry of Saul/Paul around the eastern part of the Roman empire filled the remaining chapters of the book of Acts. Barnabas and Saul had been in Antioch for about a year, meeting with the church and teaching many people.

Barnabas and Saul first sailed to Cyprus (Barnabas was a native of Cyprus, 4:36), where they preached the word at two main cities, Salamis and Paphos. At Paphos, the proconsul, Sergius Paulus, 'wanted to hear the word of God' (13:7). They then travelled to Asia Minor, where they ministered at Perga in Pamphylia and then arrived at another Antioch, called Antioch in Pisidia (13:13–14). On the sabbath they went to the synagogue, and after the reading of the law and the prophets, the synagogue officials invited them to give a 'word of exhortation', or, as we would say, 'preach a sermon' (13:14–15). This sermon was so striking that the people urged Paul and Barnabas to speak again on the next sabbath, while some people followed them to their lodging to hear more about the Lord Jesus (13:42–43).

Here is a major theme of the book of Acts, that of enquirers and unbelievers, Jews from the synagogue, Gentile converts to Judaism, and other Gentiles, hearing about the Lord Jesus Christ. We find this happening many times in Acts, from Peter's preaching on the day of Pentecost in Jerusalem in chapter 2 to Paul's ministry in Rome in chapter 28.

Almost the whole city gathered, because God's plan is that the gospel goes to both Jews and Gentiles, and because God's Spirit has been poured out on all, so that 'everyone who calls on the name of the Lord shall be saved' (2:21). It is a word or a message that needed to be heard, and so Acts is a New Testament collection of sermons, just as Deuteronomy is an Old Testament sermon collection.

What did hearing 'the word' mean? 'The word' meant the message about Jesus Christ. It is very instructive to read in Acts 13 the expressions that are equivalent to 'the word of the Lord' in verse 44. They are 'the word of God' (verses 5, 7, 46), 'the teaching about [or of] the Lord' (12), a 'word of exhortation' (15), 'the message of this salvation' (26), 'the good news' of 'what God promised to our ancestors [and] has fulfilled for us' (32–33), and 'the grace of God' (43). We find a similar list of equivalents in Acts 20, in Paul's address to the elders of the church at Ephesus: 'the message' (verse 20), 'repentance towards God and faith towards our Lord Jesus' (21), 'the good news [gospel] of God's grace' (24), 'the kingdom' (25), 'the whole purpose of God' (27), 'the truth' (30), and 'the message of his grace' (32).

In summary, it is a word or message that must be heard, received, believed. Its origin is God, its content is the Lord Jesus Christ, and its qualities are salvation, grace, and truth.

We should not think that if we are fortunate enough to have many churches where people gather to hear the word of God, then we are in a similar situation to that recorded in Acts. Splendid and miraculous as it is to have churches filled with people who want to hear the word of God, and preachers to teach the word of God, Acts paints a bigger picture. An evangelical church is not only true to gospel doctrine, but also effective in gospel practice, as unbelievers hear the evangel, the word of God. For unbelievers gathered to hear God's word: 'The next sabbath almost the whole city gathered to hear the word of the Lord' (13:44).

The word spoken for Jews and Gentiles

The usual pattern for Paul was to go first to the synagogue to preach and teach the Jews and then, after some Jews have been converted, to go to the Gentiles. The Gentile converts to Judaism in the synagogue would often be receptive to his message, but the basic structure of his ministry was 'to the Jew first and also to the Greek' (Rom. 1:16). This pattern is clearly presented here in chapter 13, just as it is also evident in his ministry in Rome (Acts 28:23–31).

What was done to communicate 'the word'? Sometimes, in this chapter, it was by preaching in the synagogue on the sabbath day (see also Acts 17:1–3, 18:4, 7, 19; 19:8; etc.). At Philippi, Paul spoke the word at the place of prayer by the river, and also in prison (Acts 16:13, 31); in Athens, in front of the Areopagus (Acts 17:22); in Ephesus, in the synagogue, then in the hired lecture hall of Tyrannus (19:8–9), and also 'from house to house' (20:20); and in Rome, in his own hired lodging (28:23). In summary, in places of traditional religious and philosophical discussion, in other people's houses and in his own lodging, and wherever he found people to listen.[1]

What was the content of 'the word'? We find some indications in the sermon in Acts 13. This is the first account in Acts of the content of Paul's preaching of 'the word'. It matched Peter's sermon on the day of Pentecost (Acts 2), and Jesus' first sermon at Nazareth (Luke 4). It is the only sermon in Acts which includes the language of 'justification' (Acts 13:38–39), which Paul later developed in Romans.[2]

---

1. See Green, *Evangelism*, for an excellent study of various aspects of evangelism in Acts, and the implications for our church life.
2. Johnson, *Acts*, p. 155.

The word spoken from the Old Testament

[handwritten margin note: Problem with 2 ways to Live etc?]

These sermons in Acts did not begin with the story or events of the life of Christ. Rather, they began with the story of God's plan with his people in Old Testament times. The word that was preached was based on the words of God in the Old Testament. Peter preached in Acts 10:43: 'All the prophets testify about him [Jesus Christ] that everyone who believes in him receives forgiveness of sins through his name.'

Paul's sermon here in Acts 13 was based on a summary of Old Testament history, Psalms, and Habakkuk. He began with God's choice of Israel, his making them into a great nation, his deliverance from Egypt, his patience with them in the wilderness, his gift of the land, his gift of Saul as king, and then his gift of David (verses 17–22). Paul then developed the theme of King David as 'the man after [God's] heart, who will carry out all my wishes', and pointed out that it is from David's posterity that 'God has brought to Israel a Saviour, Jesus, as he promised' (22–23). Just as Jesus was promised through David, he was also promised in the words of John the Baptist (24–25).

God's message of repentance and salvation had been sent to this generation of God's people, because this generation, in fulfilment of the words of the prophets, had not recognized Jesus, had not understood the words of the prophets, had asked Pilate to have him killed, and had taken Jesus down from the tree and buried him in a tomb (26–29). God, however, raised him from among the dead, and he had appeared to his disciples, witnesses of his resurrection (13:30–31). So here is the good news: what God promised to our ancestors he has fulfilled for us, their children, by raising Jesus, as promised in the Psalms and in Isaiah. For David died, but Jesus died and then was raised by God (32–37). Paul concluded:

'Beware, therefore, that what the prophets said does not happen to you:

'Look, you scoffers!
  Be amazed and perish,
For in your days I am doing a work,
  A work that you will never believe, even if someone tells you.' (13:40–41)

As Paul wrote in Romans, the gospel came to the Gentiles through the prophetic writings of the Old Testament:

Now to God who is able to strengthen you according to my gospel and the proclamation of Jesus Christ, according to the revelation of the mystery that was kept secret for long ages but is now disclosed, and through the prophetic writings is made known to all the Gentiles, according to the command of the eternal God, to bring about the obedience of faith – to the only wise God, through Jesus Christ, to whom be the glory for ever! Amen. (Rom. 16:25–27)

Here is a simple but profound lesson: Paul used the Bible to preach the gospel. He did this not just because it was culturally appropriate, but because he believed that the words of God, the Scriptures, were an evangelistic instrument provided by God. Even in his sermon in Athens he provided a summary of crucial Old Testament teaching about the nature of God, and fundamental Old Testament lessons about the relationship between God and humanity. Why do we fail to use the God-written Bible for our evangelism?

What was their response to Paul's 'word of encouragement'?

But when the Jews saw the crowds, they were filled with jealousy; and blaspheming, they contradicted what was spoken by Paul. Then both Paul and Barnabas spoke out boldly, saying, 'It was necessary that the word of God should be spoken first to you. Since you reject it and judge yourselves to be unworthy of eternal life, we are now turning to the Gentiles. For so the Lord has commanded us, saying,

"I have set you to be a light for the Gentiles,
    so that you may bring salvation to the ends of the earth."'
(Acts 13:45–47)

Why were the Jews jealous? We read that 'when the Jews saw the crowds, they were filled with jealousy' (verse 45). As David Williams commented, 'This could mean that they resented the success of the missionaries. A more likely meaning, however, is that they were jealous of their own privileged position.'[3] This would certainly fit in with Paul's expectations in Romans: 'But through their stumbling [that is, Jews finding it hard to believe in Christ] salvation has come to the Gentiles, so as to make Israel jealous' (Rom. 11:11).

Paul claimed that this turning to the Gentiles was in fulfilment of the prophecy in Isaiah (Acts 13:47). The ministry of the apostles was fulfilling the ministry of Jesus, the servant of the Lord. What was promised through him was carried forward through the preaching of Paul and the other apostles. In John Stott's words, 'Luke has already recorded how this verse was applied to Jesus by Simeon (Luke 2:32) and will soon record Jesus applying it to Paul (Acts

---

3. Williams, *Acts*, p. 227.

26:17–18) . . . the Lord's suffering servant is the Messiah, who gathers around him a Messianic community to share in his ministry to the nations.'[4]

Praising the word

Then we read: 'When the Gentiles heard this, they were glad and praised the word of the Lord; and as many as had been destined for eternal life became believers' (Acts 13:48).

The Gentiles were glad not only to hear the word of the Lord, but also to hear that their inclusion in the people of God was promised by God in his promise of his Servant in Isaiah. It was clear in the Old Testament that God's plan of salvation and blessing was to include all nations, as we see in God's promise to Abram ('in you all the families of the earth shall be blessed', Gen. 12:3), in the praise-filled and evangelistic psalms ('Praise the LORD, all you nations! Extol him, all you peoples!', Ps. 117:1), and in the prophets ('Turn to me and be saved, all the ends of the earth!', Isa. 45:22).

It is instructive to notice the language used to describe the comparison between the response of the Jews and that of the Gentiles in this passage. Of the Jews, Paul says, 'You reject [the word of God] and judge yourselves to be unworthy of eternal life' (verse 46); and we read of the Gentiles, 'As many as had been destined for eternal life became believers' (48). Those who rejected the word were responsible for that rejection, and God was responsible for acceptance of that word.[5]

Both responses are described in terms of attitudes to 'the word of God'. According to Paul, addressing the Jews in the synagogue, 'The word of God [was] spoken first to you . . . you reject it' (46). Of the Gentiles, Luke wrote: 'They were glad and praised the word of the Lord' (48).

No doubt they praised God, and no doubt they praised the Lord Jesus, but here they are described as having 'praised the word', the message of salvation through Christ Jesus. They 'praised the word', for the word is the God-given means by which the deeds and message of salvation had been communicated to them, and also the means by which God had enabled their response. In praising 'the word of God' they were praising the God who not only promised his plan of salvation to include the Gentiles, but also achieved that plan through the death and resurrection of Jesus Christ, and also effectively com-

---

4. Stott, *Acts*, p. 227.

5. The statements here need to be understood in the light of Paul's complementary statements in Rom. 9:1–32.

municated that plan through the 'word of God' that Paul preached. It is God's plan, God's salvation through Christ, and God's word.

The word spread throughout that region

Not only was the word praised, but the word also spread, as the message of Jesus Christ was taught and preached: 'Thus the word of the Lord spread throughout the region' (13:49). It is typical of Luke's comments about the progress of the gospel, the 'word of God': 'But many of those who heard the word believed; and they numbered about five thousand' (4:4); 'The word of God continued to spread; the number of the disciples increased greatly in Jerusalem, and a great many of the priests became obedient to the faith' (6:7); 'Now those who were scattered went from place to place, proclaiming the word' (8:4). At least 30% of the text of Acts consists of apostolic preaching of the word.[6]

Dennis Johnson detects four themes in the sermon proclamations of 'the word' in Acts: (1) Jesus, crucified and risen to life, is the Messiah and Saviour promised in the Scriptures, who has brought the kingdom of God among us. (2) Jesus the Messiah bestows the blessings of the kingdom. (3) Jesus the Messiah will come again to judge and to deliver. (4) People must repent and trust in the name of Jesus for salvation.[7]

'Word growth' achieves church growth. 'Word growth' fulfils Jesus' plan for the gospel to go 'to the ends of earth' (1:8). 'Word growth' fulfils God's promises in the Old Testament about the inclusion of the Gentiles in the family of God, God's promise to pour out his Spirit 'upon all flesh' (2:17). 'Word growth' is gospel growth (20:24, 'the good news [gospel] of God's grace'), and 'word growth' is kingdom growth (Acts 28:31).

Not only was the word of God rightly praised (13:48), but also, as we have seen, it seems to have had an energy of its own: 'Thus the word of the Lord spread throughout the region' (13:49). We should not think of the word of God as having its own energy independent of God. Rather, God continues to work and speak through his word; he continues to achieve powerful and effective communication whenever it is spoken and heard. We find the same kind of language used of the gospel elsewhere in the New Testament: 'the

---

6. Johnson, *Acts*, 11.

7. Johnson, *Acts*, pp. 143–154. Johnson also gives perceptive insights into how the apostles and others preached the gospel in Acts in a world of religious pluralism (chapter 10), and civil religions (chapter 11).

gospel . . . is the power of God for salvation to everyone who has faith' (Rom. 1:16). It is not that the word, the gospel, has power independent of God, but that God always speaks through his words, and so his words are always his powerful and effective instruments or agents.

How did all this activity of speaking and hearing the word come about?

There are many answers to this question, including God's salvation plan (2:17–21; 8:32–38; 15:15–17), the commands of the Lord Jesus (Luke 24:44–53; Acts 1:8), and the promptings of the Holy Spirit (13:2, 4). In terms of human responses to this plan and work of God, it came about through the determination to do the ministry of the word, and to pray. We find these priorities in Luke's account in Acts 6:

> And the twelve called together the whole community of the disciples and said, 'It is not right that we should neglect the word of God in order to wait at tables.
> Therefore, friends, select from among yourselves seven men of good standing . . . whom we may appoint to this task, while we, for our part, will devote ourselves to prayer and to serving the word.' (6:2–4)

This decision of the apostles to devote their time and attention to prayer and serving 'the word' was immediately productive, not only in word growth but in church growth: 'The word of God continued to spread; the number of the disciples increased greatly in Jerusalem, and a great many of the priests became obedient to the faith' (6:7).

It was followed by accounts of two of those set apart to wait at tables. In chapter 7 Stephen witnessed to his faith in Jesus Christ at his martyrdom, and in chapter 8 Philip converted and baptized the Ethiopian.

As James explained, 'For in every city, for generations past, Moses has had those who proclaim him, for he has been read aloud every sabbath in the synagogues' (Acts 15:21); so now Christ is proclaimed through the reading and preaching of the Old Testament, and through the witness of the apostles.

In this chapter we have seen from Acts the centrality of the word of God in the life and mission of the church of God. We have also seen that word as a word about Jesus Christ, a word from the Old Testament interpreted in the light of its fulfilment in Christ. It was and is a word for Jews and Gentiles, a word that spread through the ministry of many, and a word that is praised because of its gospel power.

16. RECEIVING GOD'S WORDS WRITTEN FOR HIS PEOPLE BY HIS SPIRIT ABOUT HIS SON

HEBREWS

Receiving God's words

We find in Hebrews a summary of what that the Bible teaches about itself, namely, that we should receive God's words written for his people, by his Spirit, about his Son. Hebrews is a sustained exhortation to receive those words with faith and obedience.[1] Hebrews summons us to hear the speaking God. It begins: 'Long ago God spoke to our ancestors in many and various ways by the prophets, but in these last days he has spoken to us by a Son' (1:1–2).

When we first read these words, we might think that the contrast between 'to our ancestors' and 'to us' means that the Old Testament is redundant for New Testament believers. However, that is not the case, for the author makes extensive use of the Old Testament as the source of the words with which God continues to address his people throughout the letter. Here are some examples:

---

1. Adam, *Hearing*, pp. 99–105.

- In chapter 1, God has spoken to our ancestors through the prophets, and to us by a Son. The proof of the divinity of the Son is the words of God in Old Testament Scripture.
- In chapter 2, we are warned: 'Therefore we must pay greater attention to what we have heard, so that we do not drift away from it' (2:1). The God who speaks wants a people that listens to and receives his words.
- In chapter 3, we are warned to hear the words of God spoken by the Holy Spirit long ago through David, and still spoken to us today. Here the writer exemplifies how the Old Testament applies today, and also explains why this is the case, and what it means. Then the writer tells us that 'the word of God is living and active, sharper than any two-edged sword, piercing until it divides soul from spirit, joints from marrow; it is able to judge the thoughts and intentions of the heart' (4:12).
- In chapter 5, the writer tells his readers that they need someone to teach them again 'the basic elements of the oracles of God' (5:12), and in chapter 6 he describes the hearing of the gospel as having 'tasted the goodness of the word of God' (6:5).
- We read in chapter 6 that the security of our salvation depends on God's words, namely his promise to Abraham and his oath, 'I will surely bless you and multiply you' (6:14). He did this so that, 'through two unchangeable things, in which it is impossible that God would prove false, we who have taken refuge might be strongly encouraged to seize the hope set before us' (6:18).
- Similarly, in chapter 7, Jesus became high priest by God's oath: 'The Lord has sworn and will not change his mind, "You are a priest for ever"' (7:21, quoting Ps. 110:4).
- The promise of the new covenant is that God will 'put [his] laws in their minds, and write them on their hearts' (8:10). The gospel is described as a 'promised eternal inheritance' (9:15).
- In chapter 12, the writer links God speaking at Mount Sinai and God speaking now. The application is the same: 'See that you do not refuse the one who is speaking; for if they did not escape when they refused the one who warned them on earth, how much less will we escape if we reject the one who warns from heaven!' (12:25).
- The letter ends with an injunction: 'Remember your leaders, those who spoke the word of God to you' (13:7).

The author uses the language of God speaking as a metaphor for all the various forms of revelation in the Old Testament and in Christ. However, the metaphor of speaking derives its power from the power of words to communicate.

Furthermore, the 'many and various ways by the prophets' included verbal revelation, and the revelation through Jesus Christ also included words. Our access now to the 'many and various ways' in which God has spoken is not because we can see those visions, or perceive the angelic messenger, or receive the bread from heaven, or enter the tabernacle, or see the high priest, or return to Jerusalem. We are like the subsequent generations in Old Testament times, for whom all these events and words were recorded. Our means of access to all this revelation to our ancestors in the faith is by means of the Old Testament Scriptures.

The author assumes that the words of the Old Testament can be rightly understood to come from the mouth of God the Father, God the Son, and God the Spirit. We find this in 1:5, when he attributed the words of Psalm 2 to God the Father: 'You are my Son: today I have begotten you.' In 2:13 he attributes the words of Isaiah 8 to God the Son: 'Here am I and the children whom God has given me.' In 3:7 the words of Psalm 95 were described as spoken by the Holy Spirit: 'Therefore, as the Holy Spirit says . . .' In the pages of Hebrews, we cannot avoid the God who has spoken. The speaking God requires a listening people.

Here in Hebrews we also find the idea of the power of God's words. We might have thought that a human heart, hardened by unbelief (3:12) and by the deceitfulness of sin (3:13), would be impenetrable. That is not so. For the word of God is able to pierce hardened human hearts. The word of God has this power because of the nature of God. In 4:12, 'Indeed, the word of God is living and active, sharper than any two-edged sword, piercing until it divides soul from spirit, joints from marrow; it is able to judge the thoughts and intentions of the heart.'

In the next verse, 4:13, he links that power to the power and character of God: 'And before him no creature is hidden, but all are naked and laid bare to the eyes of the one to whom we must render an account.' As Spicq wrote, 'the word was truly in the place of the omniscient and omnipresent God, and received its power and its qualities only from him.'[2]

The new covenant in the blood of Christ means the fulfilment of the prophecy of Jeremiah in transformed hearts, as explained in Hebrews 8: 'This is the covenant that I will make with the house of Israel after those days, says the Lord: I will put my laws in their minds, and write them on their hearts' (8:10).

And the writer of Hebrews links this work of God in the human heart, promised by the Holy Spirit, to the forgiveness of sins by the single offering

---

2. Spicq, as quoted in Hughes, *Hebrews*, p. 167.

of Christ on the cross (Heb. 10:14–18). Sanctification means forgiveness of sins, and the transformation of the heart. God's words are living, active, and powerful in every generation of God's people, achieving the same aim as when God first spoke them.

Notice that here the writer says that the Spirit's words lay us bare, whereas we often think that our task is to lay bare the words and thoughts of Scripture. Desiring to lay bare the words and thoughts of Scripture is good, if done humbly, and with a desire to learn all that God has put into the text. However, the real power of Scripture is found when it reads us, when it lays us bare. In the words of Richard Shumack, 'The Scriptures are profoundly existential . . . in purpose and effect. They question us as to how we define ourselves in the light of God's self-revelation, rather than the other way around.'[3]

Some submit the text of the Bible to a hostile interrogation, when they assume that the writers of the Bible are trying to hide something, either consciously or unconsciously. As Kevin Vanhoozer has argued, we should treat texts with the same respect we should show to people.[4] We should respect the human authors of Scripture, as well as its divine author.

It is right for us to work hard to 'lay bare' the text of Scripture, to ask good questions about all the dimensions of the meaning and impact of the text. However, we should also let the text 'read' us, and not put up barriers against the words of the Spirit in Scripture; we should let the text have its full God-planned and God-empowered impact on our thoughts and lives.

Furthermore, the writer of Hebrews believed that God's words in the Old Testament still had contemporary power, that they still remained God's speech. For Hebrews often refers to the Old Testament as God's present words: 'as the Holy Spirit says . . .' (Heb. 3:7; Ps. 95:7); 'the Holy Spirit also testifies to us . . . saying . . .' (Heb. 10:15; Jer. 31:33); and 'have you forgotten the exhortation that addresses you as children . . .' (Heb. 12:5; Prov. 3:11–12). God lives and endures for ever, and therefore so do his words, whenever they were spoken.

Gregory the Great was one of the famous preachers of the early church. Just as Hebrews described the word of God as a sword, so Gregory likened the words of God in the mouth of a preacher to darts, arrows, thorns, nails, swords, knives, hammers, and battle-axes.[5] Or think of God's question through Jeremiah, 'Is not my word like fire . . . and like a hammer that breaks a rock in pieces?' (Jer. 23:29).

---

3. Shumack, *Bible*, p. 42.

4. Vanhoozer, *Meaning*.

5. Straw, *Gregory*, 211

How then should we respond to the words of God? We should receive them, and believe them with enduring faith. God is the God who speaks, so the idea of receiving God's words is central to Hebrews. There are a number of phrases which express different nuances of the same basic idea. Here are some of those phrases: 'received the good news' (Heb. 4:6), 'seize the hope set before us' (6:18), 'received the promises' (7:6), 'through faith and patience inherit the promises' (6:12), 'received the knowledge of the truth' (10:26), and 'you need endurance, so that . . . you may receive what was promised' (10:36). All these are ways of paying careful 'attention to what we have heard' (2:1), and therefore of 'not refus[ing] the one who is speaking' (12:25).[6]

Receiving God's words is central to Old and New Testament faith and practice. We find that the writer connects other ideas with receiving God's words:

> For you need endurance, so that when you have done the will of God, you may receive what was promised. For yet
>
> > 'in a very little while,
> > > the one who is coming will come and will not delay;
> > but my righteous one will live by faith.
> > > My soul takes no pleasure in anyone who shrinks back.'
>
> But we are not among those who shrink back and so are lost, but among those who have faith and so are saved. (10:36–39)

Here we see that those who 'receive what was promised' 'live by faith', and so 'are saved'. This then connects with the great examples of faith in chapter 11. To receive the words of God is to believe. To believe the promise is to receive it.

Yet we also find the tension inherent in the gradual unfolding of the plan of God. For Abraham had 'received the promises' (7:6; 11:17). Yet while he had received them in the sense that he had heard them, believed them, and acted on them, yet he did not receive all that was promised. 'By faith he stayed for a time in the land he had been promised, as in a foreign land' (11:9). For all these Old Testament believers knew of these promises, and lived by them, but did not receive all of what was promised. 'All of these died in faith without having received the promises, but from a distance they saw and greeted them' (11:13). They lived before the coming of Christ, and so lived before the fulfilment of

---

6. Notice too the variety of forms of God's words which are received: 'the promises' (7:6; 6:12), 'the law' (7:11), and 'the good news' (4:6).

all of God's promises. 'Yet all these, though they were commended for their faith, did not receive what was promised, since God had provided something better so that they would not, without us, be made perfect' (11:39–40). Believers in Christ have 'better promises' of a 'new covenant' (8:6; 9:15). So, then, 'Let us hold fast to the confession of our hope without wavering, for he who has promised is faithful' (10:23).

The writer of Hebrews was concerned that his readers had become 'dull in understanding' (5:11). They 'ought to be teachers', but needed to learn again 'the oracles of God' (5:12). Their immaturity was evident in their moral igno-rance: they were 'unskilled in the word of righteousness', and unable 'to dis-tinguish good from evil' (5:13–14). He wanted his readers to receive God's words, 'so that you may not become sluggish, but imitators of those who through faith and patience inherit the promises' (6:12).

Receiving God's words is at the heart of the message of Hebrews.

Receiving God's words written for his people

A robust theology of the Bible depends on the idea that there is one people of God, and that the accumulated Scriptures of this one people are God's con-tinuing words written for his people.

Not only is this developed fully in Hebrews, but the practical application of it is seen in the ways in which the author uses the Old Testament. Hebrews bring together the ideas of one salvation history, one biblical theology, one gospel, and one Scripture of the one people of God.

Here we focus again on 3:7 – 4:12. What should we think of the writer's use of the Old Testament, in assuming that what God said to his people in the time of David was relevant, so many years later, to Christian believers? And, for that matter, what should we think of the writer of Psalm 95, assuming that what happened many years before, when God's people were in the wilderness, would be of contemporary relevance? Is it just a matter of the creative use of a relevant story, wherever it comes from? Would a story from Chinese litera-ture (if the writer of Psalm 95 had known it) have been as useful? Would our use of a story from the Brothers Grimm, or from a contemporary film, have served the same function?

The answer is that the stories and words from the Bible have a particular relevance to the people of God in the land, and to the people of God in the time of the writer of Hebrews, as also to Christian believers, the people of God, today. For these are not stories and words from a different family, with different ancestors, but from our family, our ancestors. For the Bible is about the one people of God in every generation, and the Bible is for the one people of God in every generation. Here is God's accumulated and definitive verbal revelation for his people. The tabernacle built by Moses in the desert, and the priesthood of Aaron and of Melchizedek and the ritual of sacrifices and especially of the Day of Atonement are not just accidentally useful illustrations of the person and work of Christ, our great high priest. They are, as Calvin wrote of the temple, the visible sign of the Christ to come: 'The people were preserved by the visible temple in hope of the coming Christ.'[7]

Throughout the Old Testament God formed and built one people of God, and prepared them for the coming of Christ. The shape of believing obedience to God in the Old Testament is the same shape as believing obedience to God and to Christ in the New Testament.

There is, as the writer of Hebrews told us, one household of God, with Moses as its servant: 'Now Moses was faithful in all God's house as a servant, to testify to the things that would be spoken later' (3:5). And if Moses' ministry was of verbal witness to the greater and later revelation, then Christ's ministry is to rule over that house, and 'we are his house if we hold firm the confidence and the pride that belong to hope' (3:6).

There is a real equivalence between the promise of the Old Testament and the evangel of the New Testament, for their essential content is the same: the former looks ahead to fulfilment in Christ, the latter proclaims the accomplishment in Christ of what was promised.[8]

So the constant use of quotations from the Old Testament pointing forward to Christ is making a theological point: the Old Testament gospel is the New Testament gospel, for it looked forward to the coming of Christ as Priest and Son, the new covenant, and fulfilment of the Day of Atonement in the cross of Christ.

Similarly, the unity of the people of God in both Old Testament and New Testament times is demonstrated in the great list of those who lived by faith in Hebrews 11. It is not just that they provide instructive examples, but that God's great work of redemption begun with them will be completed with us (11:39–40). This assumption about the unity of God's house, the people of God, is the basis for the idea of one collection of Holy Scriptures, one word of God, one gospel.

We see this in Hebrews' biblical theology of 'God's rest'. There was the one rest of God, spoken of in Genesis 2, promised to God's people in the wilderness

---

7. Calvin, *Commentaries*, 15, p. 332, on Hag. 1:7–8.

8. Hughes, *Hebrews*, p. 156.

in the form of rest in the promised land, and lost by nearly all that generation. God's rest was still the subject of God's promise even to his people who had entered the land, a sure sign that there was more to God's rest than entry into the land. For the rest, like the land itself, pointed forward to a heavenly rest ('a sabbath rest still remains for the people of God', 4:9). Rest in the land was a fore-taste of eternal rest, just as in chapter 11 the promised land was a promise of 'the city that has foundations, whose architect and builder is God' and 'a better country . . . a heavenly one', and the 'heavenly Jerusalem' (11:10, 16; 12:22). God's promise of rest did not merely have an earthly fulfilment, but points to permanent fellowship with God for eternity. We too are invited to enter that rest through Christ our great high priest.

God's people in the wilderness, like us, had the gospel preached to them, and they provide us with a vivid picture of the dangers of not believing the gospel.

> Now who were they who heard and yet were rebellious? . . . And to whom did he swear that they would not enter his rest, if not to those who were disobedient? So we see that they were unable to enter because of unbelief . . . For indeed the good news came to us just as to them; but the message they heard did not benefit them, because they were not united by faith with those who listened. (3:16 – 4:2)

For of all those who left Egypt, only Caleb and Joshua entered the promised land.[9] For all the others, 'unbelief passed into action'.[10] The message they heard, literally the 'word of hearing', had no good effect, because their response to the gospel was not faith and obedience, but unbelief and disobedience.

David Gooding wrote: 'These statements could not be plainer; it was the gospel which they did not believe. They heard it; but it did them no good because they never did believe it.'[11] The gospel, then as now, brings the moment of decision. The message benefits only those who believe. Disobedience here means total rejection, not momentary turning away. The progression of the argument here is relentless. On the part of man, heedlessness leads to sin, sin leads to disobedience, and disobedience leads to unbelief. The response of God to this is firstly exasperation, secondly disgust, then the sentence of death, and finally a vow of perpetual exclusion from his rest.[12]

---

9. Num. 14:28–32.

10. Westcott, *Hebrews*, p. 87.

11. Gooding, *Kingdom*, p. 113.

12. Montefiore, *Hebrews*, p. 80.

These arguments are all the more forceful because we are the same people of God. As John Owen wrote, 'It is a dangerous condition, for children to boast of the privilege of their fathers, and to imitate their sins.'[13] And of the wilderness generation he wrote, 'Their mercies are our encouragements, and their punishments our warnings.'[14]

God's words are more serious for us than they are for God's people in the Old Testament, for greater revelation brings greater responsibility, and greater responsibility brings greater judgment. 'Anyone who has violated the law of Moses dies without mercy "on the testimony of two or three witnesses". How much worse punishment do you think will be deserved by those who have spurned the Son of God, profaned the blood of the covenant by which they were sanctified, and outraged the Spirit of grace?' (10:28–29).

So the message of Psalm 95 is not arbitrarily applied to the readers of Hebrews. There is one people of God, and one 'rest', promised in the Old Testament and realized in the New. This unity and gradual revelation of God is the basis for the accumulation of writings that come together to form the Holy Scriptures.

Furthermore, the writer did not make Psalm 95 into timeless truths, but pointed to its significance within its historical context and within the gradual revelation in the Bible about the nature of the rest that God promises to share with his people: 'Since therefore it remains open for some to enter it, and those who formerly received the good news failed to enter because of disobedience, again he sets a certain day – "today" – saying through David much later, in the words already quoted, "Today, if you hear his voice, do not harden your hearts"' (4:6–7).

We have here both history and theology: that is, the gradual revelation of the gospel in events in history and in the accumulated Holy Scriptures, including creation, the wilderness wanderings, the promised land, and eschatological hope. The writer of Hebrews used the account of the generation who fell in the wilderness as a warning and an encouragement to his readers. If the lesson of history is that 'no one learns from history', then the writer hopes that a better future lies in store for his readers, that they will indeed learn from the sacred record of the sacred history. 'Let us therefore make every effort to enter that rest, so that no one may fall through such disobedience as theirs' (4:11).

The robust biblical theology of the Bible in Hebrews means that the central themes of salvation through Christ were promised in the Old Testament, and

---

13. Owen, *Hebrews*, vol. 4, p. 51.

14. Ibid., p. 36.

also that the writer was able to use the Old Testament for encouragement and instruction for New Testament believers.

Moses had a distinct and unique role in salvation history, yet he was also an example of faith for present-day believers. Indeed, in chapter 11, it is in Moses' unique leadership in salvation history in the events of the exodus that he provides all believers with an example to imitate: 'By faith Moses, when he was grown up, refused to be called a son of Pharaoh's daughter, choosing rather to share ill-treatment with the people of God than to enjoy the fleeting pleasures of sin. He considered abuse suffered for the Christ to be greater wealth than the treasures of Egypt, for he was looking ahead to the reward' (11:24–26).

Just as Old Testament believers provide us with examples of faith, so too Esau in chapter 12 provides a warning of unbelief: 'See to it that no one becomes like Esau' (12:16). Words addressed in the Old Testament to Joshua, 'I will never leave you or forsake you' (Heb. 13:5, from Josh. 1:5), are rightly addressed now to all believers. And the words of Proverbs are as applicable now as they were then: 'My child, do not regard lightly the discipline of the Lord, or lose heart when you are punished by him; for the Lord disciplines those whom he loves, and chastises every child whom he accepts' (Heb. 12:5–6; Prov. 3:11–12). We too can receive God's words written for his people.

Receiving God's words written for his people by his Spirit

Hebrews clearly associated the words of the Old Testament with the ministry of the Holy Spirit: 'Therefore, as the Holy Spirit says, "Today, if you hear his voice, do not harden your hearts as in the rebellion"' (3:7–8). The writer claimed that the words of Psalm 95 are the words of the Holy Spirit. He implied that those words were Holy Spirit words, but more than that, he claimed that the Holy Spirit continued to speak those words.

The writer of Hebrews respected both the divine origin of Scripture, namely the Holy Spirit, and also its human authorship. That is, the words of Psalm 95 are what the Holy Spirit says (3:7), and also what God was saying 'through David' (4:7).[15] He did not take the words out of their historical setting and make them into a timeless truth. He used their historical setting to show their continuing relevance. What God had said in the past, he was still saying.

---

15. Bruce, *Hebrews*, pp. 75–76, wrote that the exact relationship of David to Ps. 95 is not clearly that of author, but this does not change the force of the claim that Hebrews' use of Ps. 95 depends on its address to the people of God in the land.

And, as we have seen, the application to Christian believers is not arbitrary, because present-day believers are the same household as Old Testament believers. These are no alien words, for they belong to those who are receiving the fulfilment of all the hopes and promises of the Old Testament, fulfilled in Christ.

The contemporary speaking of the Holy Spirit through these words from Psalm 95 is the powerful word of God, living and active (4:12). In the words of John Owen: 'But whatever authority, efficacy, or power the word of God was accompanied withal . . . when it was first spoken by the Holy Ghost, the same it retains now it is recorded in Scripture, seeing the same Holy Ghost yet continues to speak therein.'[16]

The Holy Spirit, who inspired these words, still speaks them today; what God said is what God is still saying. The Bible is the contemporary message of God's Spirit to God's people. As Chris Green has written, we should believe that 'God had this Sunday, this congregation and this sermon in mind when he inspired the original passage'.[17]

P. E. Hughes wrote that for the writer of Hebrews, 'the message of Scripture is the voice of Holy Spirit'.[18] See 10:15–17, with its triple reference to the work of the Holy Spirit in the words of the Old Testament, as one who *testifies*, *says*, and *adds*: 'And the Holy Spirit also *testifies* to us, for after *saying*, "This is the covenant that I will make with them after those days, says the Lord: I will put my laws in their hearts, and I will write them on their minds", he also *adds*, "I will remember their sins and their lawless deeds no more."'

Furthermore, the author makes it clear that the God-ordained structure of the tabernacle and the ritual of the tabernacle is also the result of the work of the Spirit: 'By this the Holy Spirit indicates that the way into the sanctuary has not yet been disclosed as long as the first tent is still standing' (9:8). The Spirit teaches that the Old Testament sanctuary points beyond itself, to a more glorious fulfilment in Christ.

For Hebrews, the work of the Holy Spirit in the words of the Old Testament was not completed when those words were first written down. For those words still remain what the Holy Spirit says, even though many years later, and even though now addressing New Testament believers. Hebrews often refers to the Old Testament as God's present words: 'Have you forgotten the exhortation that *addresses* you as children . . .?' (12:5; Prov. 3:11–12).

---

16. Owen, *Hebrews*, 4, p. 21.

17. Green, *Word of Grace*, p. 119.

18. Hughes, *Hebrews*, p. 141.

God lives and endures for ever, and therefore so do his words, whenever they were spoken.

To hear what the Holy Spirit says through those Old Testament Scriptures is to hear the voice of God today. For the 'today' of the readers of Hebrews is the present time, as the Holy Spirit speaks these words written for them, and as the writer of Hebrews reminded them of these words written for them. As we see in the next verses, the readers of the letter are also meant to use these words to one another as they encourage one another.

There are many signs of hardened hearts, not least in the way we treat other people, when we harden our hearts against them. However, the particular issue in Psalm 95 and Hebrews 3 is that of hearts hardened against God, refusing to hear his voice through the words of the Holy Spirit. Hardening your heart is later described as having an evil, unbelieving heart that turns away from the living God (3:12), and as the sins of disobedience and of unbelief (3:18–19). There seems to be no remedy for hearts hardened against God, except the words of the Spirit, sharper than any two-edged sword (3:7; 4:12). Of course, those who are hard on God will be soft on sin, and that is why Psalm 95 and Hebrews 3 speak so strongly and persistently.

Then how did the writer warn his readers against hardening their hearts? By using the words of the Holy Spirit in Psalm 95, in which God warned the people of God in David's day, and by using the frightening examples of the way God's people acted while in the wilderness on their way from Egypt to the promised land: 'Therefore, as the Holy Spirit says, "Today, if you hear his voice, do not harden your hearts as in the rebellion, as on the day of testing in the wilderness, where your ancestors put me to the test, though they had seen my works for forty years"' (3:7–10).

The frightening examples were of those who hardened their hearts in the rebellion at Meribah and Massah (Exod. 17:7). Just as the people of God fell in the wilderness, so they might fall in the promised land (as Ps. 95 warns), or in the days of New Testament believers (Heb. 3:8).

When the people of God failed in the past, then what was God's reaction, and how might that prompt the readers of Hebrews to respond to the voice of God through the Holy Spirit? 'Therefore I was angry with that generation, and I said, "They always go astray in their hearts, and they have not known my ways." As in my anger I swore, "They will not enter my rest"' (3:10–11).

Here is the most solemn of warnings: apostasy is met with the anger of God, and with his determination that he will not share his rest with such people. We find in God's statement to Moses in Numbers 14:22–23: 'None of the people who have seen my glory and the signs that I did in Egypt and in the wilderness, and yet have tested me these ten times and have not obeyed my voice, shall see the land that I swore to give to their ancestors; none of those who despised me shall see it.'

John Owen pointed out four 'aggravations', four ways in which their behaviour aggravated him:[19]

1. They had seen plenty of signs of God's provision; they had seen 'my works' (9). They had seen many miraculous examples of God's gracious deliverance of his people. The works of God had not increased their faith.
2. They had seen these signs for a whole generation: they had seen my works 'for forty years' (9–10). God's continued works had not increased their faith.
3. Their constancy in behaviour: 'They always go astray in their hearts' (10). Their response was not occasional, but was habitual, indeed constant and universal.
4. Their attitude pervaded a whole generation: it was 'your ancestors', 'that generation' (9, 10). In Owen's words, 'A multitude joining in any sin gives it thereby a great aggravation'.[20]

God had sworn an oath, 'They will not enter my rest' (3:11). 'God gave the same firmitude and stability unto his threatenings that he doth unto his promises.'[21]

To hear God's voice is to hear the Holy Spirit speaking through the Scriptures, and to heed his warnings, given by means of his words to his people in David's day, by warning them by the example of the people of God in the wilderness in the time of Moses.

As we have seen, Stephen Charnock developed the idea of 'practical' or 'secret atheism'. It is the kind of unbelief found in a believer who no longer lives by faith. He based it on words from Psalm 14:1, 'Fools say in their hearts, "There is no God."' Here are some of his comments:

All sin is founded in secret atheism. Atheism is the secret of every sin . . . Actions are a greater discovery of a principle than words. The testimony of works is louder and clearer than that of words and the frame of men's hearts must be measured rather by what they do than by what they say . . . Many, if not most actions, materially good in

---

19. Owen, *Hebrews*, 4, pp. 17, 73, 88.
20. Ibid., p. 51.
21. Ibid., p. 95.

the world, are done more because they are agreeable to self than as they are honourable to God.[22]

And what is the remedy for the evil, unbelieving heart? Not, as we might expect, intense introspection about our deepest motives, but the even more painful mutual exhortation by fellow believers:

> But exhort one another every day, as long as it is called 'today', so that none of you may be hardened by the deceitfulness of sin. For we have become partners of Christ, if only we hold our first confidence firm to the end. As it is said,
>
> 'Today, if you hear his voice,
>
> do not harden your hearts as in the rebellion.'
>
> (3:13–15)

The remedy is not personal introspection, but corporate care, both exhorting and being exhorted. This is not the ministry of leaders, but all of all members, a corporate spirituality of mutual exhortation. This difficult ministry must be carefully and prayerfully undertaken, and must be done with humility and not arrogance, for, as John Owen wrote, 'it is an easy thing to spoil the best duty in the manner of its performance'.[23] What a tragedy when people are confirmed in sin's deceitfulness because the ministry of mutual exhortation has been done out of arrogance or voyeurism. However, it is also true that some exhortation will not succeed, just because people are too hardened and too deceived.

Why do we need this ministry from our fellow believers? Because we have an evil heart, that is, an unbelieving heart, programmed against trusting the words of God.

When do we need this ministry from our fellow believers? Every day, that is, as long as the day of opportunity lasts. 'Each day is a fresh "Today".'[24] We can see that our author regards this danger 'not as a remote possibility, but as a present peril'.[25]

How wide should this ministry extend? The clear answer is that it must be universal, for everyone must be cared for, that 'none of you' may turn away from the living God.

---

22. Charnock, *Discourses*, pp. 46–105.

23. Owen, *Hebrews*, 4, p. 140.

24. Bruce, *Hebrews*, p. 67.

25. Montefiore, *Hebrews*, p. 77.

For how long do we need this ministry from our fellow believers? On every 'today', that is, until the return of Christ. For we must hold our first confidence firm to the end (3:14).

Rather than turning away from God, we should approach him. And our approach to God is by the blood of Jesus, our great high priest, that is, by his sacrifice of himself on the cross. We should come with a true heart, not hardened against God, but pierced by his word, and so with full assurance of faith, not unbelief or disobedience.

God's words are powerful in our mouths, for the benefit of our fellow believers. Hebrews is itself an example of the power of words of exhortation, words of encouragement. God's words, spoken by his Spirit, are effective means that God uses for the preaching of the gospel, and for the edification and encouragement of believers.

Hebrews uses the principles of application outlined above in its exposition of Psalm 95 in 3:7 – 4:13.

The Bible was written 'to them, to us, and for them, for us'.

Hebrews did this when the writer paid attention to the two generations of God's people in the Old Testament. The first generation 'left Egypt under . . . Moses' (3:16, and see 3:16 – 4:2), and the other generation was that addressed by David in Psalm 95 (4:7–8). Yet the writer worked to show how these words addressed to God's people so many years ago also applied to his readers.

Biblical theology

One example of this is the biblical theology of 'rest' which included unfolding the meaning of 'rest' in Genesis 2, in Psalm 95, and for Christian believers (3:7 – 4:11). Furthermore, as 'rest' in part referred to 'rest' in the promised land, this also related to his biblical theology of the land which he develops in 11:13–31, the land of promise, which foreshadowed 'the city that has foundations, whose architect and builder is God' (11:10). A coherent theology of 'rest' and the promised land forms an important foundation of the theology of Hebrews.

Text in immediate context

The writer of Hebrews made use of the immediate context when he developed the key phrases of Psalm 95:7b–11 in the context of that Psalm.

The message of the particular book of the Bible

The writer paid attention to the whole book of Psalms in his study of Psalm 95 by placing the psalm in the context of the Davidic background to the Psalms. This principle is not extensively used in Hebrews.

Pastoral intelligence or awareness

The author of Hebrews wrote with the pastoral needs of his readers in mind. This helped to determine the shape of his message, which parts of the Old Testament he chose and expounded, and the level of confrontation and encouragement that he used in different places throughout the letter.

However, we, in different situations, need immense pastoral intelligence to know when to use or preach Hebrews. For because of the strong warnings in Hebrews against sin (5:11 – 6:12; 10:26–31; 12:25–29), we need to be clear about what sins we should apply these warnings to. I take it that 'wilfully persist[ing] in sin' of 10:26 is not a small matter, but a complete rejection of Jesus Christ and his atonement. It would be pastorally disastrous to preach this passage and imply that some lesser sin deserved the same judgment.

However, it would still be good to use Hebrews to encourage enduring faith, or a good grasp of the connection between Old and New Testaments. It would be less useful in encouraging world mission.

Educative intelligence

The letter of Hebrews served an educative as well as immediately pastoral purpose. It contained a sustained biblical theology, doctrine of Christ, doctrine of salvation, doctrine of revelation, and doctrine of the people of God. Hebrews contained educative substance as well as pastoral immediacy.

Corporate application

Hebrews was addressed to the corporate condition of the people of God, to their common strengths and knowledge, as well as their shared weaknesses. The author was more concerned about their common life than about the response of individuals. He wanted a culture of mutual care and a ministry of mutual encouragement: 'exhort one another every day . . . See to it that no one fails to obtain the grace of God' (3:13; 12:15). He encouraged them: 'we have confidence to enter the sanctuary by the blood of Jesus' (10:19).

Variety of styles of writing and variety of motivations

The author of Hebrews used varied motivations and styles of writing in his selection of material from the Old Testament. These included the promises and warnings from the Psalms, the promises and warnings of the narratives and prophets, and the exhortation from Proverbs. He used stories of faith and the lack of faith. He used sustained themes such as the tabernacle, priesthood and sacrifice, and the promised land.

What are these words doing? What did God want to result from these words?
It is clear in Hebrews that the author believed in the power of the word of God
to achieve results. It is 'living and active . . . able to judge the thoughts and
intentions of the heart' (4:12). The letter is full of the results that the writer
expects from the words that he has written. He writes for transformation, not
just information.

Understanding different kinds of 'application'

The writer of Hebrews intended immediate corporate and personal application of the letter to his readers. If the same group read the letter again twenty
years later, they would need to think more carefully about its application.
However, even if they did not need the immediate application of its message,
it would still be useful for providing insight into the relationship between the
Old and New Testaments, to encourage enduring faith, and to understand that
God's grace must not be ignored or rejected.

Hebrews provides an excellent model of the good use and application of
the Scriptures.

Receiving God's words written for his people by his Spirit about his Son

P. E. Hughes wrote that Hebrews was 'a Christological treatise'.[26] What then
is the revelation of God about his Son, so richly supported and demonstrated
from the Old Testament Scriptures?

The divine dignity of the Son is evident in Hebrews 1. We read of the Son
that he was one whom God

> appointed heir of all things, through whom he also created the worlds. He is the
> reflection of God's glory and the exact imprint of God's very being, and he sustains
> all things by his powerful word. When he had made purification for sins, he sat down
> at the right hand of the Majesty on high, having become as much superior to angels
> as the name he has inherited is more excellent than theirs. (1:2–4)

His divine dignity was demonstrated by a collection of texts from the Old
Testament that show Christ's superiority to angels, and his unique divine
character as the Son of God. 'For to which of the angels did God ever say,

---

26. P. E. Hughes, 'The Christology of Hebrews', p. 19.

"You are my Son; today I have begotten you"? Or again, "I will be his Father, and he will be my Son"?' (1:5).

Just as the divinity of Christ was demonstrated in Hebrews 1, so was Christ's humanity in Hebrews 2.

> For the one who sanctifies and those who are sanctified all have one Father. For this reason Jesus is not ashamed to call them brothers and sisters, saying,
>
> > 'I will proclaim your name to my brothers and sisters,
> >   in the midst of the congregation I will praise you.'
>
> And again,
>
> > 'I will put my trust in him.'
>
> And again,
>
> > 'Here am I and the children whom God has given me.'
> > (2:11–13)

The major teaching about Christ in Hebrews is that he is our high priest.

> So also Christ . . . was appointed by the one who said to him,
>
> > 'You are my Son,
> >   today I have begotten you';
>
> as he says also in another place,
>
> > 'You are a priest for ever,
> >   according to the order of Melchizedek.'
> > (5:5–6)

Christ is not only the priest, but also the sacrifice:

> But when Christ came as a high priest of the good things that have come, then through the greater and perfect tent (not made with hands, that is, not of this creation), he entered once for all into the Holy Place, not with the blood of goats and calves, but with his own blood, thus obtaining eternal redemption. (9:11–12)

Christ is also the representative human being (2:5–9), and the Son who rules over God's house, his people (3:1–6). Just as Moses inaugurated the first covenant with blood of forgiveness, so Jesus offered his own blood once for all at the end of the age (9:18–28). Whereas priests in the old covenant offered their sacrifices day after day, Christ offered a single sacrifice for sins, once for all, and whereas the priests served in the earthly sanctuary, so Christ served in the heavenly sanctuary, in heaven itself (9:23–28). There Christ lives for ever, seated at the right hand of God: 'But when Christ had offered for all time a single sacrifice for sins, "he sat down at the right hand of God", and since then has been waiting "until his enemies would be made a footstool for his feet"' (10:12–13).

So in these last days, God has spoken to us by his Son, but the language that God used to interpret and explain his Son was the language of the Old Testament, fulfilled in Christ.[27]

Indeed, the main use of the Old Testament in Hebrews is to point to Christ, and to point us to Christ. The word of God that points to our sin also points to our Saviour. The Old Testament that shows us our hardness of heart also shows us the softness and sympathy of our Saviour, who sympathizes with our many weaknesses. And if God swore that 'They shall not enter my rest' in Psalm 95 (Heb. 4:3), he also said in Psalm 2:7, 'You are my Son, today I have begotten you', and in Psalm 110:4, 'You are a priest for ever, according to the order of Melchizedek' (Heb. 5:5–6). So let draw near to our God through our Saviour, with full assurance of faith, by means of the blood of Christ, and confident in our great high priest, in Jesus, whose blood speaks a better word than the condemning blood of Abel (10:19–22; 12:24).

And just as God has spoken through the Old Testament, and the Spirit continues to speak through that Old Testament fulfilled in Christ, so also the words of exhortation found in the words of Hebrews and repeated in the words of mutual encouragement and in the teaching of church leaders are also the words of God to his people (3:7, 13; 13:7, 22). The message of Hebrews is of Christ, God's majestic Son.

Hebrews gives us almost a summary of the whole Bible's teaching on itself. It teaches the centrality of 'good hearing' among the people of God, and that the Holy Spirit continues to speak the old words of Scripture, so that when we receive them we receive the voice of God. We receive God's words by the Spirit both directly in Scripture and indirectly in mutual encouragement and exhortation. We share the Old Testament Scriptures with the saints of the old covenant. We learn that the Spirit used human authors for Scripture, and that these words are powerful, living, active, and effective. We learn that the

---

27. See these themes developed in a broader way in Calvin's theology in Adam, *Hearing*, chapter 4.

Scriptures lead us to Christ, as they tell us of Jesus, our great high priest. The writer of Hebrews wants us to stop drifting away, turning away from the living God, being dull in understanding, persisting in sin after we have received the knowledge of the truth, or refusing the God who is speaking (2:1; 3:12; 5:11; 10:26; 12:25). Instead, we are called to receive God's words written for his people by his Spirit about his Son.

Part 6

JESUS AND THE BIBLE IN JOHN'S GOSPEL

17. GOD'S WORDS IN THE OLD TESTAMENT

JOHN 5

Christ is the message and focus of the Bible. He was also the teacher who accepted, assumed, taught, and practised the divine authority of the Old Testament, the divine authority of his own teaching, and the divine authority that will be found in the words of his apostles, the New Testament.[1] In this Part we will see how Christ implicitly and explicitly authenticated the Old Testament (John 5), taught the significance of his own words (John 8 and 17), and authenticated the New Testament to be written by his apostles as they were taught by the Spirit of truth (John 14 – 16). We will also note the significance of Jesus' prayer in John 17 for our understanding of God's words, which are true and powerful in bringing people to believe in Christ, to know God, and also in sanctifying his people and protecting them from the evil one.

We will find the close connection between the Father, the Son, and the apostles, especially in the message handed on from the Father to the Son, from the Son to the disciples, and then by the disciples who later became the apostles of the risen Christ to others, including ourselves. In Jesus' words to his disciples,

---

1. See further on this theme, Wenham, *Christ and Bible*, and, more briefly, McDonald, *I Want to Know*, pp. 84–99, and Jackman, *I Believe*, pp. 59–68.

'Very truly, I tell you, whoever receives one whom I send receives me; and whoever receives me receives him who sent me' (John 13:20).

For Jesus, as the one who has come down from heaven, is the one who can speak of heavenly things: 'Very truly, I tell you, we speak of what we know and testify to what we have seen; yet you do not receive our testimony. If I have told you about earthly things and you do not believe, how can you believe if I tell you about heavenly things?' (John 3:11–12).

For the Gospel of John, the gospel of the incarnate Word of God includes many words of that Word of God. 'It is God the only Son, who is close to the Father's heart, who has made him known' (John 1:18). It was by his teaching and signs, death and resurrection, recorded in John's Gospel, that we have access to the Son's 'making known' of the Father.

To receive is to believe, as we see in these two sentences: 'Whoever believes in me believes not in me but in him who sent me' (John 12:44), and 'Whoever receives me receives him who sent me' (John 13:20). To receive is to believe: to believe is to receive.

In John 5 we find what Jesus taught about the Old Testament, and how it pointed to him.

The Father's verbal witness to Jesus in the Old Testament

> And the Father who sent me has himself [witnessed] on my behalf. You have never heard his voice or seen his form, and you do not have his word abiding in you, because you do not believe him whom he has sent.
>
> You search the scriptures because you think that in them you have eternal life; and it is they that [witness] on my behalf (John 5:37–39)

Jesus' contemporaries had never heard God's voice or seen his form. Yet they could have received his word, and that word or message could have dwelt in them. It did not. That was evident because, if God's word had dwelt in them, then they would have believed in the one sent by God. Though they studied God's Scriptures, his verbal witness to Christ, 'his word' is not in them. Just as eyewitnesses and 'earwitnesses' give their witness to what has happened in the past, so God, through the writings of the Old Testament, gave witness to what would happen in the future, in the coming of Christ. If they had received 'his word', they would have believed in Jesus, because those Scriptures and that word testify about him. God's testimony to Jesus was found in the Scriptures, as those Scriptures pointed to Jesus and his work. The irony is that Jesus' contemporaries searched the Scriptures that were the Father's 'testimony' or words of witness to his Son, and yet they did not come to Jesus to receive eternal life. They missed both witnesses: the word of God in the Scriptures, and the works of God that Jesus came to do. Furthermore, the Old Testament as a 'testimony' or 'witness' (verse 39) is the 'testimony' of the Father (37). 'Testimony' or 'witness' in John's Gospel is a legal term. It means convincing evidential vindication, rather than merely supportive sentiment.

We find this theme expanded in 1 John:

> If we receive human testimony, the testimony of God is greater; for this is the testimony of God that he has testified to his Son . . . Those who do not believe in God have made him a liar by not believing in the testimony that God has given concerning his Son. And this is the testimony: God gave us eternal life, and this life is in his Son. (1 John 5:9–11)

Why did they not believe in Jesus and receive life from him? The painful answer to this question is that they preferred the honour and praise that came from their fellow human beings to that honour and praise that come from God. 'I have come in my Father's name, and you do not accept me . . . How can you believe when you accept glory from one another and do not seek the glory that comes from the one who alone is God?' (John 5:43–44).

This is a familiar theme in John's Gospel. In John 12 John explains that many of the Jewish leaders believed in Jesus, but would not confess their faith, 'for they loved the praise from men more than praise from God' (12:43 [my trans.]). Unbelief comes from a deep dependence on human affirmation, because this need blinds people, and stops them turning to God for his affirmation and for his 'Well done.' The deep source of unbelief here is not intellectual confusion or misunderstanding, nor is it moral disobedience. It is the deep need to be praised by people, which precludes wanting God's praise and honour. The fact that they did not want God's praise shows that they did not love God. For if they loved God, then his approval would have been their chief goal. This guilt was exposed by the fact that they did not accept the one who had come in his Father's name to do his work, the one promised in the Old Testament.

Moses' writings and Jesus' words

Rather than setting their hopes on Jesus, the one now sent by God, they set their hopes on Moses. However, Moses would accuse them and not rescue them, because Moses wrote about Jesus. Clearly, they did not believe what

Moses wrote, for if they had, they would have believed in Jesus. Since they did not believe what Moses wrote, how could they believe what Jesus said to them?

So we see that the witness of the Father to the Son was found in the Old Testament Scriptures. Those Scriptures witness to Jesus, and do so by pointing to the work that Jesus is doing, in showing his glory, and revealing and explaining the Father. Some of Jesus' contemporaries did not believe either Moses' writings or Jesus' sayings. They studied the Scriptures, but missed the message.[2]

Furthermore, as we discover elsewhere in John's Gospel, if people do not keep Jesus' word, then that word will be their judge on the last day. For Jesus said, 'On the last day the word that I have spoken will serve as judge' (John 12:48). This is a remarkable claim, because God is the judge. However, we read in John 5:22 that 'the Father . . . has given all judgement to the Son', and so people will then be judged by their response to Jesus' words. Those who reject Jesus' words will be condemned not only by the words of Jesus, but also by Moses – 'your accuser is Moses' (5:45) – because Moses 'wrote about me' (5:46).

There are of course two serious and related warnings in these verses.

The first is that it is possible to study the Scriptures and still not turn to Jesus, to whom the Father witnesses in the Scriptures. In John 5 it was Jesus' contemporaries who made this mistake, as they read the Old Testament. No doubt it is possible to make the same mistake with the New Testament.

The second serious warning is related to the first, because it explains why those early readers of the Old Testament missed its meaning. It is the danger of desiring the approval of our human contemporaries, and so failing to desire the approval or praise of God: a common but fatal human failing. We cannot have God's approval if we desire the approval of other people. We may receive that approval and feel falsely secure, or fail to achieve it and then feel falsely undervalued. Either way we are in trouble, because the fundamental problem is that we should not be looking to people for this approval, but to God. We cannot have both.

---

2. More fully, in John 5 the Father has provided three forms of witness: John the Baptist, Jesus' works, and the Scriptures = Moses). Our access to these witnesses is in the Scriptures of the Old Testament and John's Gospel.

18. JESUS' OWN WORDS AND TEACHING

JOHN 8 AND 17

In John chapters 8 and 17 we see the centrality of Jesus' teaching in his ministry, and in the disciples' response to Jesus and to the Father. How could people in Jesus' day respond positively to him? They could watch what he did, they could observe the signs and miracles that he provided, they could believe what he taught, and they could practise what he preached. The positive response that Jesus hoped for was that they would receive his words, for his words conveyed the meaning of his life, the interpretation of his signs, the content of his teaching, and the lifestyle that he demanded. The content of his words was not only about his own significance, but also a revelation of the Father, for 'it is God the only Son . . . who has made him known' (John 1:18). To reveal the Son was to reveal the Father, for the essential revelation of the Father was as the Father of the Son.

For Jesus' words explained the meaning and significance of his incarnation and revelation, his actions and his signs. For the people who saw and met Jesus, their response to his words defined their response to him. For people who did not or could not meet Jesus, his contemporaries and those who were alive after him, response to his words still defined their response to him.

John 8: My word brings freedom

'Continue in my word'

Conversion to Christ meant life-long learning. No wonder that Jesus said to the Jews who had believed in him, 'If you continue in my word, you are truly my disciples' (8:31).

For to continue in Jesus' word meant to continue to learn from him and his teaching: true disciples were those who were committed to life-long learning from Jesus, their rabbi or teacher. Even those who doubted Jesus' miracles or divine nature could at least have valued his teaching: a minimalist Christology would still value Jesus the teacher.

Believing Jesus' teaching should lead us to understand and value his miracles and believe in his divine nature. It is also true that those who accept Jesus' divinity and miracles should also continue in his word or teaching. There is no graduation from this school!

Jesus elsewhere taught the dramatic and powerful effects of what he called 'my word'.

It is life-giving, and delivers people from the judgment of God: 'Very truly, I tell you, anyone who hears my word and believes him who sent me has eternal life, and does not come under judgement, but has passed from death to life' (John 5:24). As the Father has granted to the Son the power to raise the dead, so the Son exercised that power through his word. 'My word' also makes people Jesus' disciples, branches of the true vine: 'I am the true vine, and my Father is the vine-grower . . . You have already been cleansed by the word that I have spoken to you. Abide in me as I abide in you' (John 15:1, 3–4). So people became students in Christ's school when they believed Jesus' words, and they continued as his disciples as they continued in this teaching.

The truth will make you free

Jesus said to the Jews who had believed in him, 'If you continue in my word, you are truly my disciples; and you will know the truth, and the truth will make you free' (8:31–32).

Jesus' words bring about knowing the truth, and that truth brings about freedom. Here again we see the power of words, the power of the truth, for these words and this truth make people free. Freedom is achieved by the death and resurrection of Christ the Son, but is applied to us as we receive his words and truth. Truth is found in Jesus' words, and truth brings freedom. Just as Jesus is himself 'the truth' (John 14:6), and just as Jesus says to the Father, 'Your word is truth' (John 17:17), so that truth is powerfully conveyed through the truth of Jesus' own words. And these words of truth 'will make you free'.

Jesus' hearers responded: 'We are descendants of Abraham and have never been slaves to anyone. What do you mean by saying, "You will be made free"?' Jesus answered them, "Very truly, I tell you, everyone who commits sin is a slave to sin" ' (8:33–34).

So the freedom worked by truth is freedom from sin, and from the slavery of sin. The phrase 'The truth will make you free' has become a slogan, taken to mean that truth sets us free from error. While that is generally true, and while that is also true of Jesus' teaching, the freedom that Jesus refers to here is freedom from the slavery of sin, for 'everyone who commits sin is a slave to sin'. Here is freedom not from outer forces, or from wrong opinions, but from the self-induced slavery to sin that results from acts of sin. These are deeper issues than abstract ideas of truth and error.

The Son will make you free

How is it that the truth of Jesus' word makes people free? The answer is that it is the Son who sets people free, and his words are the effective means of conveying and bringing about that freedom. The words of Jesus are his powerful and effective tools or instruments that convey power to set free, and Jesus himself is the origin of that power. 'So if the Son makes you free, you will be free indeed' (8:36).

The ultimate sin is that of rejecting the word of Jesus, and so rejecting him. Although Jesus' hearers claimed that they were free because they were Abraham's descendants, Jesus replied, 'I know that you are descendants of Abraham; yet you look for an opportunity to kill me, because there is no place in you for my word' (8:37). Jesus' word has come to them, but has found no place in them, and so, because of the significance of Jesus' word, they reject it and plan to kill him. Yet in rejecting him, they are rejecting not only him but also the Father, because, as Jesus explains, 'I declare what I have seen in the Father's presence; as for you, you should do what you have heard from the Father' (8:38).

'You cannot accept my word'

They may have thought that all they were doing was assessing the words of one more deluded rabbi, but in fact they were part of a cosmic battle, for they were siding either with the devil or with God the Father. If accepting and receiving Jesus' word has radical implications, so too rejecting Jesus' word also has radical implications. For, Jesus claimed, 'now you are trying to kill me, a man who has told you the truth that I heard from God' (8:40). And in rejecting Jesus and his message, they were rejecting the Father: 'If God were your Father, you would love me, for I came from God and now I am here. I did not come on my own, but he sent me. Why do you not understand what I say? It is because you cannot accept my word' (8:42–43).

If they were not shaped and formed by God the Father and God the Son, then they were being formed and shaped by the devil. There is no neutral ground, no place where they could avoid commitment and alignment. For they either followed Jesus, in receiving his word and truth, or they followed the devil, and showed that they were his children.

The devil is a liar and the father of lies

The devil is not only a murderer, encouraging them to kill Jesus, but he is also the father of lies. The idea that we can be non-aligned in matters of religion is ridiculous. As Jesus made clear, either we are following the truth of his teaching, or we are enmeshed in lies, and those lies ultimately come from the devil. 'He was a murderer from the beginning and does not stand in the truth, because there is no truth in him. When he lies, he speaks according to his own nature, for he is a liar and the father of lies. But because I tell the truth, you do not believe me' (8:44–45).

In a world captive to lies, Jesus' weapon is the truth.

The words of God, the word of Jesus

Ultimately, to reject the word of Jesus is to reject Jesus, to reject Jesus is to reject the words of God, and to reject the words of God is to reject God. 'If I tell the truth, why do you not believe me? Whoever is from God hears the words of God. The reason you do not hear them is that you are not from God' (8:46–47).

There is an inescapable link between 'the words of God' and 'God'. Any who claim to be connected to God must be connected to his words, because, of course, his words bear witness to Jesus his Son. If they had believed the words of God they would have believed in Jesus and accepted him. They showed by their actions that they belonged to the devil, and not to God. They were exposed by their reaction to Jesus and his word.

The word of Jesus not only sets people free and delivers them from judgment, but also gives eternal life. For the devil is death-dealing, and the Son is life-giving. As the Father had granted the Son to have life himself (5:26), and as he is the resurrection and the life (11:25), so he conveys life to those who keep his word: 'Very truly, I tell you, whoever keeps my word will never see death' (8:51). Freedom from sin and eternal life are Christ's gifts to those who believe his word, and so trust in him, the eternal Son of the Father.

So the words of Jesus brought either freedom or condemnation, because Jesus had spoken the words that the Father had told him to speak. However, if the words of Jesus brought the danger of final condemnation, they also brought the promise of intimacy with both the Father and the Son. For Jesus also said, 'Those who love me will keep my word, and my Father will love them, and we will come to them and make our home with them' (14:23).

Relationships are established and preserved by words, and those who love the Lord Jesus will keep his word, receive the Father's love, and be indwelt by the Father and the Son.

'Sanctify them in the truth: your word is truth' (John 17)

In John 17 we also gain an extraordinary insight into the mind and heart of Jesus as he prepared to leave his disciples and prepared for his death and resurrection. Here we focus our attention on verses 6–18, Jesus' prayer for his disciples.

As Jesus began his prayer for his disciples, he described them in remarkable terms. He began by describing the relationships between himself and the disciples, and between the Father and himself, in terms of the disciples receiving the words that Jesus had passed on to them from the Father:

> 'I have made your name known to those whom you gave me from the world. They were yours, and you gave them to me, and they have kept your word. Now they know that everything you have given me is from you; for the words that you gave to me I have given to them, and they have received them and know in truth that I came from you; and they have believed that you sent me.' (17:6–8)

Jesus has given the words that he received from the Father to the disciples whom he also received from the Father. It is not just the general message that Jesus passes on from the Father ('the word'), but verbal transmission ('the words'). In so doing he has revealed the Father to them, and also shown them that he came from the Father. The disciples received the words Jesus gave them and accepted them, obeyed the word of the Father, and knew that everything that Jesus had came from the Father. Just as the works that Jesus did were the ones that he saw the Father doing (John 5:19), so the words that Jesus spoke were those given him by the Father. So they knew with certainty that Jesus came from the Father, and that the Father had sent him (17:6–8). Furthermore, because Jesus and the Father share all things in this way, Jesus himself was glorified through the disciples.

The same ideas are found in verses 11–19. Here Jesus prayed that the Father would 'protect them' by the power of his name, the name that the Father gave to his Son. As Jesus has protected them by that name, or revelation, so now he prayed that the Father would continue to protect them by his name. As Jesus prayed that they would be protected from the evil one, so he also prayed, 'Sanctify them in the truth; your word is truth' (17:17).

So it is the revelation, the word of the Father in the words of the Father that the Father gave to the Son, the name or word of the Father, which is the truth by which the Father will sanctify, protect, and set apart the disciples. And this work of sanctification is based on the power of Jesus' own self-sanctification, as he went to the cross ('I sanctify myself', 17:19), in order that the disciples may be truly sanctified.

Jesus formed a community of the word. While he wanted people to search the Scriptures because they testified to him, he also wanted his disciples to hear and receive his own words because they came from the Father: 'My teaching is not my own. It comes from him who sent me' (John 7:16 [my trans.]); 'I do nothing on my own but speak just what the Father has taught me' (8:28 [my trans.]). 'I am telling you what I have seen in my Father's presence' (8:38 [my trans.]).

Then in John 17 we have found that Jesus claimed that his own teaching came from the Father, and that not only 'the word' but also 'the words' that he received from the Father were 'the words' that he gave to his disciples. It was these words from the Father received from the Son that enabled those disciples to believe in Jesus, as the one sent by the Father, and who came from the Father. As John wrote of the apostolic witness: 'We are from God. Whoever knows God listens to us, and whoever is not from God does not listen to us. From this we know the spirit of truth and the spirit of error' (1 John 4:6).

Then Jesus prayed that his Father would 'sanctify them in the truth', because 'your word is truth' (17:17). Again we find the theme of the power of God's word, and especially its power to sanctify the disciples. The Holy Spirit's holy words will make God's people holy or sanctified. Jesus also is God's agent of sanctification, and achieved this through his own sanctification, that is, by setting himself the holy task of going to the cross: 'And for their sakes I sanctify myself, so that they also may be sanctified in truth' (17:19).

These words give us a clear insight into the central role of words in Jesus' ministry to his disciples.

19. JESUS, THE SPIRIT OF TRUTH, AND THE NEW TESTAMENT

JOHN 14 – 16

In the words of the historian Adolf Harnack, 'No greater creative act can be mentioned in the whole history of the Church than the formation of the apostolic collection and the assigning to it of a position of equal rank with the Old Testament.'[1]

Is there any evidence that Jesus expected that there would be more 'Holy Scriptures', written by his disciples, which would have the same status as the 'Holy Scriptures' of the Old Testament?

This is an important question, for Jesus warned his disciples about future messengers: 'Then Jesus began to say to them, "Beware that no one leads you astray. Many will come in my name and say, 'I am he!' and they will lead many astray . . . False messiahs and false prophets will appear and produce signs and omens, to lead astray, if possible, the elect"' (Mark 13:5–6, 22).

With this warning in mind, should we accept the writings of the apostles?

I believe that the answer is yes, and that the creation of these new Holy Scriptures is explained and promised by Jesus in his teaching about the coming of the Advocate, the Spirit of truth. For if the New Testament books do not

---

1. As quoted in Webster, *Word and Church*, p. 11.

come from Christ and lead us to Christ, then we should not read them, because they will lead us away from Christ.

This is a crucial issue in understanding the Bible. It is easy to show how Jesus authenticated the Old Testament and his own teaching. How did he authenticate the New Testament? We find the answer in chapters 14 – 16 of John's Gospel.

There are five statements in Jesus' teaching about the Spirit of truth in these chapters.

'The Father . . . will give you another Advocate . . . the Spirit of truth'
  (14:16–17).
'The Advocate, the Holy Spirit . . . will teach you everything, and remind you
  of all that I have said to you' (14:26).
'The Advocate . . . the Spirit of truth . . . will testify [about me]' (15:26–27).
'The Advocate . . . I will send . . . to you . . . will prove the world wrong
  about sin and righteousness and judgement' (16:7–11).
'The Spirit of truth . . . will guide you into all the truth; for he . . . will speak
  whatever he hears, and he will declare to you the things that are to come.
  He will glorify me, because he will take what is mine and declare it to you'
  (16:13–14).

The ministry of the Holy Spirit will be a ministry of words, and will include being an 'interpreter or exegete, teacher, prophet or legal counsel'.[2]

Here Jesus taught the disciples about the way in which the Spirit would direct them in their preaching and teaching ministry, and, as part of that ministry, bring about the writing of the Gospels, Acts, the epistles, and the book of Revelation. For the apostles were Jesus' representatives, and they taught, preached, and wrote God's words. Just as the Gospels were based on the 'witness' of the disciples who had been with Jesus, so they would also be part of the 'witness' or 'testimony' of the Spirit to Jesus Christ. The idea of witness in the New Testament is primarily that of a legal witness,[3] and this ties in with Jesus' description of the Spirit as an advocate, or legal counsel.

When Jesus sent out his disciples, he gave them this assurance, 'Whoever receives you receives me and he who receives me receives the one who sent me' (Matt. 10:40 [my trans.]). Later, the apostles, including Paul, would be apostles of the risen Christ. Paul was 'an apostle of Christ Jesus by the will of

---

2. Hamilton, *God's Presence*, p. 87.
3. Bauckham, *Eyewitnesses*, p. 385.

God' (Eph. 1:1). And Paul wrote: 'Hold to the standard of sound teaching that you have heard from me, in the faith and love that are in Christ Jesus. Guard the good treasure entrusted to you, with the help of the Holy Spirit living in us' (2 Tim. 1:13–14).

If Jesus did not intend the authoritative teaching and writing ministry of his apostles, then we should not accept the New Testament. If he did intend it, here is the evidence in John 14 – 16.

There were four important features of this process.

The Father and the Son will send the Spirit of truth

Just as the Old Testament teaching came from the Father, and as Jesus' own teaching came from the Father, so too this further revelation will come from the Father and the Son, for it is the Father and the Son who will send another Advocate, the Spirit of truth (14:16; 16:7).

Just as the word of the Father is truth, ('your word is truth', 17:17), and as Jesus himself is the truth ('I am . . .the truth', 14:6), so too the Spirit will bring truth (14:17, 15:26; 16:13). The task of the Spirit is to bring the truth, and to guide the disciples into all truth (16:13). There is one truth, because all the truth that is revealed comes from the Father.

The 'Advocate' is 'another Advocate' (14:16), and so is like Jesus, and will continue Christ's care for his disciples after his death, resurrection, and ascension, especially in teaching them.

This Advocate will 'prove the world wrong about sin and righteousness and judgement' (16:8). D. A. Carson suggests that the best way to understand this is to think of the Spirit's work as that of convincing the world itself of its mistakes in these vital areas, and so as preparatory to repentance and then faith in Christ. Sin, righteousness, and judgment are all about the world's misunderstanding of Christ and his death and resurrection: sin, because of unbelief; righteousness, because of Jesus' death and resurrection; and judgment, because the world's ruler is condemned by Jesus' death (16:9–11).[4] This convicting and convincing work of the Spirit is seen in apostolic preaching in Acts, when people are 'cut to the heart', because 'God has made him both Lord and Messiah, this Jesus whom you crucified' (Acts 2:37, 36).[5]

---

4. Carson, *John*, pp. 537–538, and see also John 12:31.
5. See also Acts 13:28–30.

The Spirit will point to Christ

The Spirit of truth, the Advocate, would come from the Father in response to the prayers of Jesus: 'I will ask the Father' (14:16). However, Jesus also taught that the Father would send the Spirit 'in my name' (14:26), and that the Spirit would also come from Jesus: 'When the Advocate comes, whom I will send to you from the Father . . .' (15:26). The Advocate was to be given by the Father in answer to the request of the Son (14:16); he was to be sent by the Father in Christ's name (14:26); he was to be sent by Christ from the Father (15:26); he would come from the Father (15:26); and would be sent by Christ (16:7). It is not that there would be two revelations from the Father, one through Jesus, and the other through the Spirit. For the Spirit would come from the Father and from the Son.

Furthermore, the Spirit 'will teach you everything, and remind you of all that I have said to you' (14:26), 'will testify [about me]' (15:26), and 'will glorify me, because he will take what is mine and declare it to you' (16:14). The Spirit would bring a Christocentric revelation, and not a new revelation which would make the Father's revelation through Jesus redundant. The Spirit would come from the Lord Jesus, speak about Christ, remind them of Christ's words, and so glorify Christ. If the Spirit was to 'remind you of all that I have said to you' (14:26), then these words must apply to Jesus' original disciples, those who had heard his teaching.

How else do we see these promises fulfilled than in the preaching of the apostles and in the creation of the books we call the New Testament? What else is the New Testament but the result of the fulfilment of these promises? Here we see the result of the ministry of the Spirit of truth, as the Spirit taught all things to the apostles, reminded them of Jesus' teaching as they wrote the Gospels, helped them to testify to Christ and bring glory to him, guided them into all truth, and told them what was yet to come in the life of the church and in the return of Christ.

If the Scriptures of the Old Testament were the Father's testimony to Christ ('they testify on my behalf', 5:39), then the Scriptures of the New Testament would also be the testimony of the Father to Christ, because it is the Father who would send the Holy Spirit: 'he will give you another Advocate' (14:16). And this Holy Spirit would also testify of Jesus, and this testimony to Jesus Christ would also be through his disciples: 'he will testify [about me]', and 'you also are to testify because you have been with me from the beginning' (15:26–27). The joint testimony of the Spirit of truth and the disciples is found in their preaching and teaching, and ultimately in the books of the New Testament. As Martin Foord has shown, we should add to the apostles their fellow workers, those who jointly wrote some of the letters, and the prophets of the New Testament church.[6]

Paul wrote of the message of Christ crucified that 'God has revealed [it] to us through the Spirit' (1 Cor. 2:10). Peter wrote of those who 'brought you good news by the Holy Spirit sent from heaven' (1 Pet. 1:12). This is 'the faith . . . once for all entrusted to the saints', that 'most holy faith' which God has given them (Jude 3, 20). The apostolic teaching and writing consituted the fulfilment of these promises.

The Holy Spirit will do this work after Christ's death and resurrection

The Holy Spirit will do this work in the period after the death and resurrection of Christ. This is clear in the following phrases: 'On that day you will know that I am in my Father' (John 14:20); 'If I do not go away, the Advocate will not come to you; but if I go, I will send him to you' (16:7–8); 'When the Spirit of truth comes, he will guide you into all the truth' (16:13); 'A little while, and . . . you will see me' (16:16); and 'I have said these things to you in figures of speech. The hour is coming when I will no longer speak to you in figures, but will tell you plainly of the Father' (16:25–26).

These words were addressed specifically to the disciples there present with Jesus. We must avoid a facile application of the words to ourselves. Of course, it is true that the Spirit works in subsequent generations to open the Scriptures and teach us about Christ, and that we are also guided by the Spirit. However, here in John 14 – 16 we find teaching about the coming of the Spirit of truth on that first generation of apostles and prophets, in the church 'built on the foundation of the apostles and prophets' (Eph. 2:20).

Of course, it is also true that the Holy Spirit is at work when anyone becomes a believer. New birth comes through the internal work of the Spirit, and the Spirit works in every believer to help them understand and receive the gospel of Jesus Christ. As John wrote, 'But you have been anointed by the Holy One, and all of you have knowledge' (1 John 2:20). However, we should not confuse the specific work of the Spirit in the creation of apostolic teaching and the New Testament with his general work in all believers.

---

6. Foord, *Weakest Link*, p. 11.

We can see the evidence of this activity of the Spirit in the New Testament

Are then any signs of this process happening in John's Gospel itself? Here are some indications.

Reference back to the historic revelation in Christ

Here are some of the references back to that revelation. 'We have seen his glory' (1:14). To see the glory of Christ included being eyewitnesses of his signs or miracles: 'Jesus did this, the first of his signs, in Cana of Galilee, and revealed his glory; and his disciples believed in him' (2:11). It also included being witnesses of his death and resurrection: 'His disciples did not understand these things at first; but when Jesus was glorified, then they remembered that these things had been written of him and had been done to him' (12:16). For it was the privilege of those who accompanied Jesus, who saw his glory and received his words, to authenticate the history of his revelation. 'This is the disciple who is testifying to these things and has written them, and we know that his testimony is true' (21:24). Just as at every stage in the unfolding revelation of the Bible, it was the original participants in the works and words of God who could witness to what God had done and said.[7]

Words that describe the Old Testament are also used to describe John's Gospel

Words applied to both the Old Testament and John's Gospel include 'witness' or 'testimony', 'scripture' or 'writing', and the idea of 'keeping' the words of Christ.

When Jesus promised that the Holy Spirit would come after his death and resurrection, he used the word 'witness' to describe both the ministry of the Spirit and the ministry of the disciples: 'When the Advocate comes, whom I will send to you from the Father, the Spirit of truth who comes from the Father, he will testify on my behalf. You also are to testify because you have been with me from the beginning' (15:26–27).

Jesus used the same word 'witness' to describe the Old Testament Scriptures: 'They witness about me'; and of Moses: 'he wrote about me' (5:39 [my trans.], 46). John used the same word 'witness' to describe what he saw and heard, and also to describe his written record. He wrote in 19:35, 'He who saw

---

7. It is common to claim that this happened in the 'Johannine community'. My claim is that it happened in all the churches through the ministry of the apostles.

this has testified so that you also may believe. His testimony is true, and he knows that he tells the truth.'

As we have already seen in 21:24, to 'testify' or 'witness' to the revelation is to write it down: 'This is the disciple who is testifying to these things and has written them.' This matches the language of Isaiah 8, where 'testimony' refers to the teaching of the prophet. As David Peterson wrote: ' "Bind up the testimony; seal the teaching among my disciples" suggests the securing of Isaiah's message from tampering and addition, committing it to the care of his disciples.'[8]

Richard Bauckham has shown that we should not think that the Gospels are the products of the post-Pentecost church and its theological priorities, questions, and creativity, but that they are based on the eyewitness account of Jesus and his ministry. He demonstrates this with particular reference to John's Gospel.[9]

Similarly, in John's Gospel the word 'scripture' or 'writing' refers to the Old Testament, and so should be 'Scripture'. It occurs twelve times, and always assumes the significance and authority of the Old Testament, and that it will be fulfilled in Jesus Christ. We read in 19:36–37: 'These things occurred so that the scripture might be fulfilled, "None of his bones shall be broken." And again another passage of scripture says, "They will look on the one whom they have pierced." '[10]

So also the Greek verb 'to write' is used of the Old Testament ten times, as for example in 6:45: 'It is written in the prophets, "And they shall all be taught by God." '[11]

Even what Pilate caused to be written about Jesus Christ on the cross, 'The King of the Jews', cannot be changed: 'Pilate answered, "What I have written I have written" ' (19:22).[12] Pilate's writing is an unconscious prophetic word which matches the word of Caiaphas, the high priest: 'It is better for you to have one man die for the people' (11:50).

It is in this context of the power of the prophetic word of testimony that we should read John's words: 'But these are written so that you may come to believe that Jesus is the Messiah, the Son of God' (20:31), and, 'This is the disciple who is testifying to these things and has written them' (21:24).

---

8. Peterson, *Christ*, pp. 72–73, commenting on Isa. 8:16.

9. See Bauckham, *Eyewitnesses*, chapters 14–17.

10. The other ten references are 2:22; 5:39; 7:38, 42; 10:35; 13:18; 17:12; 19:24, 28; and 20:9.

11. The other nine references are 1:46; 2:17; 5:46; 6:31; 8:17; 10:34; 12:14, 16; and 15:25.

12. The Greek word for 'write' occurs six times in 19:19–22.

The characteristic positive response to the words of Christ in John's Gospel is to 'keep' them. Jesus promised, 'Very truly, I tell you, whoever keeps my word will never see death' (8:51), 'If you love me, you will keep my commandments' (14:15), and 'If you keep my commandments, you will abide in my love, just as I have kept my Father's commandments and abide in his love' (15:10).

This language is also found in the Old Testament. To 'keep' God's words or commandments is to do two things. To 'keep' them is to practise them, and to 'keep' them is to preserve them and to pass them on to others. This is what Jesus called his disciples to do. He wanted them to 'keep' his words, that is, to do what he said. He also wanted them to 'keep' them, to preserve them either in their memories or in writing, so that others could hear them or read them. Jesus' disciples should do this, because Jesus' words were the word of the Father: 'Those who love me will keep my word, and my Father will love them, and we will come to them and make our home with them. Whoever does not love me does not keep my words; and the word that you hear is not mine, but is from the Father who sent me' (14:23–24).

So, then, it follows that if Jesus' disciples are to 'keep his word', those who hear or read the testimony of Jesus' disciples must 'keep' their 'word'. As Jesus said to his disciples, 'Remember the word that I said to you, "Servants are not greater than their master." If they persecuted me, they will persecute you; if they kept my word, they will keep yours also' (15:20).

These are all signs that Jesus' direct teaching and Jesus' teaching through the Holy Spirit in his disciples would come to have the value of the Old Testament as Holy Scriptures.

The writers of the New Testament books were certainly aware of their responsibility as those who received and passed on this revelation from the Holy Spirit. Luke began Acts with words that imply that Jesus would continue to teach his church after his ascension: 'I wrote about all that Jesus did and taught from the beginning until the day he was taken up to heaven' (Acts 1:1–2). As early as Acts 2 the church was meeting together, devoted to 'the apostles' teaching' (Acts 2:42). Peter's vision in Acts is an example of being 'guided into truth' (Acts 10:1 – 11:18).

There are many examples of how the writers of the books of the New Testament recognized the outpouring of the revelation of the Spirit of truth in the church after the death and resurrection of the Lord Jesus Christ and the coming of the Spirit at Pentecost. Paul wrote that he had been 'called to be an apostle, set apart for the gospel of God', and that 'we have received grace and apostleship to bring about the obedience of faith among all the Gentiles' (Rom. 1:1, 5). He claimed that he did not receive his gospel from humans: 'I received it through a revelation of Jesus Christ' (Gal. 1:12). He wrote of his 'understanding of the mystery of Christ . . . not made known to humankind, as it has now been revealed to his holy apostles and prophets by the Spirit' (Eph. 3:4–5). Paul ministered 'by word and deed, by the power of signs and wonders, by the power of the Spirit of God' (Rom.15:18–19). Paul was a minister of the new covenant, a 'ministry of the Spirit' (2 Cor. 3:8). No wonder he was able to equate 'the gospel', 'the standard of sound teaching', 'the good treasure', 'what you have heard from me through many witnesses', and 'the word of truth' (2 Tim. 1:8, 13–14; 2:2, 15).

So, too, the writer of Hebrews referred to this revelation of the Spirit received after people heard Jesus Christ on earth: 'It was declared at first through the Lord, and it was attested to us by those who heard him, while God added his testimony by signs and wonders and various miracles, and by gifts of the Holy Spirit, distributed according to his will' (Heb. 2:3–4).

Though this is more revelation than Jesus taught his disciples, it is revelation about the incarnation, ministry, death, resurrection, and ascension of Jesus Christ, and not about a new set of God's saving actions. It is revelation which further illuminated the gospel of Christ, and the implications of that gospel, of that Christ.

For example, although the death and resurrection of Christ happened at the time of the Passover, Hebrews shows that Christ's death is also explained by the Day of Atonement. In Colossians Paul explains the significance of Christ in creation, and that Christ's death was God's work to reconcile all things to himself. The book of Revelation is another example of this process of revelation. It was a revelation of Christ, mediated through Christ, and a revelation of Christ, the Lion of the tribe of Judah, the slain but standing Lamb, the one who ransomed people for God through his blood, from every tribe and language and people and nation, Jesus, who is King of kings and Lord of lords. Furthermore, he equated the words of the glorious and ascended Christ to each of the seven churches with what the Spirit is saying to those churches (Rev. 1 – 3). And 'the testimony of Jesus is the spirit of prophecy' (19:10).

The unity of the revelation that Christ gave to his disciples and that the risen Christ gave through his apostles is supported by the fact that the Spirit of truth is sent by Christ, that the Spirit's teaching is Christocentric, linked to what Jesus told his disciples, and that it mediates the revelation that belongs to Christ. As David Jackman wrote: 'It is a promise to the apostles, who were the personally commissioned witnesses of the Risen Christ, and the result is the sure and certain testimony, which is our New Testament.'[13]

---

13. Jackman, *I Believe*, p. 65, and see pp. 64–68. See also Carson, *John*, pp. 541–542.

Christ's verbal revelation was given in two stages. The first was his teaching given to his disciples when he was on earth, including his teaching recorded in the Gospels, and referred to in Acts 1.[14] The second stage was the revelation given through the Spirit to his apostles. This second stage includes the writing of the Gospels, Acts, the epistles, and the book of Revelation. It is all 'new-covenant' revelation, expanding the meaning of Christ and his blood of the covenant.[15] In the words of early church leader Didymus, 'He puts off the greater [things] for a future time, such things as they could not understand till the Cross itself of their crucified Head had been their instruction.'[16]

The significance of Christ was explained before it happened, in the Old Testament, and then further explained not only in Jesus' teaching to his own disciples, but also after the events of his life, death, and resurrection in the teaching of his apostles and prophets in the New Testament.

This last claim is of great importance. If Jesus did not send the Spirit of truth to the apostles to direct them, then we should not treat their writings as his words. If, however, that was his purpose, we should receive their words as his words. Those who received Christ's messengers received Christ's message. If that was true of those sent out in Jesus' name during his earthly ministry, was it not also true for those apostles of the risen Christ?

We can apply words of Kevin Vanhoozer to this process. He used them about the canon of the Bible, but I want to use them about the New Testament. For the New Testament is 'Christ's own Spirit-borne commissioned testimony to himself'.[17]

However, we should recognize that there are different views about the application of Jesus' words about the Spirit, 'he will guide you into all the truth' (John 16:13). Does this mean that the Spirit will guide the apostles into all the truth? Or is it a promise to all believers from Pentecost until the return of Christ? And if it is this promise, then should those whom the Spirit is guiding into all the truth continue to receive the books of the Old and New Testaments, or should they leave them behind, treat them as documents of lesser truth, or interpret them only in the light of 'all the truth' revealed at a later time? This question is more broadly understood as that of the relation-ship between the Bible and any further words or messages of God which may be thought to apply to all believers in all places at all times.

---

14. Also including his sayings recorded in Acts 20:35 and 1 Tim. 5:18.

15. 2 Cor. 3:4–18; Heb. 8 – 10; Matt. 26:26–29.

16. In Thomas Aquinas, *Catena*, p. 506.

17. Vanhoozer, *Drama*, p. 194.

Who are those whom the Spirit of truth will guide into all the truth? What is the content of that truth into which they will be guided? There are three main views.

The Roman Catholic and Eastern Orthodox view

First, the position of the Roman Catholic and Eastern Orthodox churches (also held by some Pentecostals) is that in addition to the Bible, the Holy Spirit has continued to guide the church into all the truth. In this view, the Bible is incomplete, for it is less than 'all the truth' that the Spirit will teach. According to this view, God has continued to do his saving works and words over the last 2,000 years: he has revealed new truths, and supported them with new miracles. This spirituality of the Word will include not only the words of the Bible, but also words given to the church since Bible times, whether recognized by pope, patriarch, or council of the church, or given by a prophet in a local church. In this view the Bible provides the basics, but maturity will be found in the greater truth that comes after the Bible. Frank Moloney quotes these words from the documents of the Second Vatican Council: 'God, who spoke in the past, continues to converse with the spouse of his beloved Son. And in the Holy Spirit, through whom the living voice of the Gospel rings out in the Church – and through her to the world – leads believers to the full truth, and makes the Word of Christ dwell in them in all its richness.'[18]

Furthermore, in this view there are two powerful roles for tradition, for the fullness of truth. One is to interpret the Bible, and the other is to add to the Bible. The combination of these two views unfortunately makes it even easier for the tradition to distort or muffle the Scriptures. Of course, this happens very frequently within Protestant, Reformed, and Evangelical churches as well. At least the Roman Catholic Church, and the Pentecostal traditions which follow this view, are honest and open about what is happening!

The Quaker and liberal view

Secondly, the view of the Quakers and liberal groups is that revelation comes direct from God today (Quakers), or that the most significant revelation comes direct from God today (liberals). It is that the Spirit guides us now into all the truth, and does so with present and immediate words. The Spirit may include some language from the Bible and from church traditions, but other parts are now obsolete and irrelevant. Our task is to discern what God is saying at the present time, in what is happening in the world around us, in the 'second text'

---

18. Moloney, *Living Voice*, p. 243, quoting from *Dei Verbum*, p. 8.

of God's current actions in the world, or deep within our own consciousness. It believes that the Spirit gives us the contemporary words of God, and these present words may make some words of God in the Bible obsolete and irrelevant.[19]

The evangelical and Reformed view

Thirdly, the position of evangelical and Reformed Christians is that the promise of Jesus to his disciples was that the Holy Spirit would guide those disciples into all the truth, and that the result of this would be the books of the New Testament. In this view, all God's saving words and works are found within the Bible, and within that period of revelation of the Old and New Testaments. So this view will focus entirely on the Bible for the content of the knowledge of God, and treat the Bible as the only words of God addressed to all people and all churches in every age. It also expects to find that biblical faith works, and so to find corroborative evidence in the lives and ministries of the saints. It expects that the witness of the Spirit within the believer and within the church will correspond to his external witness in Scripture.

This view was well expressed in the words of John Calvin: 'Yet this . . . is the difference between the apostles and their successors: the former were sure and genuine scribes of the Holy Spirit, and their writings are therefore to be considered oracles of God; but the sole office of others is to teach what is provided and sealed in the Holy Scriptures.'[20]

My own view is this last one.[21] Of course, the Holy Spirit continues to help us to understand and receive the words of the Bible, given by that same Spirit so long ago. The Holy Spirit continues to illuminate our minds, and helps us to receive the words of God in the Bible with clarity and joy. We can say that the Spirit does guide us into the truth, but not in the sense that Jesus meant in John 16:13. The Spirit does not guide us into more truth additional to that found in the Bible. We are to 'guard the good treasure' entrusted to us 'with the help of the Holy Spirit living in us' (2 Tim. 1:14). In this view, as we look back in history for the work of God in Christ that saved us, so we look back to his work through the Spirit, the Bible, that tells us of our Christ, and the salvation he won.

Furthermore, God is able to bring specific messages to churches and individuals at any time. However, they must be checked in the light of Scripture

---

19. For the Quaker version see Adam, *Word and Spirit*.
20. Calvin, *Institutes*, 4.8.9, p. 1157.
21. Adam, *Hearing*, pp. 37–42.

and assessed, and not accepted without investigation (see 1 Cor. 14:29). They will not be accepted as infallible, or added to God's cumulative words, or applied to all churches for all time.

This view continues to assert that the theological creativity of the New Testament came from Jesus Christ, rather than being a later product of the New Testament churches or leaders. The four Gospels are based on eyewitness and 'earwitness' accounts of Jesus' life and ministry, rather than just expressing the priorities and creativity of the churches.[22] The Gospels show what Jesus did and said. They were, of course, written later, but they record and communicate what they portray of the life, ministry, and teaching of Christ consciously and accurately. And the Holy Spirit, who guided the apostles into all the truth and helped them to preach, teach, and write down that truth, was the one promised and sent by the Lord Jesus Christ.

We find in 1 John a good summary of the process by which the apostles passed on the message they had received, and also of the results of that passing on, namely, fellowship between the readers of 1 John, and the Son and the Father. John wrote:

> We declare to you what was from the beginning, what we have heard, what we have seen with our eyes, what we have looked at and touched with our hands, concerning the word of life – this life was revealed, and we have seen it and testify to it, and declare to you the eternal life that was with the Father and was revealed to us – we declare to you what we have seen and heard so that you also may have fellowship with us; and truly our fellowship is with the Father and with his Son Jesus Christ. We are writing these things so that our joy may be complete. (1 John 1:1–4)

---

22. See Bauckham, *Eyewitnesses*.

20. RECEIVING GOD'S WORDS, WRITTEN FOR HIS PEOPLE, BY HIS SPIRIT, ABOUT HIS SON

My aim here is to show how the teaching of Jesus Christ in John's Gospel supports the four foundations of a biblical theology of the identity and purpose of the Bible, and so also supports our summary phrase, 'Receiving God's words, written for his people, by his Spirit, about his Son.'

John's Gospel gives two distinct perspectives on these foundations: one is that of the historical Jesus and his ministry up to his death and resurrection, including his teaching, and the other is that of John, the author of the Gospel, as he wrote from a later time, recording Jesus' teaching but also making reference to this later perspective.

John's Gospel makes a distinctive contribution to what the whole Bible teaches on the foundation of a doctrine of Scripture. However, we should not expect to find evidence in John's Gospel for every claim referred to in this book.

Receiving, believing and keeping God's words

John's Gospel is about revelation: 'The Word became flesh and lived among us . . . the only Son, who is at the Father's side, has made him known [explained, exegeted or narrated him]' (1:14, 18 [my trans.]). The Son made the Father known by all that he did: his presence, his signs, his relationships, his teaching, and his death and resurrection. Our access to all of those elements of revelation is by means of words, the words of John's Gospel, which narrate his signs, his relationships, his teaching, and his death and resurrection. His teaching was an essential part of that revelation: 'Very truly, I tell you, we speak of what we know and testify to what we have seen; yet you do not receive our testimony. If I have told you about earthly things and you do not believe, how can you believe if I tell you about heavenly things?' (3:11–12).

Those who received his teaching came to know the Father and the Son. For Jesus said to the Father about the disciples: 'The words that you gave to me I have given to them, and they have received them and know in truth that I came from you; and they have believed that you sent me' (17:8).

He explained: 'My teaching is not my own. It comes from him who sent me' (7:16 [my trans.]). For his task was to pass on the words of the Father to his disciples. 'I do nothing on my own, but I speak just what the Father has taught me' (8:28 [my trans.]). 'I am telling you what I have seen in my Father's presence' (8:38 [my trans.]). And he called his disciples his friends, 'because I have made known to you everything that I have heard from my Father' (15:15).

Conversely, those who refused to receive Jesus' word would be judged by that word: 'The one who rejects me and does not receive my word has a judge; on the last day the word that I have spoken will serve as judge' (12:48).

To receive Jesus' words meant to believe in him, and to believe in the Father who sent him. 'Whoever believes in me believes not in me but in him who sent me' (12:44), and 'whoever receives me receives him who sent me' (13:20). To receive is to believe: to believe is to receive. To believe or trust Jesus' word is to begin to believe or trust him. So the royal official whose son was ill first of all 'believed the word that Jesus spoke to him' (4:50). Then, after his son was healed, 'he himself believed, along with his whole household' (4:53).

Furthermore, to receive Jesus' words is to 'keep them'. In the Bible to 'keep' words or commands is, as we have seen, to obey them and to preserve them so that others too may obey them. It is a word that refers both to the obedience of the original hearers, and also to the preservation of the words for future readers and hearers. 'Keeping Christ's words' is a fundamental task of his disciples.

Jesus taught the power of his words as instruments of his grace: 'You have already been cleansed by the word that I have spoken to you' (15:3); and, 'the truth will make you free' (8:32). He prayed that the Father would sanctify the disciples by his word of truth: 'sanctify them by the truth', because 'your word is truth' (17:17).

His words brought life: 'Very truly, I tell you, anyone who hears my word and believes him who sent me has eternal life, and does not come under judgement, but has passed from death to life' (5:24); and 'Very truly, I tell you, whoever keeps my word will never see death' (8:51).

He taught that 'the scripture cannot be annulled' (10:35), and that the fulfilment of Scripture in Judas' betrayal of him would bring about faith: 'But it is to fulfil the scripture, "The one who ate my bread has lifted his heel against me." I tell you this now, before it occurs, so that when it does occur, you may believe that I am he' (13:18–19).

The theme of the fulfilment of the Old Testament is prominent in the narrative of Jesus' death. The soldiers cast lots for his clothing 'to fulfil what the scripture says'; Jesus' words 'I am thirsty' fulfilled the Scripture; and Jesus' bones were not broken, John asserts, in order that two texts of 'scripture' might be fulfilled (19:24, 28, 36–37).

Receiving and believing Jesus' words helped to establish relationships between the Father, the Son, and the disciples. 'Those who love me will keep my word, and my Father will love them, and we will come to them and make our home with them' (14:23).

Jesus' words were spirit and life, words of eternal life. For Jesus said:

'The words that I have spoken to you are spirit and life' . . . Jesus asked the twelve, 'Do you also wish to go away?' Simon Peter answered him, 'Lord, to whom can we go? You have the words of eternal life. We have come to believe and know that you are the Holy One of God.' (6:63, 67–69)

Jesus taught the significance of the words of the Old Testament, his own words, and words of his disciples. Those who receive, believe, and keep God's words will believe in God and in his Son, Jesus Christ.

Written for his people

In John there are two aspects of this theme of the Bible being 'written for God's people'.

The Old Testament
In terms of direct references to the Old Testament writings, John's Gospel focuses mainly on the law of Moses.[1] 'The law . . . was given through Moses; grace and truth came through Jesus Christ' (1:17).

---

1. On another level, for example, the book of Ezekiel was also formative, though without direct references, with its themes of temple, shepherds, and water.

In Jesus' teaching, the task of Moses' writings was to be a witness to his identity: 'they . . . testify on my behalf' (5:39). And this witness to Christ is so clear that 'if you believed Moses, you would believe me, for he wrote about me' (5:46). And if Jesus' hearers do not believe what Moses wrote, then they will find it hard to believe Jesus' words. 'But if you do not believe what he wrote, how will you believe what I say?' (5:47).

The great tragedy is that, despite the fact that the Jews had received Moses and his writings, they missed the message. 'You search the scriptures because you think that in them you have eternal life; and it is they that testify on my behalf. Yet you refuse to come to me to have life' (5:39–40). The Scriptures in which they had set their hope would be their condemnation. 'Do not think that I will accuse you before the Father; your accuser is Moses, on whom you have set your hope' (5:45).

Indeed, their commitment to Moses and his teaching was so strong that on one occasion Jesus referred to Moses' writings as 'your law' (10:34). It was natural for them to assess matters by the Scriptures, even if some missed their main message. We find this in the disagreement between Nicodemus and the other leaders. Both parties appeal to Scripture:

> Nicodemus, who had gone to Jesus before, and who was one of them, asked, 'Our law does not judge people without first giving them a hearing to find out what they are doing, does it?' They replied, 'Surely you are not also from Galilee, are you? Search and you will see that no prophet is to arise from Galilee.' (7:50–52)

The vital role of the Old Testament Scriptures written for his people is clearly recognized in John's Gospel. It is reflected in Jesus' conversation with the woman from Samaria, when he said to her, 'You worship what you do not know; we worship what we know, for salvation is from the Jews' (4:22).

Jesus' teaching
If in John's Gospel the people of God look back to the Old Testament Scriptures, they were also being reformed by the teaching of Jesus.

Here are two examples of this. While God's people in the Old Testament had thought of themselves as God's vine, now Jesus was the true vine, and his disciples were now the reformed people of God. 'My word' makes people Jesus' disciples, branches of the true vine: 'I am the true vine, and my Father is the vine-grower . . . You have already been cleansed by the word that I have spoken to you. Abide in me as I abide in you' (John 15:1, 3–4). While they had valued the temple, now Jesus was to be the temple: 'Destroy this temple, and in three days I will raise it up' (2:19). Significantly, John records that after Jesus' resurrection, 'his disciples remembered that he had said this; and they believed the scripture and the word that Jesus had spoken' (2:22). (Notice here that John combined the role of the Old Testament Scriptures and Jesus' teaching.)

God's people were now constituted by the reception of Jesus' teaching: 'What I speak, therefore, I speak just as the Father has told me' (12:50), and 'If you continue in my word, you are truly my disciples' (8:31). For those who follow the Good Shepherd 'listen to my voice' (10:16).

Future teaching including John's Gospel

Jesus also promised future teaching by the Spirit of truth. This included the writing of John's Gospel. The Old Testament is often referred to in John's Gospel by the phrase 'it is written', or as 'scripture': literally, 'what is written'. John explained that he too had written: 'these are written' (20:31); and 'This is the disciple who is testifying to these things and has written them, and we know that his testimony is true' (21:24).

We look at this theme in the next section.

By his Spirit

The great focus on the Spirit as the agent of God's truth in John's Gospel is about the future ministry of the Spirit in the verbal revelation to be given to the disciples in their ministry as apostles after the death and resurrection of Christ, some of which was to be written down and preserved in the New Testament.

Jesus Christ is described as the one on whom John the Baptist saw the Spirit descend and remain (1:33), and as 'he whom God has sent [who] speaks the words of God, for he gives the Spirit without measure' (3:34).[2] However, the Gospel's focus on the verbal revelation of the Spirit was not in the teaching that Jesus Christ gave before his death and resurrection, but on a future ministry, as we have seen.

---

2. There is no reference to the work of the Spirit in the Old Testament. In fact the statement is made, 'for as yet there was no Spirit, because Jesus was not yet glorified' (7:39). This should be read in context as meaning that full experience of the indwelling Spirit would happen only after the atonement and glorification of Christ.

I will not repeat what we have just found out about this ministry of the Spirit. However, there are two points that are worth making as we are now considering this ministry of the Spirit in the context of other biblical evidence about the verbal revelatory role of the Spirit.

The Spirit and verbal revelation
This ministry of the Spirit will be a verbal ministry. For the Spirit will 'teach you everything', and 'remind you of all that I have said to you' (14:26); 'will testify on my behalf' (15:26), 'prove the world wrong about sin and righteousness and judgement' (16:7–11), 'guide you into all the truth', and 'speak whatever he hears, and will declare to you the things that are to come' (16:13). This supports the evidence that we have seen elsewhere in the Bible, that a major ministry of the Spirit is the communication of words. That is also supported by the way Jesus referred to the Spirit: 'another Advocate', and 'the Spirit of truth' (14:16, 17).

The Spirit will continue the verbal teaching ministry of Jesus after his resurrection.

The connection between Jesus' earthly teaching, and what the Spirit will teach later
John's Gospel, like the other Gospels, is both an account of Jesus' earthly life and ministry, and also that account seen from a later perspective. It is true to what happened, and also true to the growth in understanding that happened later, guided by the Spirit.[3]

It is instructive to notice how Jesus asserts that the Spirit will help the disciples both to remember what Jesus had told them and to understand the deeper implications of that teaching. For the Spirit will 'remind you of all that I have said to you' (14:26); and will 'take what is mine and declare it to you' (16:14–15). And the Spirit will also 'teach you everything' (14:26); and 'guide you into all the truth' (16:13). So the Spirit will both help to preserve the past – that is, what Jesus had taught them – and also teach more of the significance of Christ. In the words of Don Carson: 'The Spirit of Truth . . . is

---

3. There is much debate among New Testament scholars about the balance between the two perspectives. Some think, as I do, that both have been preserved, and others that the earthly life of Jesus is invisibly hidden behind a creation of the later church, community, or author. If this is the case, and the theological content of John 14 – 16 is a product of the early church, or, more narrowly, of the Johannine community, then that at least makes it clear that some at least in the early church believed that their theological creativity was the product of the Holy Spirit.

doing little more than fleshing out the implications of God's triumphant self-disclosure in the person and work of his Son.[4]

The distinction between what Jesus told the disciples and what they understood during his earthly life, on the one hand, and what they understood when they were taught by the Holy Spirit sent by the Father and Son, on the other, is instructive. 'His disciples did not understand these things at first; but when Jesus was glorified, then they remembered that these things had been written of him and had been done to him' (12:16), and 'This is the disciple who is testifying to these things and has written them, and we know that his testimony is true' (21:24). Indeed, this ministry of the Spirit is also a continued teaching ministry of Jesus Christ through the Spirit after his ascension: 'I have said these things to you in figures of speech. The hour is coming when I will no longer speak to you in figures, but will tell you plainly of the Father' (16:25). As Kevin Vanhoozer observes: 'Jesus Christ is the *content* of the Scriptural witness, the one who *interprets* the Scriptural witness, and the one who *commissions* the New Testament witness.'[5]

In John's Gospel, all truth comes from the Father, whose 'word is truth' (17:17); all truth is found in the Son, who is 'the truth' (14:6); and all truth comes through the Spirit of truth (16:13): the Son speaks the words the Father has given him, and passes them on to the disciples (17:8).

About his Son

John's Gospel is about Jesus Christ, the Word and Son of God: 'But these are written so that you may come to believe that Jesus is the Messiah, the Son of God, and that through believing you may have life in his name' (20:31). It is about Christ the Word and Son of God, because it is in the Son that the Father was made known: 'If you know me, you will know my Father also' (14:7). John's Gospel is about Jesus Christ, whose identity is made clear through his signs and his words.

Not only is John's Gospel about Jesus Christ, but, as we have seen, the Old Testament, mainly referred to as Scripture, or Moses, also points us to Christ. Jesus said of the Old Testament Scriptures, 'they witness to me', and, 'If you believed Moses, you would believe me, for he wrote about me' (5:39, 46).

---

4. Carson, *John*, pp. 541–542.

5. Vanhoozer, *Drama*, p. 195. He continues: 'Jesus Christ is both the material and the formal principle of the canon: its substance and its hermeneutic.'

John's Gospel is about Christ, and the Old Testament is also about Christ.

Finally, in John's Gospel we also have the promise of the teaching role of the Spirit that resulted in the writing of that Gospel, and also in the teaching and preaching of the apostles, and the writing of the other books of the New Testament. As Jesus promised, this teaching would also be about himself. For Jesus taught that the Spirit would: 'remind you of all that I have said to you', 'testify about me', and 'glorify me' (14:26; 15:26; 16:14).

From John's Gospel we learn that the Bible is God's word about his Word, the Lord Jesus Christ, and that that we should 'receive God's words written for his people by his Spirit about his Son'.

Avery Dulles perceptively described two possible weaknesses in our view of Jesus Christ, in words written in 1963:

> The adventures of non-Catholic biblical criticism of the past century make it evident that he who rejects the Christ of faith will soon end up by reducing the Jesus of history to a pale figure without religious significance. Conversely, he who makes light of the flesh-and-blood Jesus of history in the name of a more spiritual faith will end up prostrating himself before a timeless myth. If we are true to the Gospels, we shall insist on retaining both fact and interpretation, both history and faith.[6]

A crucial aspect of the history of Jesus was his teaching, as his title 'Rabbi' makes clear. We should not make light of that teaching, lest we end up serving only a timeless myth. We should also accept the fullness of the biblical revelation about Jesus Christ, lest we end up serving only a pale figure, without any long-term theological significance.

The default position for many today is not the Jesus of history or the Christ of faith, but the Christ of personal experience. However, we set aside the Jesus Christ of history at our peril, as he himself taught us. One essential aspect of the historical Jesus Christ was his teaching, and that teaching included information about his own words and message, the significance of the Old Testament, and the future teaching of the Holy Spirit through Christ's apostles. For Jesus wants to say of his followers today, as he said of his disciples, that they 'received' his words (John 17:8). We have seen in Part 6 that Jesus affirmed the Old Testament, his own teaching, and the teaching of the apostles who would receive the Spirit of truth, preach and teach the gospel, and then write the books of the New Testament. We would be

---

6. Dulles, *Apologetics*, p. 57.

foolish to ignore or reject the teaching of our Rabbi, Christ, Lord, and Saviour.

Conclusion

In this book we have found that God has spoken in human words to his people, and that some of his words have been written down for all the people of God. God's words are powerful and effective, and it is the duty and joy of the people of God to receive his words.

I have expounded a biblical theology of the Bible by means of the phrase 'Receiving God's words written for his people by his Spirit about his Son.' The theology of the Bible depends on four theological foundations: a doctrine of receiving God's verbal revelation ('Receiving God's words'), a doctrine of the people of God, or ecclesiology ('written for his people'), a doctrine of the Holy Spirit, or pneumatology ('by his Spirit'), and a doctrine of Jesus Christ, or Christology ('about his Son'). These doctrines provide an effective and convincing theological basis for receiving the Bible as the word and words of God.

We have also seen the many connections and relationships between Jesus Christ and the Bible. I have argued that the doctrine of the incarnation, of the Son of God taking on humanity, is itself a basis for believing that God can speak human words, as indeed he did in Christ.

We have also recognized the crucial role of the Holy Spirit in verbal revelation, and not least in the verbal revelation that is the Scriptures. The Scriptures were written at different times, and each part was relevant to the age in which it was written, and has also been preserved by God for his people in every age. We have found much evidence that the Bible treats itself as the words of God.

Without the Bible, we would not know that God was and is Father, Son, and Spirit. In the pages and words of the Bible, we meet this God, and this God speaks to reveal who he is, what he has done for us, and how we should live by faith in Jesus Christ.

In his teaching and practice Jesus Christ authenticated the Old Testament, his own teaching, and the New Testament. He also lived by the Old Testament, shaped his life and actions by its teaching, and consciously fulfilled its promises. He identified the message of the Old Testament with his own teaching, and showed how that message was fulfilled in his death and resurrection, and in the proclamation of his gospel to all nations. He promised to send the Spirit of truth, who would guide and teach his disciples after his death, resurrection, and ascension.

In this book I have not attempted to defend what the Bible says about itself: all I have attempted to do is to describe it.[7]

In doing so I have pointed out that a sound theology of the Bible depends on our theology of God's capacity for verbal revelation, and our capacity to receive it. It also depends on a theology of the one people of God, and of the accumulated inherited Scriptures. It depends on the authentication of Christ, who in his teaching authenticates the Old Testament, his own teaching, and the teaching of his apostles. It depends on a theology of the Holy Spirit which connects the Spirit with the self-revelation of God, with truth, with words, and with verbal revelation. It also points to the Christ of the Scriptures: the word of the Lord speaks of the Lord of the word. It is this robust theology which supports Scripture's own theology and invitation: to receive God's words written for us, written for his people, by his Spirit, about his Son.

---

7. There is more evidence in the Scriptures about the nature of those Scriptures than there is about many other doctrines, such as the nature of the Holy Spirit, the nature of ordination or the sacraments, or the role of the State.

BIBLIOGRAPHY

ABRAHAM, WILLIAM J., *The Divine Inspiration of Holy Scripture* (Oxford University Press, 1981).

ACHTEMEIER, PAUL J., *Inspiration and Authority: Nature and Function of Christian Scripture* (Hendrickson, 1999).

ADAM, PETER, 'God's Powerful Words: Five Principles of Biblical Spirituality in Isaiah 55', *Southern Baptist Journal of Theology*, 10/4 (2006), pp. 28–37.

— *Hearing God's Words*, New Studies in Biblical Theology (Apollos, 2004).

— 'The Preacher and the Sufficient Word', in David Jackman and Christopher Green, *When God's Voice Is Heard: Essays on Preaching Presented to Dick Lucas* (Inter-Varsity Press, 1995), pp. 27–42.

— *Speaking God's Words* (Inter-Varsity Press, 1996; Regent, 2004).

— *'To Bring Men to Heaven by Preaching': John Donne's Evangelistic Sermons* (The Latimer Trust, 2006).

— *Word and Spirit: The Puritan–Quaker Debate* (St. Antholin's Lectureship, 2001).

BACOTE, VINCENT, MIGUÉLEZ, LAURA C., and OKHOLM, DENNIS L., *Evangelicals and Scripture: Tradition, Authority and Hermeneutics* (InterVarsity Press, 2004).

BAKER, DAVID L., *Two Testaments, One Bible: A Study of the Theological Relationship between the Old and New Testaments*, revised edition (Apollos, 1991).

BARKER, PAUL A., *The God Who Keeps Promises* (Acorn, 1998).

— *The Triumph of Grace in Deuteronomy: Faithless Israel, Faithful Yahweh in Deuteronomy*, Paternoster Biblical Monographs (Paternoster, 2004).

BARR, JAMES, *The Bible in the Modern World* (SCM, 1973).

— *Fundamentalism*, second edition (SCM, 1981).

BARRETT, C. K., *The First Epistle to the Corinthians*, Black's New Testament Commentaries, second edition (Adam and Charles Black, 1971).

BARTOW, CHARLES L., *God's Human Speech: A Practical Theology of Proclamation* (Eerdmans, 1997).

BAUCKHAM, RICHARD J., *Bible and Mission: Christian Witness in a Postmodern World* (Paternoster and Baker, 2003).

— *Jesus and the Eyewitnesses: The Gospels as Eyewitness Testimony* (Eerdmans, 2006).

— *Jude, 2 Peter*, Word Biblical Commentary, 50 (Word, 1981).

— *Scripture and Authority Today* (Grove, 1999).

BAYER, OSWALD, 'Hermeneutical Theology', *Scottish Journal of Theology*, 56/2 (2003), pp. 131–147.

BERKOUWER, G. C., *Holy Scripture*, Studies in Dogmatics (Eerdmans, 1982).

BLOESCH, DONALD G., *Holy Scripture: Revelation, Inspiration and Interpretation* (InterVarsity Press, 1994).

— *A Theology of Word and Spirit: Authority and Method in Theology* (InterVarsity Press, 1992).

BONHOEFFER, DIETRICH, *Meditating on the Word*, trans. and ed. David McI. Gracie (Cowley, 2000).

— *Reflections on the Bible: Human Word and Word of God*, ed. Manfred Weber, trans. M. Eugene Boring (Hendrickson, 2004).

BRAY, GERALD, ed., *Documents of the English Reformation* (Fortress Press, 1994).

BRIGGS, RICHARD, *Reading the Bible Wisely* (Baker Academic, 2003).

BROWN, RAYMOND, *The Message of Nehemiah: God's Servant in a Time of Change*, The Bible Speaks Today (Inter-Varsity Press, 1998).

BRUCE, F. F., *The Canon of Scripture* (InterVarsity Press, 1988).

— *The Epistle to the Hebrews* (Eerdmans, 1964).

BULLINGER, H., *Bullinger's Decades*, ed. T. Harding (Cambridge University Press, 1849).

BURROUGHS, JEREMIAH, *Gospel Worship* (Soli Deo Gloria Publications, 1990).

CALVIN, JOHN, *Calvin's Sermons on Timothy and Titus* (Banner of Truth, facsimile of the 1579 edition, 1983).

— *Commentaries*, 1–22 (Baker Book House, 1981).

— *Institutes of the Christian Religion*, 1–2, trans. Ford Lewis Battles, Library of Christian Classics (Westminster Press, 1960).

CAMERON, NIGEL M. de S., ed., *The Challenge of Evangelical Theology: Essays in Approach and Method* (Rutherford House, 1987).

CARSON, D. A., *The Cross and Christian Ministry: An Exposition of Passages from 1 Corinthians* (Baker and Inter-Varsity Press, 1993).

CARSON, D. A., *The Gospel According to John* (Inter-Varsity Press and Eerdmans, 1991).

CARSON, D. A., and BEALE, G. K., eds., *Commentary on the Use of the Old Testament in the New* (Baker and Apollos, 2007).

— and WOODBRIDGE, JOHN D., eds., *Scripture and Truth* (Inter-Varsity Press, 1983).

CHARNOCK, STEPHEN, *Discourses upon the Existence and Attributes of God* (Bohn, 1845).

CHILDS, BREVARD S., 'Speech-Act Theory and Biblical Interpretation', *Scottish Journal of Theology*, 58.4 (2005), pp. 375–392.

CLINES, DAVID J. A., *The Theme of the Pentateuch*, JSOTS (JSOT Press, 1982).

CLOWNEY, EDMUND P., *The Unfolding Mystery: Discovering Christ in the Old Testament* (Inter-Varsity Press, 1988).

COLE, GRAHAM, 'At the Heart of a Christian Spirituality', *Reformed Theological Review*, 52 (1993), pp. 49–61.

COUNTRYMAN, WILLIAM, *Biblical Authority or Biblical Tyranny? Scripture and the Christian Pilgrimage* (Fortress, 1982).

CRAGG, KENNETH, *The Lively Credentials of God* (Darton, Longman & Todd, 1995).

CRAIGIE, PETER, *Psalms 1–50*, Word Biblical Commentary, 19 (Word, 1983).

CRANFIELD, C. E. B., *The Epistle to the Romans*, International Critical Commentary, 1–2 (T. & T. Clark, 1975, 1979).

CRANMER, THOMAS, 'The First Part of the Exhortation to the Reading of Holy Scripture', in *Certain Sermons or Homilies* (SPCK, 1864).

DONNE, JOHN, *Essays in Divinity*, ed. Evelyn M. Simpson (1952; Clarendon, 1967).

— *The Sermons of John Donne*, ed. Evelyn M. Simpson and George R. Potter, 10 vols (University of California, 1953–62).

DULLES, AVERY, *Apologetics and the Biblical Christ* (Burns & Oates, 1963).

DUMBRELL, W. J., *Covenant and Creation: An Old Testament Covenantal Theology* (Paternoster and Lancer, 1984).

— *The Faith of Israel: A Theological Survey of the Old Testament*, second edition (Baker Academic, 2002).

DUNN, JAMES D. G., *The Living Word* (SCM, 1987).

— *Romans 9–16*, Word Biblical Commentary (Word, 1988).

DYCK, ELMER, *The Act of Bible Reading: A Multi-Disciplinary Approach to Biblical Interpretation* (InterVarsity Press, 1996).

EBELING, GERHARD, *Luther: An Introduction to His Thought*, trans. R. A. Wilson (Fontana, 1972).

— *Word and Faith* (Fortress, 1963).

ELLIS, E. EARLE, *The Gospel of Luke*, Century Bible, new edition (Nelson, 1966).

— *The Old Testament in Early Christianity* (Baker, 1992).

ELLUL, JACQUES, *The Humiliation of the Word*, trans. J. M. Hanks (Eerdmans, 1985).

ENNS, PETER, *Inspiration and Incarnation: Evangelicals and the Problem of the Old Testament* (Baker Academic, 2005).

FACKRE, GABRIEL, *The Doctrine of Revelation: A Narrative Interpretation*, Edinburgh Studies in Constructive Theology (Eerdmans, 1997).

FARRER, AUSTIN, *The Glass of Vision* (Dacre, 1948).

— *Interpretation and Belief* (SPCK, 1976).

FEE, GORDON D., *The First Epistle to the Corinthians*, NICNT (Eerdmans, 1987).

FLANNERY, AUSTIN, ed., *Vatican Council II: The Conciliar and Post Conciliar Documents* (Dominican Publications, 1975).

FOORD, MARTIN, *The Weakest Link? The Canon and the Infallibility of Scripture* (unpublished paper, 2005).

FORSYTH, P. T., *The Person and Place of Jesus Christ* (Independent Press, 1961).

FRANCE, R. T., *Jesus and the Old Testament: His Application of the Old Testament Passages to Himself and His Mission* (Tyndale, 1971).

FRYE, NORTHROP, *The Great Code: The Bible and Literature* (Harvest and HBJ, 1982).

GOLDINGAY, JOHN, *Models for Scripture* (Eerdmans, 1994).

GOLDSWORTHY, GRAEME, *According to Plan: The Unfolding Revelation of God in the Bible* (Inter-Varsity Press and Lancer, 1991).

— *Gospel-Centred Hermeneutics: Biblical-Theological Foundations and Principles* (Apollos, 2006).

— *Preaching the Whole Bible as Christian Scripture* (Eerdmans, 2000).

GOODING, DAVID, *True to the Faith: A Fresh Approach to the Acts of the Apostles* (Hodder and Stoughton, 1990).

— *An Unshakeable Kingdom: The Letter to the Hebrews Today*, Living Word Series (Inter-Varsity Press, 1989).

GREEN, CHRIS, *The Word of His Grace: A Guide to Teaching and Preaching from Acts* (Inter-Varsity Press, 2005).

GREEN, CHRISTOPHER, and JACKMAN, DAVID, *When God's Voice Is Heard: Essays on Preaching Presented to Dick Lucas* (Inter-Varsity Press, 1995).

GREEN, JOEL B., *The Gospel of Luke*, NICNT (Eerdmans, 1997).

GREEN, MICHAEL, *Evangelism in the Early Church* (Hodder and Stoughton 1973).

— *2 Peter and Jude*, Tyndale New Testament Commentaries, revised edition (Inter-Varsity Press and Eerdmans, 1987).

GREIDANUS, SIDNEY, *Preaching Christ from the Old Testament: A Contemporary Hermeneutical Method* (Eerdmans, 1999).

GROSHEIDE, F. W., *Commentary on The First Epistle to the Corinthians*, NICNT (Eerdmans, 1983).

GRUDEM, WAYNE A., 'Scripture's Self-Attestation and the Problem of Formulating a Doctrine of Scripture', in D. A. Carson and John D. Woodbridge, eds., *Scripture and Truth* (Inter-Varsity Press, 1983), pp. 19–59.

HAMILTON, JAMES M., Jr, *God's Indwelling Presence: The Holy Spirit in the Old and New Testaments* (B. & H. Academic, 2006).

HANSON, R. P. C., and HANSON, A. T., *The Bible Without Illusions* (SCM/Trinity Press, 1989).

HARMON, ALLAN M., *Commentary on the Psalms* (Mentor, 1998).

HATCH, EDWIN, *The Influence of Greek Ideas and Usages upon the Christian Church*, The Hibbert Lectures 1888, ed. A. M. Fairbairn, sixth edition (Williams & Norgate, 1897).

HELM, PAUL, *The Divine Revelation: The Basic Issues*, Foundations for Faith (Marshall, Morgan and Scott, 1982).

— and TRUMAN, CARL, eds., *The Trustworthiness of Scripture: Perspectives in the Nature of Scripture* (Apollos, 2002).

HICKS, PETER, *Evangelicals and Truth: A Creative Proposal for a Postmodern Age* (Apollos, 1998).

HODGE, CHARLES, *A Commentary on the First Epistle to the Corinthians*, Geneva Series (Banner of Truth, 1964).

HUGHES, P. E., 'The Christology of Hebrews', *Southwestern Journal of Theology*, 28/1 (1985), pp. 19–27.

— *A Commentary on the Epistle to the Hebrews* (Eerdmans, 1987).

JACKMAN, DAVID, *I Believe in the Bible* (Hodder & Stoughton, 2000).

JAMES, P. D., *The Skull Beneath the Skin* (Warner Books, 1982).

JENSEN, P. F., *The Revelation of God*, Contours of Christian Theology (IVP, 2002).

JODOCK, DARRELL, *The Church's Bible: Its Contemporary Authority* (Fortress, 1989).

JOHNSON, DENNIS E., *The Message of Acts in the History of Redemption* (P. & R., 1997).

JOSIPOVICI, GABRIEL, *The Book of God: A Response to the Bible* (Yale University Press, 1988).

KELLY, J. N. D., *The Epistles of Peter and of Jude*, Black's New Testament Commentaries (Adam & Charles Black, 1969).

KELSEY, DAVID H., *The Uses of Scripture in Recent Theology* (SCM, 1975).

KIDNER, DEREK, *Ezra and Nehemiah*, Tyndale Old Testament Commentaries (Inter-Varsity Press, 1979).

KNIGHT, GEORGE W., *The Pastoral Epistles*, NIGTC (Eerdmans and Paternoster, 1993).

LANE, WILLIAM L., *Hebrews: A Call to Commitment* (Hendrickson, 1985).

LAW, DAVID R., *Inspiration*, New Century Theology (Continuum, 2001).

LAWSON, STEVEN J., 'The Pattern of Biblical Preaching: An Expository Study of Ezra 7:10 and Nehemiah 8:1–18', *Bibliotheca Sacra*, 158 (2001), pp. 451–466.

LAZARETH, WILLIAM H., *Reading the Bible in Faith: Theological Voices from the Pastorate* (Eerdmans, 2001).

LEIGHTON, ROBERT, *A Practical Commentary of the Epistle General of 1 Peter*, 2 vols (Religious Tract Society, n.d.).

LLOYD-JONES, D. M., *Expository Sermons on 2 Peter* (Banner of Truth, 1983).

LONG, THOMAS G., *Preaching and the Literary Forms of the Bible* (Fortress, 1989).

LONGENECKER, RICHARD, *Biblical Exegesis in the Apostolic Period* (Eerdmans, 1977).

Longman, Tremper, III, *Literary Approaches to Biblical Interpretation*, Foundations of Contemporary Interpretation (Academie and Apollos, 1987).

— *Reading the Bible with Heart and Mind* (NavPress, 1997).

Lucas, Dick, and Green, Christopher, *The Message of 2 Peter and Jude*, The Bible Speaks Today (Inter-Varsity Press, 1995).

McComiskey, D. S., *Lukan Theology in the Light of the Gospel's Literary Structure*, Paternoster Biblical Monographs (Paternoster, 2004).

McComiskey, Thomas Edward, *The Covenants of Promise: A Theology of the Old Testament Covenants* (Inter-Varsity Press, 1985).

McConville, J. G., *Ezra, Nehemiah and Esther*, Daily Bible Study Series (Westminster John Knox, 1985).

McDonald, H. D., *I Want to Know What the Bible Says About the Bible* (Kingsway, 1979).

— *Ideas of Revelation: An Historical Study A. D. 1700 to A. D. 1860* (Macmillan, 1959).

— *Theories of Revelation: An Historical Study 1860–1960* (George Allen & Unwin, 1962).

McGowan, A. T. B., 'The Divine Spiration of Scripture', *Scottish Journal of Evangelical Theology*, 21/2 (2003), pp. 199–217.

McKim, Donald A., ed., *The Authoritative Word: Essays on the Nature of Scripture* (Eerdmans, 1983).

Macquarrie, John, *Principles of Christian Theology* (SCM, 1966).

Marshall, I. Howard, *Beyond the Bible: Moving from Scripture to Theology* (Baker and Paternoster, 2004).

— *Biblical Inspiration* (Eerdmans, 1983).

Moloney, Francis J., *The Living Voice of the Gospel* (Collins Dove, 1986).

Moltmann, Jürgen, *The Crucified God* (SCM, 1977).

Montefiore, H. W., *The Epistle to the Hebrews*, Black's New Testament Commentary Series (A. & C. Black, 1964).

Morris, Leon, *I Believe in Revelation* (Hodder & Stoughton, 1976).

Motyer, J. Alec, *Look to the Rock: An Old Testament Background to Our Understanding of Christ* (Inter-Varsity Press, 1996).

— *The Message of Exodus: The Days of Our Pilgrimage*, The Bible Speaks Today (Inter-Varsity Press, 2005).

— *The Prophecy of Isaiah* (Inter-Varsity Press, 1993).

Mounce, William D., *Pastoral Epistles*, Word Biblical Commentary, 46 (Nelson, 2000).

O'Donovan, Oliver, *On the Thirty-Nine Articles: A Conversation with Tudor Christianity* (Paternoster, 1986).

Old, Hughes Oliphant, *The Reading and Preaching of the Scriptures in the Worship of the Christian Church: The Biblical Period*, 1 (Eerdmans, 1998).

Origen, 'Commentary on Matthew', in Allan Menzies, ed., *Ante-Nicene Fathers*, 10, fifth edition (T. & T. Clark and Eerdmans, 1986), pp. 411–512.

Orr, James, *Revelation and Inspiration* (Duckworth, 1910).

OSWALT, JOHN N., *The Book of Isaiah, Chapters 40–66*, NICOT (Eerdmans, 1998).

OWEN, JOHN, *An Exposition of the Epistle to the Hebrews, with Preliminary Exercitations*, 1–7, ed. W. H. Goold (1854–5; Banner of Truth, 1991).

PACKER, J. I., *'Fundamentalism' and the Word of God* (1958; Inter-Varsity Press, 1996).

— *God Has Spoken* (Baker, 1988).

— *Honouring the Written Word of God: Collected Shorter Writings of J. I. Packer* (Paternoster, 1999).

— *Keep in Step with the Spirit*, new expanded edition (1984; Inter-Varsity Press, 2005).

PARKER, T. H. L., *The Oracles of God* (Lutterworth, 1947).

PETERSON, DAVID, *Christ and His People in the Book of Isaiah* (Inter-Varsity Press, 2003).

PETERSON, EUGENE H., *Eat This Book: A Conversation in the Art of Spiritual Reading* (Eerdmans, 2006).

— *Working the Angles: The Shape of Pastoral Integrity* (Eerdmans, 1987).

PINNOCK, CLARK H., *Biblical Revelation: The Foundation of Christian Theology* (Moody, 1971).

POYTHRESS, VERN S., *God-Centred Biblical Interpretation* (P. & R., 1999).

RAMM, BERNARD, *Protestant Biblical Interpretation*, third revised edition (Baker, 1970).

RICOEUR, PAUL, *Essays on Biblical Interpretation*, ed. Lewis S. Mudge (Fortress, 1980).

RIDDERBOS, HERMAN, *Studies in Scripture and Its Authority* (Eerdmans, 1978).

ROSNER, BRIAN, 'Written For Us: Paul's View of Scripture', in Philip E. Satterthwaite and David. F. Field, eds., *A Pathway into the Holy Scriptures* (Eerdmans, 1994), pp. 82–105.

SATTERTHWAITE, PHILIP E., and WRIGHT, DAVID F., eds., *A Pathway into the Holy Scriptures* (Eerdmans, 1994).

SCHNABEL, E. J., 'Scripture', in T. D. Alexander and Brian S. Rosner, eds., *New Dictionary of Biblical Theology* (Inter-Varsity Press, 2000), pp. 34–43.

SCHNEIDERS, SANDRA M., *The Revelatory Text: Interpreting the New Testament as Sacred Scripture* (Michael Glazier, 1999).

SCHÖKEL, LUIS ALONSO, *The Inspired Word: Scripture in the Light of Language and Literature* (Burns & Oates and Herder & Herder, 1967).

SHUMACK, RICHARD, *The Bible on the Bible* (unpublished monograph, 2005).

SONTAG, SUSAN, *Against Interpretation and Other Essays* (Picador, 1966).

SPONG, JOHN SHELBY, *Rescuing the Bible from Fundamentalism* (HarperSanFrancisco, 1991).

SPRIGGS, DAVID, *Feasting on God's Word: From Frozen Food to Gourmet Banquet* (Bible Reading Fellowship, 2002).

STEPHENS, W. P., *The Holy Spirit in the Theology of Martin Bucer* (Cambridge University Press, 1970).

STONEHOUSE, N. B., and WOOLLEY, PAUL, eds., *The Infallible Word* (P. & R., 1967).

STOTT, JOHN, *Calling Christian Leaders* (Inter-Varsity Press, 2002).

— *Christ the Controversialist: The Basics of Belief*, Christian Classics (Inter-Varsity Press, 1996; Tyndale Press, 1973).

— *Evangelical Truth: A Personal Plea for Unity* (Inter-Varsity Press, 1999).

— *The Message of Acts: To the Ends of the Earth*, The Bible Speaks Today (Inter-Varsity Press, 1990).

— *The Message of Romans: God's Good News for the World*, The Bible Speaks Today (Inter-Varsity Press, 1994).

STRAW, CAROLE, *Gregory the Great: Perfection in Imperfection* (University of California Press, 1988).

SWINBURNE, RICHARD, *Revelation: From Metaphor to Analogy* (Clarendon, 1992).

THOMAS AQUINAS, *Catena Aurea: Commentary on the Four Gospels Collected out of the Works of the Fathers*, IV/2 (Parker, 1845).

THOMPSON, J. A., *Deuteronomy*, Tyndale Old Testament Commentaries (InterVarsity Press, 1974).

THOMPSON, MARK D., *A Clear and Present Word: The Clarity of Scripture*, New Studies in Biblical Theology (Apollos and InterVarsity Press, 2006).

— *A Sure Ground on Which to Stand: The Relation of Authority and Interpretive Method in Luther's Approach to Scripture*, Paternoster Biblical and Theological Monographs (Paternoster, 2004).

— *Too Big for Words? The Transcendence of God and Finite Human Speech*, Latimer Studies (Latimer Trust, 2006).

THRONTVIET, MARK A., *Ezra–Nehemiah*, Interpretation (John Knox, 1992).

TIDBALL, DEREK, *The Message of Leviticus: Free to be Holy*, The Bible Speaks Today (Inter-Varsity Press, 2005).

TORRANCE, T. F., *The Trinitarian Faith* (T. & T. Clark, 1995).

TRUEMAN, CARL R., *The Claims of Truth: John Owen's Trinitarian Theology* (Paternoster, 1998).

TURRETIN, FRANCIS, *Institutes of Elenctic Theology*, 1–3, trans. G. M. Giger (P. & R., 1992, 1994, 1997).

VANHOOZER, KEVIN J., *The Drama of Doctrine: A Canonical Linguistic Approach to Christian Theology* (Westminster John Knox, 2005).

— *First Theology: God, Scripture, and Hermeneutics* (InterVarsity Press and Apollos, 2002).

— 'God's Mighty Speech-Acts: The Doctrine of Scripture Today', in Philip E. Satterthwaite and David. F. Field, eds., *A Pathway into the Holy Scriptures* (Eerdmans 1994), pp. 143–181.

— *Is There a Meaning in This Text?* (Apollos, 1998).

VIRKLER, HENRY A., *Hermeneutics: Principles and Process of Biblical Interpretation* (Baker, 1981).

VOS, GEERHARDUS, *Redemptive History and Biblical Interpretation: The Shorter Writings of Geerhardus Vos*, ed. Richard B. Gaffin (P. & R., 2001).

WALLACE, RONALD S., *Calvin's Doctrine of Word and Sacrament* (Oliver & Boyd, 1953).

WARD, TIMOTHY, 'The Incarnation and Scripture', in David Peterson, ed., *The Word Became Flesh: Evangelicals and the Incarnation* (Paternoster, 2003), pp. 152–184.

— *Word and Supplement: Speech Acts, Biblical Texts, and the Sufficiency of Scripture* (Oxford University Press, 2002).

WARFIELD, BENJAMIN BECKENRIDGE, *The Works of B. B. Warfield*, 1: *Revelation and Inspiration* (1927; Baker, 1981).

WEBB, BARRY, *The Message of Isaiah: On Eagles' Wings*, The Bible Speaks Today (Inter-Varsity Press, 1993).

WEBB, STEPHEN H., *The Divine Voice: Christian Proclamation and the Theology of Sound* (Brazos, 2004).

WEBSTER, JOHN, *Confessing God: Essays in Christian Dogmatics*, 2 (T. & T. Clark, 2005).

— *Holy Scripture: A Dogmatic Sketch*, Current Issues in Theology (Cambridge University Press, 2003).

— *Word and Church: Essays in Christian Dogmatics* (T. & T. Clark, 2001).

WEEKS, NOEL, *The Sufficiency of Scripture* (Banner of Truth, 1988).

WELLINGS, MARTIN, *Evangelicals Embattled: Responses of Evangelicals in the Church of England to Ritualism, Darwinism and Theological Liberalism, 1890–1930* (Paternoster, 2003).

WELLS, PAUL RONALD, *James Barr and the Bible: Critique of New Liberalism* (P. & R., 1980).

WENHAM, JOHN W., *Christ and the Bible* (Tyndale, 1972).

WESTCOTT, BROOKE FOSS, *The Epistle to the Hebrews*, second edition (1892; Eerdmans, n.d.).

WILLIAMS, DAVID JOHN, *Acts*, A Good News Commentary (Harper & Row, 1985).

WILLIAMSON, H. G. M., *Ezra, Nehemiah*, Word Biblical Commentary, 16 (Word, 1985).

WILSON, LINDSAY, *Joseph Wise and Otherwise: The Intersection of Wisdom and Covenant in Genesis 37–50*, Paternoster Biblical Monographs (Paternoster, 2004).

WOLTERSTORFF, NICHOLAS, *Divine Discourse: Philosophical Reflections on the Claim that God Speaks* (Cambridge University Press, 1995).

WOODBRIDGE, JOHN D., and McCOMISKEY, THOMAS EDWARD, eds., *Doing Theology in Today's World: Essays in Honor of Kenneth S. Kantzer* (Zondervan, 1991).

WORK, TELFORD, *Living and Active: Scripture in the Economy of Salvation*, Sacra Doctrina (Eerdmans, 2002).

WRIGHT, CHRIS, *Knowing Jesus through the Old Testament: Rediscovering the Roots of Our Faith* (Marshall Pickering, 1992).

— *The Mission of God: Unlocking the Bible's Grand Narrative* (Inter-Varsity Press, 2006).

WRIGHT, G. ERNEST, *God Who Acts: Biblical Theology as Recital*, Studies in Biblical Theology, 8 (SCM, 1952).

WRIGHT, N. T., *Scripture and the Authority of God* (SPCK, 2005).

YOUNG, E. J., *Thy Word is Truth* (Banner of Truth, 1963).

ZIMMERMAN, WOLF-DIETER, and SMITH, RONALD GREGOR, eds., *I Knew Dietrich Bonhoeffer* (Collins, 1966).

INDEX OF MAJOR BIBLE PASSAGES

INDEX OF THEOLOGICAL THEMES AND TOPICS

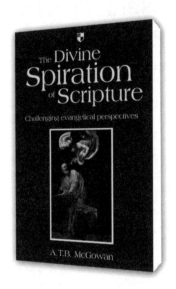

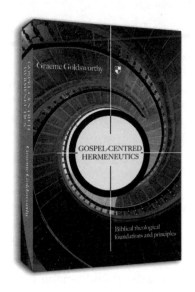

NEW STUDIES IN BIBLICAL THEOLOGY

NSBT

Series Editor: D. A. Carson

Hearing God's words

Exploring biblical spirituality

Peter Adam

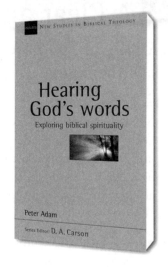

Many discussions of Christian spirituality draw on a range of traditions and 'disciplines'. However, little attention appears to have been given to the Bible itself as a source of spirituality, or to its teaching on this theme. Furthermore, a common assumption is that the evangelical tradition has little to offer in the area of spirituality.

In response, Peter Adam urges us to renew our confidence in a biblical model of spirituality, and to test our spirituality by the Bible. Drawing on Old and New Testament texts, along with significant insights from the Christian tradition, he expounds the shape and structure of a gospel-centred 'spirituality of the Word', through which we receive the life that God gives, and know God himself.

'By appealing both to the Bible and to influential voices in the history of the church (notably John Calvin), Dr Adam manages to combine biblical theology and historical theology in an admirable synthesis. His academic training, years of pastoral ministry, and now principalship of a theological college, ensure that this book simultaneously informs the mind, warms the heart and strengthens the will.'

D. A. Carson

Paperback 256 pages
ISBN: 978-1-84474-002-4

Available from your local Christian bookshop or via our website at **www.ivpbooks.com**